For my parents.

Blasphemers & Blackguards

About the author

David Ryan holds a Master's degree in History from NUI Galway and has published articles on different aspects of eighteenth- and nineteenth-century Irish history. *Blasphemers & Blackguards: The Irish Hellfire Clubs* is his first full-length publication. He currently lives in Dublin, where he works as a television researcher and writer.

Blasphemers
& Blackguards

The Irish Hellfire Clubs

David Ryan

MERRION

Dublin • Portland, Oregon

First published in 2012 by Merrion

an imprint of Irish Academic Press

2 Brookside	920 NE 58th Avenue, Suite 300
Dundrum Road	Portland, Oregon,
Dublin 14, Ireland	97213–3786, USA

© 2012 David Ryan

British Library Cataloguing-in-Publication Data
An entry can be found on request

978-1-908928-03-0 (cloth)
978-1-908928-01-6 (paper)

Library of Congress Cataloging in Publication Data
An entry can be found on request

Typeset by FiSH Books Ltd, Enfield, London
Printed and bound by CPI Group (UK) Ltd, Croydon, CR0 4YY

Contents

List of Plates

Acknowledgements

Many people have assisted me with this book. In particular I wish to thank Professor James Kelly for his encouragement and advice at an early stage of my research and for his helpful and constructive comments on drafts of the work. I would also like to thank Lea Benson, Síghle Bhreathnach-Lynch, Emer Ní Cheallaigh, Clodagh Kingston, Adrian Le Harivel, Sandra McElroy, Professor Daithí Ó hÓgáin, Dr Martyn Powell, Thomas Sinsteden and Christina Tse-Fong-Tai for their assistance with various aspects of the research, and the Earl of Rosse and Mervyn Whaley for allowing me to reproduce, respectively, portraits of the 1st Earl of Rosse and Thomas 'Buck' Whaley. I am grateful to two scholars who are no longer with us, the late A.C. Elias Jr and the late Knight of Glin, for their invaluable input and expertise on hellfire club portraiture and aspects of the hellfire club phenomenon.

Research for this study was undertaken in libraries, archives and art galleries in Ireland and Britain. I am grateful to the staff of the following institutions for their courtesy and assistance: the Dublin City Library and Archive, the National Archives of Ireland, the National Gallery of Ireland, the National Library of Ireland, the National Museum of Ireland, the Public Record Office of Northern Ireland, the Royal Irish Academy, Trinity College Dublin, the Department of Irish Folklore at University College Dublin, the British Library, the Courtauld Institute of Art, the National Archives, Kew, and the National Portrait Gallery, London.

Thanks to Cos Egan for taking me to view the remains of the

hellfire club 'turret' in Doonass, County Clare, Don McGann for the photocopies, and Eamonn, Laura, Jen, Egon, Karina and Omar for their input, help and encouragement. Thanks to Keith and Diana for accommodating me during a research trip to Belfast. Many thanks also to Joan Ryan, Judy Ryan and Marie Ryan for reading and commenting upon sections of the work at draft stage, and Michael F. Ryan for offering general advice and assistance.

I would like to thank my publisher Lisa Hyde for her positive response to an early draft of the work and for encouraging me to expand it into the present full-length study, which she has resolutely supported for publication.

Some years ago a number of people assisted me with filming for a mooted documentary on the Dublin Hellfire Club. While this project was never realized, it inspired me to continue researching the subject, the result of which is the present publication. Thanks to Colin Killeen, Duncan Lacroix, Duncan MacFadyen, Des Mulcahy, John Mulcahy and Kerrill Thornhill for their assistance with this unfinished documentary. Perhaps some day it will be completed!

Note on the Text

Prior to the adoption of the modern Gregorian calendar in Britain and Ireland in 1752, each New Year legally began on 25 March rather than 1 January. In practice, however, Gregorian or New Style dates were frequently given. For instance, many Dublin newspapers of the period listed dates between 1 January and 24 March in composite form (e.g. 10 March 1737/38). New Style is used to refer to dates throughout the text. Where Old Style dates are quoted on newspapers, documents or extracts from documents, the New Style date is given in squared brackets.

The text contains many quotations from printed or manuscript primary sources. In these quotations capitalization has been standardized. Where names of people, places, months, etc. were italicized, these have been standardized to normal font. Spelling and punctuation have been left unchanged from the original.

List of Abbreviations

Add. Ms.	Additional Manuscript
BL	British Library
DEP	*Dublin Evening Post*
DG	*Dublin Gazette*
DIB	*Dictionary of Irish Biography from the Earliest Times to the Year 2002*, 9 vols (Cambridge, 2009)
DNB	*Dictionary of National Biography*
DNL	*Dublin News-Letter*
FDJ	*Faulkner's Dublin Journal*
FJ	*Freeman's Journal*
HJ	*Hibernian Journal*
HMC	Historical Manuscripts Commission
IFC UCD	Irish Folklore Collection, Department of Irish Folklore, University College Dublin
IHS	*Irish Historical Studies*
JCKAS	*Journal of the County Kildare Archaeological Society*
JRSAI	*Journal of the Royal Society of Antiquaries of Ireland*
NAI	National Archives of Ireland
NGI	National Gallery of Ireland

NLI	National Library of Ireland
ODNB	*Oxford Dictionary of National Biography*, 60 vols (Oxford, 2004)
PO	*Pue's Occurrences*
PRIA	*Proceedings of the Royal Irish Academy*
PRONI	Public Record Office of Northern Ireland
RIA	Royal Irish Academy
SNL	*Saunders' News Letter*
TCD	Trinity College Dublin
TNA	The National Archives, Kew, London
WHM	*Walker's Hibernian Magazine*

Chapter one

Introduction

On Mountpelier Hill in south County Dublin there stands an enigmatic ruined hunting lodge. Not easy of access, it lies on the crown of the hill beyond a sloping coniferous wood and a sharp rocky incline. On finally gaining the summit, walkers attain not only a superb view of Dublin City but also access to this oddly shaped two-storey stone structure. A number of gaping holes that once accommodated doors and windows line the ground and upper floors. Entrance through a low aperture reveals a dank interior adorned with scrawled graffiti and bestrewn with rubbish. The overall impression is of a not very hospitable, and on the whole rather foreboding, edifice. The building is known as the 'Hell Fire Club' or 'Hellfire Club', after the group of eighteenth-century aristocrats and gentlemen that supposedly once met there. For over two centuries it has been the subject of popular interest and many tales and legends. It is believed that here the Dublin Hellfire Club engaged in rampant orgies, excessive drinking and gambling, and sinister Satanic rituals. The most common folklore relates to members of the club being joined in a card game by a mysterious stranger who turns out to be the Devil. Other tales refer to banquets presided over by diabolical black cats, the burning of a butler or other servant, and the destruction of the lodge by fire.[1] Mountpelier is only the most well known of a number of locations in Ireland, mainly in remote rural areas, that are associated with so-called hellfire clubs. A roofless, brick-and-stone structure adjoining the Desmond Castle in Askeaton, County Limerick, is thought to have been the meeting place of the Limerick Hellfire Club, while a crumbling folly tower that overlooks the River Shannon at Doonass, County Clare, is believed to have been the rendezvous of a similar group. A castle that once stood at Grangemellon near Athy, County Kildare, was spoken of in similar terms prior to the demolition of its final remains in the twentieth century. The fact that no documented evidence has been found to support any of these claims has not prevented these locations from being associated with nefarious practices and supernatural occurrences.[2]

In the present day, the term 'hellfire club' summons up images of a mysterious elite society engaging in debauches, orgies, occult rituals and devil worship, with supposed connections to other enigmatic groups such as the Freemasons and the illuminati. The esoteric nature of the subject has lent it an enduring appeal. As well as being the subject of a number of sensationalist 'histories',[3] the hellfire club concept has inspired works of fiction, feature films and even popular music. That reliable barometer of popularity in the digital age, the Google search, will return over a million results for the term.[4] Originally, however, 'The Hellfire Club' was the name of an exclusive society that flourished in London around 1720. Consisting of a membership drawn from fashionable, upper-class circles, the club earned notoriety through its blasphemous conduct and its mockery of Christian doctrine and ritual. Although it was suppressed by order of George I in 1721, it had made a lasting impression on eighteenth-century society.[5] Before long, the term 'hellfire club' was used to refer to any upper-class group that was thought to engage in anti-Christian, blasphemous and diabolic activities. The most famous, or infamous, of all such groups was the Order of the Knights of St Francis, or Medmenham Monks, who met near West Wycombe, Buckinghamshire, in the 1750s and 1760s. Its founder was Sir Francis Dashwood, a well-known libertine and connoisseur of art, and its members included social and political luminaries such as John Montagu, 4th Earl of Sandwich, the MP John Wilkes and the poet Paul Whitehead. Although the group never actually called itself the 'Hellfire Club' it came to be popularly known by this name, and contemporaries derided it as a nest of 'black magic, outlandish orgies, and obscene parodies of the rites of Rome'.[6] There was much hyperbole in such accounts, and the activities of the Medmenham Monks were not as outrageous as was suggested. While they did hold mock religious ceremonies in which they attired themselves in monks' habits, there is no evidence that they actually practised devil worship. Indeed, their rituals and activities centred on sex rather than Satan.[7] Other upper-class groups that engaged in activities such as aggressive and riotous conduct or unbridled sexual indulgence were often bracketed alongside the hellfire clubs. Examples include the Mohocks, a violent gang of rakes that was active in London in 1712, and the Beggar's Benison, a sex-fixated society that flourished in Scotland from the 1730s.[8]

In Ireland, the hellfire club ethos made a significant impact on the world of the ruling elite, the Anglo-Irish Protestant upper classes. Over the course of the eighteenth century, members of the elite formed a number of hellfire clubs in different parts of the country. Some of these groups modelled themselves on, and took the name of, the original London club of the 1720s. Others went by different names, but exhibited similar characteristics and can be regarded as hellfire clubs in a generic sense. The most infamous group was the Dublin Hellfire Club, or Blasters, founded in the capital around 1737. Although it existed for only a short period, its impious and aggressive conduct caused a major furore. The blasphemous outbursts of one member were so offensive that the authorities ordered his arrest early in 1738. Later that year, another member – a peer of the realm – killed a servant in a drunken rage, with the result that he was indicted and tried for murder. These scandals precipitated the dissolution of the club. However, its provocative and esoteric ways appealed to other sections of the upper classes, and a number of imitative clubs were formed in different parts of the country. Some endeavoured to revive the Dublin Hellfire Club's blasphemous practices, others dedicated themselves to dissipation, while yet others engaged in violent and aggressive conduct. Around 1738 a group of local squires established a hellfire club in County Limerick. Although little is known about this group, it was probably a sister society of the Dublin Hellfire Club, with which it shared at least one member. Over twenty years later a number of County Kildare gentlemen formed another hellfire club, supposedly holding orgies at which a seat was kept vacant for the Devil. In 1770 another regional group, known as the Holy Fathers, caused uproar by holding banquets at which they uttered 'vile oaths, imprecations and blasphemies'.[9] The closing decades of the eighteenth century witnessed the emergence of a number of upper-class groups who were notorious for offensive and aggressive conduct. In the late 1770s and early 1780s a gang of thuggish young gentlemen known as the Pinkindindies disturbed the streets of Dublin, carrying out assaults, rapes, robberies and acts of vandalism. They were succeeded a decade later by the Cherokee Club, which scandalized Dublin society through its antagonistic disruptions of public entertainments. Although they did not engage in blasphemy and diabolism, the Pinkindindies and Cherokees were rooted in the violent and hedonistic traditions of the hellfire clubs that had preceded them. For contemporaries, they represented a final flourish of the hellfire phenomenon.[10]

Over the ensuing 200 years, a growing body of myth and legend served to sustain the memory of the Irish hellfire clubs. In so doing, however, it obscured their true nature. Even ostensibly historical accounts of the subject were often little more than recitals from folklore.[11] Louis C. Jones did offer a fact-based overview of the Dublin Hellfire Club in *The Clubs of the Georgian Rakes* (1942); however, he failed to provide adequate detail on the club's activities and principles, instead padding out his account with folkloric references. Since the publication of Jones's work there have been two other full-length studies of hellfire clubs: Geoffrey Ashe's *Do What You Will: A History of Anti-Morality* (1974; republished in 2000 as *The Hell Fire Clubs: A History of Anti-Morality* and in 2005 as *The Hell-Fire Clubs: Sex, Rakes and Libertines*) and Evelyn Lord's *The Hell-Fire Clubs: Sex, Satanism and Secret Societies* (2008). Both Ashe and Lord deal almost exclusively with British hellfire clubs, and while they do engage briefly with the Irish manifestation of the phenomenon, their analyses of it are poorly

informed and vague.[12] Thus, despite the fact that a large array of folklore has developed around the Irish hellfire clubs, their actual history
has been neglected.

It is the purpose of this book to chart the origins, activities and
demise of these clubs. It will explore the careers of the wasted
libertines, violent rakes, unscrupulous womanizers, inveterate duellists,
eccentric scientists and compulsive gamblers who belonged to them. It
will also investigate the social and philosophical contexts in which the
hellfire clubs operated, revealing how the diabolism and blasphemy that
made the Dublin Hellfire Club and the Holy Fathers notorious was
prompted both by the progressive forces of the Enlightenment and the
conservatism of Church and State. It will consider the aggressive and
destructive conduct of groups such as the Pinkindindies and the
Cherokee Club, why they behaved in such a manner and why so many
of their crimes went unpunished. Finally, it will look at the development of the rich corpus of folklore that might be collectively termed
'the hellfire myth'.

Club Culture, the Enlightenment and the London Hellfire Club

To understand why the hellfire clubs emerged when they did, it is
necessary to consider some of the pivotal social and intellectual developments of the late seventeenth and early eighteenth centuries. While
these developments occurred initially in Britain, before long they were
also key influences in Ireland. The first and most obvious was the rise
of club culture as a major social phenomenon. The second was the
emergence of the great philosophical movement known as the
Enlightenment.

Clubs and societies first began to appear in large numbers in Britain
during the late seventeenth century, as groups of middle- and upper-
class men – clubs were usually exclusively male – formed associations
in which they could pursue certain aims and objectives, or simply
converse and be sociable. Many different types of club were established,

including political societies, charitable and industrious groups, intellectual and philosophical societies, and drinking clubs. Factors such as the growth of cities and towns, improved living standards and the reduced role of central government contributed to this process.[13] However, the most important development was the increased proliferation of coffee houses and taverns as locations in which men could meet and mingle. Coffee houses and taverns not only housed clubs, they also sometimes engendered them, as informal gatherings of like-minded individuals often developed into formally constituted groups and associations. Crucially, coffee houses also stimulated debate. They were repositories of printed media, and the venues to which men retired in order to discuss the social, political and religious issues of the day. As Máire Kennedy puts it, 'coffee houses were closely allied to the supply of news, transmitted orally and through the medium of newspapers and pamphlets . . . [they] were convivial spaces central to the social life of the city, associated with trade and commerce, science and natural philosophy, politics, journalism and the law, and located in the busiest part of town with a conspicuous public profile'.[14] The coffee house environment facilitated the spread of Enlightenment philosophy, which advocated a more sophisticated society based on scientific and rational principles. 'Enlighteners' committed themselves to 'emancipating mankind through knowledge, education and science, from the chains of ignorance and error, superstition, theological dogma, and the dead hand of the clergy . . . and to practical action for creating greater prosperity, fairer laws, milder government, religious tolerance, intellectual freedom, expert administration, and not least, heightened individual self-awareness'.[15] This process was heavily influenced by the scientific advances of the seventeenth century: Sir Isaac Newton, for instance, had demonstrated that miracles were incompatible with the laws of modern science. As a result of such discoveries, orthodox values that had long been held to be universal truths, such as the principles and strictures of Biblical Christianity, began to be called into question.

Enlightenment discourse provided ample fuel for debate in clubs, taverns and coffee houses. This process was encouraged by intellectuals such as Joseph Addison, whose contributions to the periodical *The Spectator* provoked debate on social, moral and philosophical issues.[16] Such debate became increasingly fashionable among members of an educated and cultured class, who 'preened themselves upon their own progressive opinions and "polite" lifestyles, picking up a smattering or more of Voltaire and Co. – maybe just as a veneer, but sometimes as part of a genuinely new way of living'.[17] Many of these self-proclaimed freethinkers were keen to express reservations about Biblical Christianity and show their appreciation for alternative ideologies such as deism.[18] For some, the logical conclusion of the realization that the earth and the universe operated according to scientific rather than divine law was atheism. This viewpoint was not without its attractions, as disbelief in an afterlife was a persuasive argument in favour of indulgence in pleasure. Since body and soul were destined for dissolution, it made sense to indulge oneself: 'why should I go without my part of pleasure, since this life is my Portion, and this my Lot, and since my time is a shadow, and after my end there is no returning'.[19] Furthermore, the Enlightenment concept of individual rights, including the right to indulge in pleasure, was taken as justification for excessive and self-indulgent behaviour.[20]

It was out of this milieu that the hellfire clubs emerged. The members of these clubs were generally wealthy, propertied men who chose to devote their time and money to hedonistic excess. First and foremost, hellfire clubs were convened for the purposes of conviviality and pleasure, and so much the better if self-indulgence could be justified by philosophical argument. Yet they also took Enlightenment criticism of religious orthodoxy to new extremes, mocking and inverting Christianity and its rituals. Churches, clergymen and social conservatives were viewed as archaic, superstitious and repressive, and, as such, fit subjects to be lampooned through blasphemy and sacrilegious behaviour. The Hellfire Club founded in London around 1720 was the prototype for a whole range of succeeding British and Irish groups. Its president, Philip, 1st Duke of Wharton, was one of the most controversial and provocative noblemen of the day. Born in 1698, he was the only son of Thomas, 1st Marquis of Wharton. In 1715 he rebelled against his father's authoritarian and controlling influence by eloping with Martha Holmes, the penniless daughter of an army officer. Following the embittered marquis's death later that year, Wharton succeeded to the title. Still a minor, he was sent to the Continent to complete his education under the watchful eye of a Calvinist tutor. Before long he wearied of the tutor's moralizing and abandoned his studies, travelling to Avignon to meet James Francis Edward Stuart, the Jacobite king-in-exile or 'Pretender'. While this flirtation with an enemy of the Hanoverian monarchy was injudicious, it did not prevent Wharton from being elevated to a dukedom following his return to England.[21] He was now regarded as one of the realm's most controversial noblemen, a reputation that was enhanced by his involvement in the notorious Hellfire Club.

Contemporaries identified the club as an ungodly society where young people met in order to, 'in the most impious and blasphemous manner, insult the most sacred principles of our holy religion, affront Almighty God himself, and corrupt the minds and morals of one another'.[22] Another account put the club's membership at forty, fifteen of whom were 'ladies of considerable quality'. The reported presence of female members is intriguing: it seems that the male-only rule by which upper-class clubs usually operated did not apply in this instance. The same account stated that the Hellfire Club held meetings to 'ridicule the Holy Trinity and the mysteries of religion by blasphemy and unrepeatable profanities'.[23] Such meetings may have been held in public places. Daniel Defoe's description in *A Journal of the Plague Year* (1722) of a group of blasphemers who met at a London tavern is thought to have been inspired by the club:

> a dreadful set of fellows . . . met there every night, [and] behaved with all the revelling and roaring extravagances, as is usual for such people to do at other times, and indeed to such an offensive degree, that the very master and mistress of the house grew first asham'd and then terrify'd at them . . . they were not afraid to blas-

pheme God, and talk atheistically... this tavern, where they held
their club, being within view of the church door, they had the
more particular occasion for their atheistical profane mirth.[24]

Yet some of the Grub Street accounts of the club's practices probably
owed more to imagination than reality, such as the much-cited story
that one of the members ordered a 'Holy Ghost pie' at a tavern. The
historian John Oldmixon acknowledged that 'the coming to particu-
lars seem'd to give greater ground to the belief of such a wicked
society, than perhaps there was cause for'.[25] Nonetheless, the widely
advertised accounts of the club's practices outraged public sensibilities,
precipitating its suppression in 1721.

Apart from Wharton's group, there may have been two other similar clubs active in London and Westminster at this time, though it is
unclear whether these were separate entities or different branches of
one organization.[26] In any event, the Wharton club was the first group
to call itself 'the Hellfire Club'. It may itself have evolved from an
earlier society. According to Oldmixon, the members of the London
Hellfire Club 'were branch'd out from the Scowrers and
Mohocks... and were guilty of the like extravagancies'.[27] He was not
the only contemporary observer to connect the London Hellfire Club
with the Mohocks, a notorious gang of gentlemen who haunted the
streets of London in 1712, violently waylaying anyone unfortunate
enough to stray into their path. The Mohocks wounded and abused
their victims in an eccentric manner. They slit the noses of some, and
manhandled others into barrels, which they then proceeded to roll
downhill. Female victims, many of whom were servants, were subjected
to particularly wanton violence. One maidservant was pulled so
violently that her arm was dislocated, while a victualler's wife was flung
onto the cobblestones, causing her to miscarry the child she was
bearing. Watchmen and isolated males were also attacked. There was
widespread public revulsion at the Mohocks' crimes and several were
brought to trial. In June 1712 four members of the gang, including Sir
Mark Cole, a baronet, and Robert Squibb, a gentleman, were

convicted. However, the sentences that were handed down to them, consisting of relatively insignificant fines, were in no way proportionate to their crimes.[28] The lenient treatment of gentleman miscreants was a common feature in the eighteenth-century courts system.

Although the activities of the London Hellfire Club and the Mohocks attracted considerable controversy, it is arguable that their Irish counterparts were even more prone to extreme and violent behaviour.[29] The eccentricities and excesses of the Duke of Wharton paled in comparison with the near-psychopathic conduct of the Dublin Hellfire Club's most notorious member, Lord Santry. Equally, the assaults and acts of vandalism perpetrated by the Mohocks were arguably less brutal and less destructive than those carried out by Dublin's Pinkindindies two generations later. That members of the Anglo-Irish Protestant elite chose to behave in such a manner was not altogether surprising. Sections of the elite had long been known for their hedonistic excesses and their willingness to resort to violence. To appreciate why this was the case, it is necessary to consider the distinctive social and political circumstances that prevailed in eighteenth-century Ireland.

The Protestant Elite in Eighteenth-Century Ireland

The shape of Irish society in the eighteenth century was determined by the wars of the seventeenth, when Catholics and Protestants struggled for mastery of the country. Having emerged triumphant in the final, decisive conflict, the War of the Two Kings (1689–91), Protestants enacted penal legislation designed to ensure that their Catholic opponents could never again threaten their supremacy. Despite the fact that Catholics comprised the majority of the population, they were subjected to a range of crippling restrictions. Having already undergone large-scale losses of property following the Cromwellian conquest of 1649–53, they suffered further confiscations under the Williamite regime, with the result that by 1703 only 14 per cent of the land in the country remained in their hands. Laws such as the *Act to*

Prevent the Further Growth of Popery (1704) ensured that those Catholics who did possess property found it difficult to extend or even retain their estates. In addition, Catholics were denied the right to vote or sit in Parliament.[30] Presbyterians also faced restrictive measures, though not to the same degree as Catholics, who were effectively reduced to the status of third-class citizens. The Protestant population, meanwhile, occupied a position of extraordinary social and political dominance. The Protestant nobility and gentry stood at the apex of society. They owned the bulk of the country's property, oversaw military and political affairs and enjoyed an unprecedented level of privilege. Only land-owning Protestants could vote, and only their interests were represented in the Irish parliament.[31] They effectively constituted an elite within an elite, one that came to be known as the Protestant Ascendancy.

Despite such dominance, all was not well within the world of the Ascendancy. Its members were gripped by a strong sense of insecurity, stemming in no small part from the very real limitations that were placed on their ability to control their affairs. The Protestants of Ireland would not have triumphed in the War of the Two Kings without the assistance of their British and continental co-religionists, and in political, legislative, economic and military terms they were heavily dependent on Britain.[32] Poyning's Law, which remained in operation until 1782, required the Irish parliament to submit legislation to the British monarch for approval before it could be enacted. As the English writer Edward Lloyd observed in 1732, 'the proceedings of Irish parliaments are in a manner only form. For not a bill can pass into a law before it be sent to London and approv'd by the king and council.'[33] Moreover, laws enacted by the English parliament ensured that Ireland's economic interests were subordinate to those of Britain. Late seventeenth-century measures such as the Cattle Acts and the Woollen Act imposed a series of prohibitive duties and bans on Irish products and commercial interests and fuelled resentment. Finally, Ireland's Protestants remained acutely conscious that the position of precedence that they had latterly attained could easily be lost. A rebellion by the dispossessed Catholic majority, or a military intervention by the Pretender, remained disconcerting possibilities even in times of apparent peace and security. As one historian noted, 'the ascendancy was always very conscious, and scared of the under-currents of the fractured society over which it presided'.[34] In the event of a Catholic rebellion or invasion, the ascendancy would be forced to have recourse to the military might of Britain.[35]

Faced with these realities, sections of the elite manifested 'a certain savagery of mind', engaging in excessive and abandoned behaviour, particularly when it came to socializing. It was not uncommon for the gentry to hold extravagant banquets at which huge quantities of food and alcohol were consumed.[36] Newcomers to the country were appalled by the inebriation that they witnessed at such feasts. The Earl of Orrery, who took up residence in Ireland in the 1730s, commented that 'drunkenness is the touch stone by which they try every man, and he that cannot or will not drink, has a mark set upon him. He is abus'd behind his back, he is hurt in his property, and he is persecuted as far as the power of malice and intemperance can go.' William James Conolly, who also moved to Ireland in the 1730s, was equally aware of the incontrovertible social obligation to drink. His wife observed that 'his head had not been enough settled to do anything for drinking you know does not agree with him 'tho he must practise it a little at his first coming into the country or he wou'd not please'.[37] For many, claret was the tipple of choice. Moralists such as George Berkeley, the Bishop of Cloyne, and the Rev. Samuel Madden commented disapprovingly on the excessive consumption of wine, with Berkeley observing that Ireland was one of Bordeaux's most avid customers.[38] Such claims are reinforced by statistics: during the 1720s, over twelve million gallons of wine were imported into the country every year.[39]

Upper-class excess and volatility did not derive solely from social and political insecurity, however. Madden felt that its origins were also to be found in 'the original customs and manners, of those who came over as adventurers in the many wars, and troubles that so frequently happened here'.[40] Indeed, some of the country's wealthiest and most prominent dynasties had been founded by Cromwellian soldiers and settlers.[41] Their militaristic origins frequently induced an aggressive approach to social interaction. On the whole, the Anglo-Irish gentry proved to be more willing to engage in violent altercations and encounters than their English counterparts. One of the strongest indications of this was in the fondness for duelling. Motivated by firmly held notions of honour and social prestige, duels occurred with increasing regularity as the eighteenth century progressed. When Edward Lloyd described Irish gentlemen as 'generous and hospitable, as well as brave in single combat with the small sword and pistol', he may well have had his tongue in his cheek.[42] It could as easily have been said that they were extravagant and quarrelsome, and many of those who deemed themselves gentlemen were justifiably criticized for coarse and ungentlemanly behaviour.

Yet it would be wrong to maintain that all members of the Protestant elite behaved in such a manner. Individuals such as Berkeley and Madden were representative of a more refined and progressive element in upper-class society. '"Improvement" was one of the great buzzwords of the eighteenth century' and much energy was directed towards economic development and the extension of 'civility'. Some even concerned themselves with academic and antiquarian pursuits, exploring the natural history, geography and antiquities of the country.[43] These industrious and moralistic Protestants were disheartened and outraged by the self-indulgent and aggressive conduct that they witnessed among their peers, particularly those who formed hellfire clubs.

Clubs and Societies in Ireland

Club culture was slower to commence in Ireland than in Britain. This was partly due to the instability of Irish society in the late seventeenth century. Even after the conclusion of the War of the Two Kings, upper-class society remained heavily militaristic, with the gentry and nobility more likely to associate with one another in the context of aggressive encounters than in the confines of clubs and societies.[44] Partly as a result of this, and partly owing to a paucity of coffee houses in towns and rural areas, club activity outside of Dublin and Cork was limited in the early eighteenth century. In the capital, however, a range of different associations began to appear, including philosophical societies, scientific societies, religious societies, political clubs, trade associations and Masonic lodges.[45] The city centre, between the Parliament House on College Green and Dublin Castle on Cork Hill, was a hive of social and recreational activity, as a 'sparse supply of public rooms obliged sundry groups to use the cheerful spaces in inns and coffee houses'. MPs, government officials and army officers met in these establishments, and so, to an increasing degree, did clubs.[46]

Many clubs and societies placed great emphasis on excessive drinking and conviviality. This was particularly evident among politically oriented societies such as the loyalist Hanover, Aughrim and Boyne clubs, who were concerned with commemorating the Protestant victory in the War of the Two Kings, the various anniversaries that were important to the Protestant succession, and the 'glorious and immortal' memory of William of Orange. Such commemorations frequently occasioned heavy drinking: a total of thirty-five healths were drunk at a banquet held in Dublin in May 1724 to celebrate the birthday of George I.[47] The Hanover Club, which met at the Rose Tavern on Castle Street, was described as being ruled over by Bacchus 'with his liquid whip'. The Earl of Orrery remarked:

> A right jolly glorious-memory Hibernian never rolls into bed without having taken a sober gallon of claret to his own share. You wonder perhaps what this animal is? It is a yahoo that toasts the glorious and immortal memory of King William in a bumper without any other joy in the revolution, than that it has given him a pretence to drink so many more daily quarts of wine...[48]

Loyal clubs were not the only political societies active in the city. There were also Jacobite groups such as the Swan Tripe Club, which frequented the Swan Tavern on Cork Hill. The club's members were accused of drinking 'seditious toasts' and of disloyal, drunken and licentious behaviour generally.[49] In a poem published in 1706, the sign of the Swan Tavern, 'In all his milky plumes, and fether'd letchery', was taken to symbolize the Roman god Jove, 'Patron of whoring, and of toping too'.[50] Although this politically motivated satire aimed to present the Swan Tripe Club in the worst possible light, it was not without some truth. Yet if its members were given to drunken and licentious conduct, the Swan Tripe Club was no different from many other eighteenth-century clubs.

The progressive and moralistic members of society, meanwhile, formed associations dedicated to the achievement of their purposes. Apart from the Dublin Society (founded in 1731), which focused on the development of industry and agriculture, the Incorporated Society (also founded in 1731) aimed at the improvement of the young through schooling, while the Physico-Historical Society (1744) endeavoured to document the natural resources, local customs and history of the country. Significant clerical participation bore witness to the moral agendas that underlay these societies, and in many ways they were diametrically opposed to the hellfire clubs.[51] Indeed, the conflict between two significant elements of upper-class society – one civil, industrious and polite, and the other raucous, extravagant and violent – can be witnessed in microcosm in the history of the hellfire clubs. Those who were involved in the latter pursued new extremes of drunken excess, blasphemy and violence. In so doing they provoked a series of major controversies.

Hellfire Clubs and Rakish Clubs

The motivations of those who established or joined hellfire clubs in Ireland can only be guessed at, and tended to vary from club to club. At least one historian has claimed that hellfire clubs were primarily convened as drinking clubs,[52] and it is true that convivial pleasure was very important to the Irish groups: drink and drinking vessels feature prominently in the group portraits of the Dublin and Limerick hellfire clubs, now in the National Gallery of Ireland. Hellfire clubs offered gentlemen companionship and the opportunity to drink heavily, gamble unrestrainedly and behave in a boisterous manner. While this in itself was not shocking – conviviality was a key constituent of eighteenth-century club life – heavy drinking helped to fuel the clubs' more controversial activities. Their meetings, for instance, were rumoured to involve a fair amount of sexual excess, as well as homosexual activity, which was a criminal offence at the time.[53] More ominously, hellfire club members, whether in groups or as individuals, were also known to have committed murders and sexual assaults.

Quite apart from this, the systematic blasphemy and mockery of Christian ritual that these clubs engaged in was highly controversial. The conservative and censorious environment that prevailed in eighteenth-century Ireland helped to motivate such activities. For decades, the civil and ecclesiastical establishments had attempted to silence the Enlightenment deists and atheists who dared to question the orthodoxies of Christianity. The hellfire clubs offered an extreme protest against this by blaspheming vociferously and flaunting diabolic symbols. Influenced by their own rudimentary appreciation of Enlightenment philosophy, they aimed to show their contempt for the traditional Christian interpretation of existence, while provoking the conservatives who adhered to that interpretation. Such disdain was even more pronounced when it came to Catholicism; the adherents of that faith were dismissed as 'silly priest-rid fools' in a letter that was attributed to a member of the Dublin Hellfire Club.[54]

Groups such as the Pinkindindies and Cherokees lacked a diabolist or blasphemous agenda; however, as raucous, upper-class groups they were often juxtaposed with the hellfire clubs. In considering the differences between these two varieties of club, it is useful to employ the libertine–rake schema outlined by Daniel Statt. While the terms 'libertine' and 'rake' are often used interchangeably, they were in fact two distinct types in the eighteenth-century social milieu. The libertine was, supposedly, a man of taste, cultivation and wit, who concerned himself with sybaritic and sexual self-indulgence, but who also had intellectual opinions. The rake, on the other hand, was 'the aggressive, the violent, the destructive' side of the libertine – an upper-class thug and vandal who operated without much intellectual exertion.[55] Broadly speaking, the Dublin Hellfire Club might be regarded as a libertines' society: its founding members were the intellectually gifted Earl of Rosse and the artist and playwright James Worsdale. Other members of the club also had intellectual pretensions, as did the Holy Fathers, who believed themselves to be too sophisticated for Biblical Christianity. Their appreciation of Enlightenment philosophy, however inchoate, led them to deny that entities such as heaven and hell existed. The Pinkindindies and the Cherokee Club, on the other hand, concerned themselves with perpetrating drunken assaults and acts of vandalism. These activities are best seen in the context of 'the violent subculture of the rake'.[56] For the purposes of this study, upper-class groups that had an agenda of blasphemy, anticlericalism and irreligion are referred to as hellfire clubs. Those that were more narrowly focused on hedonism and aggression, notably the Pinkindindies and Cherokees, are described as rakish clubs.

While the Dublin Hellfire Club of the 1730s is generally believed to have been the first Irish hellfire club, there is no definite evidence that this was case.[57] However, even if it was not, it was certainly the most well known. The cloud of scandal and shame generated by its members' excesses took some time to dissipate, and over the remainder of the eighteenth century and beyond its name was uttered with a sense of mingled awe and outrage. Nonetheless, the two individuals who established the club managed to avoid any official retribution for their actions. One of these men was an erstwhile Grand Master of the Freemasons and arguably the city's most infamous libertine: Richard Parsons, 1st Earl of Rosse. The other was an English painter and play-wright, a wit, mimic and womaniser with a knack for turning virtually any situation to his advantage: James Worsdale. Despite Worsdale's humble origins he, like Rosse, was used to the high life, mingling with the nobility and gentry in a milieu of entertainments, balls and festivities. Outside of the beau monde, however, they traversed a more insalubrious environment. For early eighteenth-century Dublin was a precarious place, fraught with poverty, danger and instability.

Chapter two

The Dublin Hellfire Club

Today, the term 'Georgian Dublin' summons up images of fine redbrick townhouses, wide boulevards, grand squares, and set-piece buildings such as the Custom House and the Four Courts. This impressive urban environment resulted largely from the projects of property developers such as Luke Gardiner (1745–98) and the work of the Wide Street Commission, which replanned the metropolis at the end of the eighteenth century, laying out iconic thoroughfares such as Parliament Street, Westmoreland Street and Sackville Street. In 1786, law and order received a vital new impetus from the establishment of a dedicated police force. In the 1730s, however, the great era of Georgian building had not yet truly commenced, and the city in which the Dublin Hellfire Club operated was more a relic of the medieval era than a harbinger of modernity: chaotically planned, socially unstable and poorly policed. Arriving in the capital, a visitor from the country would have been struck by the filth and smell of the place. Poor sanitation and rubbish-collection systems, as well as the ubiquity of horses and livestock, meant that refuse and excrement (human as well as animal) littered the streets. Scavengers, appointed by the Corporation, were responsible for keeping the streets clean, which they did with varying degrees of efficiency.[1] The piles of ordure that they gathered were deposited in the Liberties, prompting street names such as 'Dunghill Lane' and 'Dirty Lane'. The filth, which stank particularly badly in the summer months, obscured dangerous holes and fissures in the surface. Pedestrians also had to allow for the fact that the streets were laid out in a haphazard and impractical manner. The central part of the city was a maze of narrow, poorly lit alleys and laneways: Skinner Row, the main thoroughfare leading to the Liberties, was no more than fifteen or sixteen feet wide.[2] Many streets were overshadowed by tall, front-gabled houses, and, as ground floor windows admitted little in the way of daylight, the main rooms of coffee houses were usually situated on first floors to maximize the available light for reading.[3] At night-time, much of the city lay in pitch darkness. Although oil-fuelled public lighting was introduced in the late seventeenth century, its application was sporadic and those who wished to move about by night sometimes had to engage lantern-boys to light their way.[4] When the street lamps were lighted, however, Dublin could look impressive. On winter evenings, those crossing Essex Bridge from the south were confronted with 'three long vistos, resembling fire works, both up and down the river, and before your face, [i.e. along Capel Street] as you pass the bridge from the old town'. This was the commercial hub of the city: to the east of Essex Bridge, the Liffey was congested with sailing ships and smaller vessels, clustered around the old Custom House on the south bank of the river. Adjoining the bridge itself, an equestrian statue of George I, a symbol of the Protestant elite's loyalty to the ruling house of Hanover, surveyed the scene impassively.[5]

The means by which people moved through Dublin depended on their social status and financial situation. Unlike the grandees who belonged to the Hellfire Club, most of the city's 120,000 inhabitants were impoverished. While the poor generally went on foot, some were fortunate enough to have alternative means of transport, such as 'an old beggar man' who 'used to be drawn about the streets by an ass on a carr'.[6] A variety of other conveyances were available, ranging from crude carts to two-wheeled chaises to elaborate coaches drawn by four or more horses. The latter were the preserve of the nobility and gentry, who also travelled about in sedan chairs, closed vehicles seating one person, carried at front and rear by servants known as chairmen. Sedan chairs and their bearers could be hired for as little as sixpence per trip;

however, many members of the upper classes had their own chairs and chairmen.[7] Traffic congestion was an ongoing problem. As many streets were barely wide enough to allow two coaches to pass one another, the sedan chairmen and hackney coach drivers who stopped on or near busy thoroughfares to ply for hire often succeeded in bringing proceedings to a standstill.[8] It was also a noisy environment, with one contemporary singling out hackney drivers as the authors of much of the racket: 'the coachmen have so hoarse and frightful voices, and their continual lashing of their whips increase[s] their noise in such a horrid manner, that they seem so many furies in the regions of Pluto'. These sounds mingled with 'the hideous cries' of street vendors selling their wares. They, along with porters of various kinds, could be seen hunched under the burdens they carried on their backs or heads – sacks of produce, churns of milk, baskets of foodstuffs, bundles of birch twigs, baskets of dirt.[9] Most of these poor inhabitants lived out precarious existences, plagued by the lurking threat of starvation should their livelihoods fail. Whatever goods and money they possessed were under constant threat from pickpockets, sharpers, thieves and burglars. There was little prospect of assistance from the forces of law and order: the antiquated and inefficient parish watch system, another leftover of medieval times, was wholly inadequate to deal with the hordes of criminals that beset the city.

Needless to say, the nobility and gentry lived in a more salubrious world. They resided in spacious townhouses on smart new boulevards such as Henrietta Street and Molesworth Street, venturing forth to take the air at fashionable resorts like St Stephen's Green or the City Basin, a reservoir situated near St James's Street. Their concerns were the management of their estates, politics, administration and military affairs. When not at work, they attended balls at Dublin Castle, or frequented musical concerts, plays and other fashionable events.[10] The social whirlwind was at its most intense during the 'parliament winter', the six months of every second year during which the king's representative, the Lord Lieutenant, held court. During this time, the nobility and gentry flocked to attend the weekly balls and drawing-room nights that were held at Dublin Castle.[11] It was during one such season, that of 1737–38, that a number of noblemen and gentlemen came together to form the Dublin Hellfire Club. The opulent settings in which they operated seemed a world away from the squalid environment that surrounded the poor. Yet the two worlds could not be kept entirely separate, for, like other grandees, the members of the Hellfire Club employed many servants, some of whom suffered to a fatal degree from their masters' excesses. Members of the club also ventured periodically into the city's poorer quarters in search of late-night street affrays and, occasionally, prostitutes. One of the most ardent participants in these activities was the club's founder and probable president, Richard Parsons, the 1st Earl of Rosse. His reputation as one of Dublin's most hardened libertines was not undeserved.

Richard Parsons, 1st Earl of Rosse

'His boyhood bespoke, and his manhood maintained the reputation of being the most finished libertine within the four seas.'[12] This late nineteenth-century assessment of the career of the Earl of Rosse is an exaggeration, but it does give a sense of the headlong career of debauchery and excess that earned him lasting notoriety. Born around 1696, Richard Parsons succeeded to the title of 2nd Viscount Rosse following his father's death in 1703. Under the guardianship of William, Lord Berkley of Stratton, and James Butler, 2nd Duke of Ormond, he spent his boyhood and youth in England. The only surviving portrait of Rosse, painted by William Gandy, dates from this time (see Plate 2). It shows a cherubic child aged about 10, the antithesis of the dissolute libertine he later became.[13] On 7 April 1713 he requested permission from one of his guardians to enrol at Christ Church College, Oxford, which he did the following month. Placed under the watchful eye of a minder, an 'honest gentleman' by the name of Captain Williamson, the 17-year-old Rosse was restless.[14] A letter he wrote to one of his guardians, probably Ormond, several months later betrayed his desire to break free from the constraints of childhood and enter into London society:

I had ye honour of your Graces second letter which counter-
mands the leave you were pleased to give me for London, but
assurd me of that pleasure in a little time if I continue to do well,
I submit in this as I shall in all other things to your Graces pleasure and promise you my behavior shall be such as shall
recommend me to your favor, I would not have asked but most
of our young noblemen are gone or going to London.[15]

Although nothing else is known of Rosse's initial attempts to venture
onto the London social scene, he was not long in choosing a bride. On
25 June 1714 he married Mary Paulet, niece of the Duke of Bolton, at
Gray's Inn Chapel in London.[16] Two years later he moved to Ireland,
perhaps to take charge of the considerable estates he had inherited
there.[17] In August 1717 Rosse took his seat in the Irish House of Lords.
The Duke of Wharton, receiving the Irish peerage of Marquess of
Catherlough, was in attendance on the same day.[18] The two men must
have met and recognized one another as kindred spirits. They were of
a similar age and shared a liking for drink and dissipation, an underly-
ing Jacobitism and a strong disregard for orthodox religion. Each of
them later became infamous as the founder of a hellfire club.

In June 1718 Rosse was made an earl. A few months later, his wife
died at Westchester in England, having borne him two sons, Richard
and James, and a daughter, Elizabeth. The following year he married
again, to Frances, daughter of Thomas Claxton of Dublin. With her he
had another son, who died in infancy. Having settled in Dublin, the
wealthy and hedonistic earl sought ways to occupy his time.[19] Although
a member of the House of Lords, he had little interest in political affairs
and repeatedly failed to turn up for its meetings. However, he did
possess certain Jacobite sympathies, probably inherited from his forebears: his grandmother had married the Jacobite Earl of Tyrconnell,
while his father had been expelled from Parliament in 1696 for refus-
ing to support a Williamite association.[20] On 10 June 1726, the
Pretender's birthday, a Jacobite mob rioted in St Stephen's Green. It was
rumoured that on the same day Lord Rosse, wearing the Jacobite

symbol of the white rose, had provoked a duel with an army officer and been killed. Although the report was false, it suggests that the earl's Jacobite sympathies were common knowledge.[21] Nonetheless, he was prepared to renounce them for practical purposes; the following year he took the oath of abjuration in the House of Lords, denying the legitimacy of the Jacobite succession.[22]

Rosse was able to make such concessions because the appeal that politics held for him was limited at best. Described as 'eccentric and vicious, but clever and accomplished',[23] he was interested in arcane lore and mysterious practices, not to mention entertaining himself in sociable settings. It seemed inevitable, therefore, that he would become involved in a convivial and pseudo-mystical movement that was then sweeping through Britain and Ireland. Freemasonry had spread rapidly following the establishment of the Grand Lodge of England in 1717. Although Freemasons consorted with one another mainly for convivial purposes, there was a strong esoteric element to their practices. Masonic lodges 'bound their members with bizarre entrance rituals that sometimes blasphemously parodied the rites of the church'.[24] Such practices held considerable appeal for Rosse, who became Grand Master of the Irish Grand Lodge in 1725, presiding over its banquets and participating in its secret ceremonies.[25] The degree to which secrecy and mysticism were important in these rituals is evident from a contemporary description of the induction of Rosse as Grand Master on 24 June 1725:

> the Grand Lodge, composed of the Grand Master, Deputy Grand Master, (who was absent) Grand Wardens, and the masters and wardens of all the lodges, retired to the room prepared for them, where after performing the mystical ceremonies of the Grand Lodge which are held so sacred, that they must not be discover'd to a private brother; they proceeded to the election of a new Grand Master...and the proxy of the Senior Grand Warden acquainted the Society, that the Grand Lodge had chosen the Rt Hon. earl of Ross[e], Grand Master for the year ensuing...then

the officers of the Order, &c. went to the Grand Lodge Room, and conducted this new Grand Master in great state to the head of the mystical table, and [the] Mason King at Arms hung the gold trowel by the black rib[b]on about his neck.[26]

When not engaged in Masonic activities, Lord Rosse pursued an extravagant social life. For a time, at least, his finances were sufficient to support this. The income from his extensive estates in Leinster was not inconsiderable, and in 1731 he came into even greater wealth on the death of his grandmother, the dowager Countess of Tyrconnell. It was rumoured that she left a bequest of close to a million pounds, the majority of which went to Rosse.[27] Even allowing for exaggeration, the inheritance must have been massive and its recipient did not hesitate to squander it, spending extensively in taverns and gambling at the groom-porter's gaming tables in Dublin Castle. More controversially, Rosse was also known to take part in late-night affrays and other disorderly activities. Such conduct attracted the adverse notice of the more conservative elements of Dublin society. As Jack Pilkington, son of the famous poet and memoirist Laetitia Pilkington, noted,

> a nobleman could not, in so censorious a place as Dublin, lead [such] a life... without being a general topic for reproach and having fifty thousand faults invented to complete the number of those he had... his Lordship's character was torn to pieces every where, except at the groom porter, where he was a man of honour; and at the taverns, where none surpassed him for generosity.[28]

This reputation for generosity was well founded. Reports of his inheritance had occasioned 'the general joy of the citizens, that nobleman having been formerly one of their greatest benefactors'. This was only one of a number of laudable qualities that Rosse possessed. He was also extremely witty, affable and liberal, and regarded as 'a nobleman of great sprightliness and vivacity'.[29]

By the late 1730s, Rosse had drifted away from Freemasonry which, despite its rituals and secretive nature, was regarded as a highly respectable institution. Perhaps it was too respectable for Rosse, who was given to provocative conduct designed to infuriate those conservative elements that had torn his character 'to pieces'. Clergymen appear to have been the chief sufferers of his outrageous practical jokes. When the philanthropically-inclined Dr Samuel Madden visited Rosse's residence on Molesworth Street to solicit funds for a charitable cause, he encountered more than he bargained for:

> His Lordship, on being told that the doctor was in the parlour, shrewdly guessing at his business, immediately stript himself stark naked, and, and in this state, came running into the room with out-stretched arms, saying, 'worthy Dr Madden, I am glad to see you, how do you do? shake hands with me Doctor, when I heard you were here, I was in such a hurry to see you, that I would not wait to put on my clothes.' The doctor shocked at the wild spectacle, leapt up, and was for hastening out of the room; but his Lordship stopped him saying, 'my dear doctor, don't be in a hurry, tell me your business, I would be glad to do any thing to serve you.' The doctor pushed past him, but his Lordship accompanied him to the street door, where he stood for some time as a *show* to the people passing by.[30]

While the incident bore witness to Rosse's fondness for pranks, it also demonstrated his dislike of Madden, an avid critic of upper-class excess,[31] and other moralists. He regarded such people as the sanctimonious and censorious representatives of an outmoded world view, and wanted to goad and outrage them as much as possible. In the English painter James Worsdale, whose acquaintance he probably made sometime in 1737, he found a willing accomplice to help him further this agenda of provocation. The two men conceived of a club that would make drunkenness and sexual excess its ordinary business, and take blasphemy to hitherto unheard-of extremes.

James Worsdale

The son of an impoverished colour-grinder, Worsdale was born in England around 1692. As a young man he became a servant in the house of, and an apprentice to, the renowned court painter Sir Godfrey Kneller.[32] In later years he would claim to be Sir Godfrey's illegitimate son; indeed, his continual boasting that he was 'Kneller's bastard' so irritated Laetitia Pilkington that she commented: 'some people [are] so fond of family, that, to keep it up, they would prove themselves sons of whores'.[33] Although he was diminutive in stature (the engraver George Vertue described him as 'a little cringing creature') and possessed of limited artistic ability, Worsdale's garrulous, charismatic personality and his talent for mimicry won him considerable attention and a number of lucrative commissions. On occasion he even painted members of the royal family, including George II himself, and other luminaries such as Henrietta Pelham, the Duchess of Newcastle.[34]

Worsdale is also believed to have painted a conversation piece that has been variously titled *Portraits of W. Domville, Esq., and a Group of his Friends* and *W. Domville and Friends at the Hell Fire Club* (see Plate 3). The painting is stylistically similar to Worsdale's group portrait of the Dublin Hellfire Club; however, as Adrian Le Harivel notes, 'the facial expressions and gestures are more consciously refined than in Worsdale's other pictures'.[35] It also recalls the work of Sir Godfrey Kneller, indicating that if Worsdale did paint it, he may have done so at an early point in his career when he was still under Kneller's influence.[36] The painting depicts three gentlemen, only one of whom can be firmly identified: the full-lipped, rather decadent-looking man seated on the right. This is William Domvile (1686–1763), proprietor of a substantial estate at Loughlinstown, County Dublin, and scion of a prominent Protestant family that had established itself in Ireland in the early seventeenth century.[37] The fact that Domvile left Ireland permanently in 1714 in order to pursue a fashionable existence in London indicates that the painting was executed in that city. It is possible, therefore, that it depicts members of the original London

Hellfire Club, and that Worsdale had contact with this group, if only in the capacity of portrait-painter.[38] It is not known if this flirtation with London's most notorious society damaged his standing within the Kneller household. In any event, his tenure there was cut short in 1722 when he was dismissed for covertly marrying Lady Kneller's niece.[39]

Deprived of Kneller's guidance and protection, Worsdale may have initially found it difficult to build an artistic career in the unforgiving world of Georgian London. In the mid-1720s he went to Ireland,[40] where he mingled in polite society, attracting many admirers through his 'poignant table chat and conviviality'. Chief among these was Cadwallader Blayney, 7th Baron Blayney (1693–1733). It is unlikely that Worsdale profited financially from the relationship as Blayney was short of cash on a consistent basis.[41] However, the resourceful Worsdale understood that there were more ways than one for a struggling artist to raise finance. By the early 1730s he had returned to London, where he participated in various schemes, one of which involved the pre-eminent poet of the day, Alexander Pope. In May 1733 the publisher Edmund Curll received a visit from a mysterious clergyman who offered to sell him a number of Pope's letters for unofficial publication. Curll described his visitor as 'a short, squat man . . . He had on a clergyman's gown, and his neck was surrounded with a large lawn barrister's band. He showed me a book in sheets almost finished, and about a dozen original letters, and promised me the whole at our next meeting.' Curll, though suspicious of the vendor's motives, eventually printed the letters. It later transpired that Pope himself had engineered the whole affair so that he could publish a 'correct' edition of his letters in response to Curll's 'bootleg' edition: 'the stratagem effectively drew attention away from the sheer effrontery of a living poet printing his own letters, which had never been done before'.[42] The mysterious clergyman was none other than James Worsdale, who had seemingly inveigled his way into Pope's employ. It was not the last time that he put his talent for disguise and mimicry to profitable use.

Worsdale was also acquainted with a lesser-known poet, the clergyman Matthew Pilkington, husband of Laetitia. Matthew had arrived in

London in the autumn of 1732, having virtually abandoned his wife and children in Dublin. When Laetitia arrived for an impromptu visit in August 1733, her disinterested husband did his best to pawn her off on Worsdale, who made amorous advances towards her. Despite Laetitia's claims to the contrary, there may have been a dalliance.[43] If so, it was a short-lived affair, as she returned to Dublin not long afterwards. In the meantime, Worsdale and Pilkington mixed with 'a hard-drinking, heavy-gambling set' that included Edward Walpole, the son of Sir Robert Walpole.[44] The two became close friends, and Worsdale's artistic and literary career benefited considerably from Walpole's patronage. In 1735 he dedicated his play *A Cure for a Scold* to his benefactor, expressing his gratitude 'for favours of which my present happy condition is the best proof'.[45]

Two years later, Walpole was appointed secretary to the new Lord Lieutenant of Ireland, the Duke of Devonshire. On taking up office in Dublin in the summer of 1737, Walpole soon found himself in receipt of letters requesting his 'favour & protection'.[46] Unwilling to deprive himself of those same benefits, Worsdale followed his patron to Dublin. Walpole had complete access to the upper echelons of society and was well placed to introduce Worsdale to leading noblemen such as the Earl of Rosse, with whom the painter became closely associated. Worsdale also made a significant impact on the city's dramatic and artistic scene. In January 1738 *A Cure for a Scold* opened at Smock Alley Theatre, where it ran for several months. A few weeks later Worsdale secured a commission to portray no less a personage than the Lord Lieutenant himself. However, some believed that he had imported negative, as well as creative, influences into Dublin.[47] Rumours began to circulate that he and Lord Rosse had 'established a hell-fire club at the Eagle tavern on Cork hill'.[48] Another party concerned in this enterprise was a hard-drinking, unstable young nobleman, Henry, 4th Baron Barry of Santry. It was he who provided Worsdale with his next artistic commission.

Portrait of a Hellfire Club

Sometime in 1737 or 1738, five men gathered around a table in a house in Dublin or its immediate vicinity. As was evident from their splendid attire and carefully powdered wigs, they were high-ranking members of the nobility and gentry. It was also clear from their easy postures and the presence of wine, wine glasses and a punchbowl that they were well used to leisurely self-indulgence. They were members of the city's most notorious society, the Hellfire Club, and they had come together in order to pose for a group portrait. Although the Earl of Rosse was a notable absentee from the scene, most of the other members were present and the artist who was about to commit their likenesses to canvas was none other than James Worsdale. The large oil-on-canvas conversation piece that he produced (see Plate 5), which was later housed in Lord Santry's mansion, Santry Court, was probably intended to commemorate the foundation of the club.[49] It shows four men seated around a table covered by a green cloth, with a fifth standing at the rear. Two of the seated men have laid a hand on the shoulder of the adjacent person in a gesture of camaraderie. At the centre of the table is a silver punchbowl containing a straw-covered bottle of wine, and each man has a wine glass to hand. Trees can be glimpsed through an arched window to the rear, indicating a rural setting, possibly Santry Court. Lord Santry himself is seated to the left of the table in pride of place. He wears a splendid azure coat trimmed with gold, symbolic of his wealth and ostentatious lifestyle. With his right hand he strokes a spaniel; with his left he presents the other members of the club. They are identified as Colonels St George, Ponsonby and Clements, and Mr Luttrell.[50]

While it is not stated who is who, the figure standing at the rear bears a close resemblance to a 1744 mezzotint of Brigadier General Richard St George, an accomplished soldier from a military family of long standing.[51] Born in 1670, St George had an auspicious start to his career, joining Sir George St George's regiment as an adjutant on 1 July 1690, the date of the Battle of the Boyne. In 1696 he married

Elizabeth, daughter of Richard, 1st Baron Coote of Clooney. Although the union was childless, St George did father at least one illegitimate child. In 1695 he was elected MP for the borough of Galway and from 1715 he represented his family borough of Carrick, County Leitrim. These spells in Parliament did not interfere unduly with his military career as he achieved a series of promotions. On 27 June 1737 he was appointed colonel of the 20th Royal Regiment of Foot, by which time he was almost 67 years old.[52] Yet he was not the only old soldier in the group. The figure seated in the centre, attired in black, is probably Colonel Henry Ponsonby, whose familial background and career closely mirrored St George's. Born in 1685, Ponsonby belonged to an Anglo-Irish family that had risen to prominence following the Cromwellian conquest, amassing large estates in counties Kilkenny and Tipperary. In 1705 he became a captain in the 27th Foot, seeing service in the West Indies and Spain. He too pursued a political career, serving as MP for Fethard, County Wexford, from 1715 to 1727, and Innistiogue, County Kilkenny, from 1727 to 1745.[53] In 1735, after being made colonel of the 37th Foot, Ponsonby 'turned once more to soldiering in earnest'. He maintained a disciplined regiment that was commended when it was reviewed in Kilkenny in June 1736.[54] The regiment was stationed in Dublin periodically, and it was probably during these times that Ponsonby fraternized with the Hellfire Club. At the time of the club's foundation he was around 52 years old. The black-wigged man seated to his left may be Captain Henry Clements (later to achieve the rank of lieutenant colonel). Clements was considerably younger than his two military colleagues. Born in 1704, he had joined the army as an ensign in the 1720s, attaining the rank of captain in 1733. He represented the borough of Cavan in Parliament from 1729 to 1745 and was probably the most politically active member of the Hellfire Club, being nominated for thirty-seven parliamentary committees between 1731 and 1741. Clements was regarded as a handsome man. Although he was outranked by St George and Ponsonby, he derived considerable prestige from the fact that he was the brother of the prominent government official Nathaniel Clements, allowing him to stand almost on a par with senior officers and giving him access to exclusive clubs.[55]

St George, Ponsonby and Clements all belonged to significant Anglo-Irish families that had made their fortunes in the country during the seventeenth century. As senior army officers and Members of Parliament they enjoyed high rank and privilege. While they may have been attracted by the club's anti-Christian ethos – according to a contemporary, freethinking was rampant in the army[56] – they probably joined the Hellfire Club principally for the purpose of convivial recreation. None of the three officers attained the notoriety of other club members such as Rosse and Santry. The advanced age of St George and Ponsonby may have prompted them to be more circumspect in their actions than their younger club-mates. Henry Clements, also, would have been unwilling to antagonize his brother Nathaniel, on whom he relied for money.[57]

The last individual featured in the portrait, seated on the extreme right, is probably Simon Luttrell of Luttrellstown, County Dublin. Luttrell belonged to a family that had earned enduring notoriety among Irish Catholics: during the War of the Two Kings his father, the Jacobite officer Colonel Henry Luttrell, had defected to the Williamites. In 1704 Luttrell married Elizabeth Jones. She bore him two sons: Robert, and Simon, who was born in 1713.[58] Four years later Colonel Luttrell was shot and mortally wounded as he returned to his townhouse in Stafford Street, Dublin. The assassination seems to have been arranged by his first cousin, Thomas Grace, who bore Luttrell, 'from whom he received no kindness', considerable ill will, and was said to have 'declared an hatred and malice' towards his sons.[59] It is possible that such assertions were designed to mask the identity of the real party behind the assassination: Luttrell's wife was said to have orchestrated it in revenge for her husband's dalliances. The Luttrellstown estates devolved to Robert, the elder son. However, he died on his travels in Europe and the inheritance passed to Simon. Following the completion of his education at Eton, Simon embarked on the Grand Tour in the early 1730s. Accompanied by his governor

Captain Maule, he visited Florence and Siena, and probably also Rome and Naples.[60] On his return he joined an exclusive new London club, the Society of Dilettanti, which restricted membership to gentlemen who had been to Italy and declared itself to be 'desirous of encouraging at home a taste for those objects [of antiquity] which had contributed so much to their entertainment abroad'. Yet the club was 'essentially... a dining society', 'dining' denoting heavy drinking as well as eating.[61] At this time, Luttrell fraternized with Sir Francis Dashwood, later to attain prominence as president of the Medmenham Monks, the notorious hellfire club of West Wycombe. In 1737 Luttrell married Judith Maria Lawes, daughter of Sir Nicholas Lawes, the Governor of Jamaica. In the same year he attempted to sell his estates at Luttrellstown, perhaps with a view to settling permanently in England. However, another Simon Luttrell, possibly a distant relative, disputed his title to the property, lodging a bill against him in the Court of Chancery.[62] This seems to have scuppered the intended sale, and the estates remained in the possession of Simon Luttrell of Luttrellstown and his family until the end of the century. While his abortive attempts to sell the estates were underway, Luttrell was based temporarily in Dublin, where he socialized with those who shared the Dilettanti's commitment to conviviality and exclusivity. He may have made the acquaintance of the Hellfire Club through his fellow Dilettante William Ponsonby, a nephew of Colonel Henry Ponsonby.[63] Although a man of questionable character, Luttrell could be an affable companion when he chose. According to one commentator, 'a more agreeable man could scarcely be found. He was the delight of those whose society he frequented, while he resided in Dublin.'[64]

The overall impression that the painting imparts is of a group of wealthy and powerful notables, well-established members of the Protestant elite. The fact that the club included two members of the House of Lords and three members of the House of Commons might give the impression that it was a sort of retreat for politicians, like the Kit-Cat Club of early eighteenth-century London or Daly's Club of 1780s–90s Dublin (see Chapter 6). However, this is unlikely. The

Hellfire Club was a much smaller and more elite group than Daly's. Neither Rosse nor Santry was politically inclined, while Colonels Ponsonby and St George were more concerned with military matters than their duties as Members of Parliament. The club was convened principally for the purposes of conviviality. What set it apart from other convivial groups was its willingness to engage in conduct of an extreme and provocative nature that included rampant licentiousness, overt blasphemy and random acts of aggression.

The Hellfire Club At Large

Between late 1737 and early 1738, the Earl of Rosse and Lord Santry were conspicuous by their absence from meetings of the House of Lords. Santry was present on 23 November, but only pursuant to an express order of the House. He was not seen there again until March of the following year, and Rosse appeared to have given up attending altogether.[65] It is likely that both men gave themselves over to the affairs of the Hellfire Club during this period. The club quickly became notorious for its excesses, which were often conducted in public. Its heavy drinking sessions were sometimes followed by rape attempts and violence, ending in murder on at least one occasion. Many such rampages would have commenced at the club's principal meeting place, the Eagle Tavern, situated on the northern side of Cork Hill between Crane Lane and Blind Quay.[66] Although many public houses of the time were little more than crude, converted private residences, the Eagle was a well-appointed and commodious establishment that was 'reckon'd the best tavern in Dublin'. Fronted by an open court known as the lord chief baron's yard, the tavern served food as well as drink and offered long-term accommodation.[67] It also acted as a meeting place for several other elite societies, including the Aughrim and Hanover clubs and the Freemasons.[68]

Any attempt to describe what went on at the Hellfire Club's gatherings at the Eagle Tavern must be largely conjectural, as no records or minutes have survived, if indeed any were kept to begin with.

Nonetheless, a sense of their activities can be gleaned through combining what is known of eighteenth-century tavern and club life with the surviving contemporary references to the club, its members and their activities. It is likely that the tavern-keeper, Mr Lee, provided a private room for the club's meetings. Here, they would have been attended by servants, possibly their own footmen as well as waiters and 'drawers' employed by the house.[69] Dinner was probably served; the Freemasons held banquets at the Eagle and there is no reason to think that the Hellfire Club did not do likewise. However, when seated at table the club's chief concern was the consumption of alcohol. Rosse, Santry and Worsdale were known to be hardened drinkers, and it is likely that the other members also partook heavily. As the group portrait indicates, punch – prepared using citrus fruits and brandy – and claret were the beverages of choice. It seems that a set of special, commemorative wine glasses, each bearing a member's name and honorary title, were used. One such glass – Worsdale's – survives. Inscribed 'The Hell Fire Club' and 'James Worsdale Master of the Revels' (see Plate 6), it is similar to those depicted in the club portrait. An engraved illustration on the glass shows a group of men gathered around a table bearing wine bottles and a punchbowl, with one standing proposing a toast.[70] Like the group portrait, this evokes the Hellfire Club's status as a drinking club. This reputation was sustained in later years by folkloric references to the consumption of scaltheen, a 'fiery' beverage made from hot whiskey, butter and sugar (see Chapter 7). Yet the club was more than a drinking society. Historically, 'Master of the Revels' was the title given to the individual within the British royal household whose responsibility it was to organize entertainments and festivities. Its allocation to Worsdale suggests that it was his job to set out a schedule of activities for the club's evening amusement.[71] Sexual indulgence figured prominently on the list of priorities. When the club-mates had had their fill of drink, their thoughts turned to more prurient activities.

Certain eighteenth-century hellfire clubs were preoccupied, and in some cases obsessed, with sex. The best known are the Beggar's Benison, active in Scotland from the 1730s, and Sir Francis Dashwood's

Medmenham Monks. The rituals undertaken by these groups possessed a strong sexual dimension, as did the ceremonial objects they utilized. Their actual sexual activities probably did not extend beyond masturbatory practices and relations with courtesans and other females. In the case of the Medmenham Monks, however, commentators inflated these activities into graphic accounts of orgies and black masses.[72] That the Dublin Hellfire Club was also seen in this light is evident from a curious contemporary broadsheet, *An Ample Discovery of the Damnable Cabal, Commonly Known by the Name of the Hell-Fire Club* (see Plate 7). Purporting to be a letter from 'Moloch', a club member, to a prospective recruit, the broadsheet portrayed the club as a diabolic cabal of sexual excess and deviancy. Though undated, it was probably published in 1737 or 1738 when the club was at its most active. The broadsheet describes the supposed initiation procedure for new members, as overseen by 'Pluto', the club's Grand Master. According to the text, the initiate was required to swear an oath to Pluto, promising to abandon 'all that is called good, by silly priest-rid fools' and to 'let nothing share the least part of my favour, but what is solely urg'd by my most vicious and libidinous desires'. Consistent with this emphasis on sexual indulgence, the letter maintained that the newly enrolled member had 'immediately at command all his boundless wishes can desire; performance waits his will, and when he bids, 'tis done! 'Tis here, and only here, where brightest nymphs do constantly abound, to satiate our constant craving appetites; nor do we meet but when our lusts run high, and nature rallying gives new force to love.' Other 'memorable' activities are also mentioned, such as the 'sacrificing [of] a maid', a probable reference to the taking of a girl's maidenhood. An allusion to the admission of 'a molly', an effeminate or homosexual man, points to a possible homosexual dimension to the club's activities.[73] If there was such a dimension, it was not without precedent in the world of the hellfire clubs: in April 1726 several members of a 'sodomodical or hellfire society' in London were tried and convicted for the offence at the Old Bailey.[74]

It is unlikely that the Hellfire Club had any involvement in the composition or publication of the broadsheet. Its salacious tone is redolent of the work of a sensationalist or printer's hack hoping to cash in on the notoriety of the club. While the author may have drawn on rumours that were circulating as to the club's activities, its content was probably invented to enhance the broadsheet's commercial appeal. *An Ample Discovery* was aimed at the same market that avidly consumed the last speeches of condemned criminals, which were also published in broadsheet form.[75] In its reference to 'subterranean, diabolical divertisements' conducted under the aegis of Lucifer and the libertine Don Juan, who had been damned to hell, the broadsheet also highlighted the supposed satanic character of the club's proceedings. The members may have been content to allow such material to circulate, as it served to extend the sense of allure and mystique surrounding their activities. It may even have had some grounding in truth. There is a strong suggestion of the burlesque – dressing up and engaging in rituals – in the broadsheet, and such activities may indeed have been comprehended within the club. Certainly, Worsdale liked putting on costumes and playing roles, and not just on stage. The broadsheet also makes reference to the presence of 'female acquaintance[s]' at the club, and at least some of its members were in the habit of engaging prostitutes or courtesans.

The Earl of Rosse enjoyed the company of prostitutes; 'whoring' was one of the many vices of which he was accused on his deathbed by a clergyman vainly hoping to secure his repentance. It was Worsdale's job to procure female company for Rosse,[76] and while he could readily obtain common prostitutes in the brothels of Smock Alley, a stone's throw from the Eagle Tavern, it is likely that 'women of quality' were preferred. Worsdale may have directed his club-mates towards the rooms of upper-class women who, though not necessarily courtesans, were unprotected and therefore considered fair game. Laetitia Pilkington found herself in this predicament in late 1737. Her separation from her husband Matthew in October or November of that year left her isolated, vulnerable and at the mercy of Dublin's rakes and libertines. Not long afterwards she found herself besieged in her lodgings by Rosse and several 'persons of distinction', whose number may have included other members of the Hellfire Club. She described how after the party broke into the house she was forced to lock herself in the dining room to escape their attentions: 'when those worthy peers could not find me, they threaten'd to kick the landlady...being disappointed, they were forced to decamp, cursing, and vowing revenge against the woman of the house'.[77]

While Mrs Pilkington had a narrow escape on this occasion, other vulnerable females may have been less fortunate. In her memoirs, Laetitia alluded to Worsdale's philandering on several occasions.[78] In 1741, a satirical poem alleged that he was in the habit of seducing his clients' wives and mistresses while in employment as a portrait-painter: 'Must he uncensur'd artfully Procure? / Frequent, as Painter, his Employer's House? / And thence delude his Mistress or his Spouse? / True to the Lover's procreating Cause, / He breaks all Ties, all hospitable Laws, / And Pimps, resistless, while his Pencil draws.' Worsdale instituted a suit for libel in response to this, but tellingly lost his case. The enthusiasm with which he engaged in sexual liaisons is testified to by his fathering of at least five illegitimate children.[79] The sexual proclivities of the other members were probably not far removed from those of Rosse and Worsdale. Simon Luttrell, for instance, proved to be a notorious womanizer in later life, and is likely to have been more active in early manhood.[80]

Women were not the only victims of the Hellfire Club. Its members also engaged more generally in violent conduct that recalled the activities of London's Mohocks. The Earl of Rosse participated, Laetitia Pilkington's son Jack noted, in 'rackets, brawls and midnight confusion',[81] and Lord Santry was prone to sudden and unpredictable acts of aggression. Both would have had ample opportunity to get involved in affrays in the vicinity of Cork Hill, one of the more insalubrious parts of the city. The area was a matrix of narrow, winding alleys, and the aggressive conduct of its denizens, along with the absence of an effective police force, contributed to a dangerous atmosphere at night-time.[82] Cork Hill itself was crammed with a number of dubious establishments that played host to rakish gentlemen. As well as the

Eagle, there was the Cock and Punch Bowl Tavern, the Hoop Tavern, the Cockpit Royal and Lucas's Coffee House.[83] Sedan chairmen were allowed to ply for hire on Cork Hill, although it was stipulated that they must 'stand close by the houses in a range one after another', in a manner similar to that of a modern-day taxi rank.[84] These chairmen, along with waiters from Lucas's Coffee House and the Eagle, were known for their aggressive conduct. They routinely insulted and molested passers-by, whom they drenched with pails of filthy water. One chairman got more than he bargained for in 1727 when he used 'unmannerly language' towards a gentleman at the entrance to Lucas's and received in reply a sword-cut that almost severed one of his fingers.[85]

The atmosphere inside the coffee house, which was situated directly across the street from the Eagle, in Cork House, could be equally dangerous. Caustically referred to in a satirical poem as 'that fam'd place, where slender wights resort... Where exil'd wit ne'er shews its hated face, / But happier nonsense fills the thoughtless place', it was a rendezvous for rakes and duellists and a troublesome spot for the unwary.[86] Several duels were fought in its backyard and the establishment was popularly known as 'surgeon's hall', owing to the supposed frequency with which dead bodies were laid out on its tables.[87] Its notoriety persisted even after its eventual demolition in 1768: in 1773 Horace Walpole, commenting on a contemporary dramatic work, remarked that 'Persian princes love single combat as well as if they had been bred in Lucas's Coffee House.'[88] However, it is not known if members of the Hellfire Club were involved in any of the affairs of honour that took place in Lucas's or elsewhere. Although Lord Santry was said to be a duellist, notching the barrel of his pistol to mark each 'deed of blood' he had committed, there is no evidence to support the claim that it was necessary to have killed a man in a duel in order to qualify for admission to the club.[89] Indeed, Santry was known more for his aggressive conduct off the duelling field, and the casual violence he perpetrated proved fatal on more than one occasion.

Lord Santry

The excesses of Rosse and Worsdale pale into insignificance when compared with the murderous deeds of Lord Santry, the most infamous member of the Hellfire Club. Born in Dublin in 1710, he was the only son of Henry, 3rd Baron Barry of Santry, and his wife Bridget, a member of the Domvile family of Templeogue and a friend of Jonathan Swift. Lady Santry doted on and indulged her son.[90] Her husband, meanwhile, was an alcoholic who was posthumously blamed for setting his son a bad example. When the latter was indicted for murder in 1738, the Countess of Orrery remarked that 'his mother is to be pityed much, but all her ills proceed from not having a due regard for vertue in her choice of a husband, for maybe had she been only Mrs Coghill her son would have been as great a comfort to her as this lord is a shame & grief'.[91] By January 1735, the 3rd Baron had 'by hard drinking...brought himself into so great a disorder, that his life is dispaird off'. He died soon afterwards and his son succeeded as 4th Baron Barry of Santry.[92]

The new Lord Santry's inheritance was considerable, comprising estates in counties Dublin, Meath and Carlow. In October 1735 he took his seat in the House of Lords.[93] A keen horse-racing enthusiast, he was noted for his polite and rational demeanour while sober. However, he was increasingly disposed to spend his time drinking, which unleashed an altogether darker and more destructive side of his character.[94] Santry's drink-fuelled excesses were so notorious that Jonathan Swift felt compelled to confront the Lady Dowager Santry about the matter, even though he 'had hardly the least acquaintance with your Lord, nor was at all desirous to cultivate it, because I did not approve of his conduct'. Yet she was blind to her son's faults and unwilling to rebuke or restrain him. Swift was coldly rebuffed, provoking him to wash his hands of the affair: 'all I had said to you proceeded from friendship, and a desire of reforming your son. But that desire is now utterly at an end.'[95] On 8 May 1737, Santry married his bride of choice, Anne Thornton, 'a young lady of fine accomplishments, great beauty and good fortune', at Finglas. While it might have been expected that marriage would pacify the baron, his 'barbarous and cruel treatment' of his wife served only to increase his infamy.

Reportedly, Santry avoided prosecution for his various misdeeds by bribing witnesses, to the great annoyance of the general public, which was 'not a little exasperated on seeing so vicious a career pursued with impunity'.[96] It was probably in the context of Hellfire Club activities that he committed the worst of these unpunished crimes. This was an atrocity that went well beyond the bounds of normal upper-class excess: the killing of an ill and bedridden sedan chairman in a horrific and seemingly unprovoked attack:

> One of the murders laid to Lord Santry's charge was of the most wicked complexion; to wit, his having forced a poor chairman (that had been used to carry him) lying sick a-bed to drink a quart of brandy; then, with kindled spirits, he set fire to the sheets, &c. the wretch lay in, who soon expired in the most excruciating torture.[97]

The memoirist Andrew O'Reilly (1782–1862) stated that several members of the Hellfire Club were involved in this murder, the scene of which he identified as a tavern in Saul's Court.[98] Located east of Fishamble Street, not far from Cork Hill, Saul's Court was 'a mean court or ally... not within the immediate observation of the passers through the thoroughfare near at hand although it could be gained in a moment by a sharp detour from one of the most thronged quarters of the city'. The Court was principally inhabited by shopkeepers and small-scale businesspeople, the most prominent of whom was the Catholic distiller and grocer Laurence Saul.[99] His premises may have been the 'tavern' at which, by O'Reilly's account, Santry and his club-mates seized the unfortunate chairman, 'threw back his head, and poured brandy down his throat until the poor fellow could no longer swallow... and then set fire to it! The man died.'[100]

It is possible that the murder occurred as part of a mock-diabolic ritual. Certainly, other groups were known to engage in such activities. In May 1738 the Dublin press reported on a murder that took place at a 'Masonic' initiation ceremony in Philadelphia. Here, a young apprentice became the victim of his master and a number of associates. Pretending to be a Masonic group, they 'initiated' the young man in a mock ritual that involved the use of a pan of burning spirits containing raisins. One of those present 'was wrap'd in a hide to represent the Devil', and the ritual culminated with the pan of spirits being thrown over the 'initiate' with the result that he was burned to death.[101] Whether members of the Hellfire Club were aware of this incident and decided to enact something similar for their own amusement will remain a moot point. Whatever its motivation, the atrocity committed by Lord Santry became firmly embedded in folk memory, inspiring many later tales of the burning of servants during the Hellfire Club's carouses (see Chapter 7). However, Santry was not prosecuted for the crime; probably money changed hands and the affair was hushed up. Yet the public clamour against the baron's excesses could not be ignored forever, and the authorities awaited an opportunity to undertake proceedings against him.

In some respects, the club's activities were no different from those of other elements in society. Their predilection for alcohol was not unusual. Nor were their assaults on vulnerable females such as Laetitia Pilkington, occurring as they did in a male-dominated society in which women enjoyed little in the way of rights or consideration. Beyond this, however, the club did much to make itself notorious in Dublin. Lord Santry had shown himself to be a dangerous and unpredictable individual. His penchant for violence had resulted in one fatality, and it was clear that it could not be allowed to continue unchecked. In addition, thanks to the circulation of sensationalist material such as the *Ample Discovery* broadsheet, the club had earned a reputation for engaging in conduct of a sexually deviant and diabolic nature. This inevitably caused a stir in the rather reserved and censorious social environment that prevailed in the city. Soon, the club added fuel to this fire by directly invoking diabolical forces and engaging in shocking, publicly articulated blasphemy. This was largely due to its association with another English painter, a young, atheistic miniaturist named Peter Lens.

Chapter three

The Demise of the Hellfire Club

In February 1738, the Irish House of Lords ordered its Committee for Religion to undertake an investigation into the 'notorious immorality and profaneness' that was believed to be pervading society. The committee commenced an enquiry, examined a number of persons under oath and, a few weeks later, reported back to the House of Lords. They claimed to have uncovered 'an uncommon scene of impiety and blasphemy', involving 'several loose and disorderly persons' who had 'of late erected themselves into a society or club, under the name of Blasters; and used means to draw into this impious society, several of the youth of this kingdom'. A number of witnesses had testified to the extraordinary conduct of Peter Lens, a 'painter, lately come into this kingdom, who professes himself a Blaster'. Lens (and by implication the other members of the group to which he belonged) was in the habit of praying to the Devil and uttering 'the most daring and execrable blasphemies against the sacred name and majesty of God'. This caused consternation in official circles. The Committee for Religion recommended that Lens be called to account for his actions and that 'atheistical and blasphemous clubs' be investigated.[1]

It is likely that the Blasters and the Dublin Hellfire Club were one and the same. Lens had formerly been based in London, where he was well known for his atheistic bluster. Having moved to Dublin in 1737, he fraternized with Worsdale, whom he probably knew from London's artistic circles. By March of the following year Jonathan Swift was identifying the two men as leaders of the Blasters (or Hellfire Club). Lens's blasphemous outbursts and proclamations of devotion to the Devil gave an added impetus to the club's diabolic posturing, securing its reputation as a cabal of devil worshippers.[2] To understand why the club behaved in this manner, and why an atheist such as Lens would pray to the Devil, it is necessary to consider the conservative nature of society in early eighteenth-century Ireland, and how those who bridled against this conservatism came into conflict with the clergymen, moralists and other pillars who sought to defend it.

The Hellfire Club and the Enlightenment

Despite the fact that the members of the Dublin Hellfire Club routinely behaved in a raucous and aggressive manner, there is evidence that they regarded themselves as intellectuals in the mould of the Enlightenment deist Matthew Tindal (1657–1733). Tindal's *Rights of the Christian Church Asserted* (1706) had attacked the clergy, accusing them of deliberately confusing and complicating religion in order to justify their involvement in the religious lives of people. While it is not hard to see how such sentiments appealed to the anti-clerical Earl of Rosse, it appears that the Hellfire Club were also interested in – or at least affected to be interested in – other aspects of Tindal's philosophy. In *Christianity as Old as the Creation* (1730), Tindal contended that natural religion was superior to revealed or institutional religion. This controversial assertion, which provoked some thirty published ripostes from the conservative establishment, was embraced enthusiastically by the Hellfire Club. A contemporary critic of the club observed that as far as they were concerned, the doctrines of Christianity were nothing more than 'speculative opinions...which piece of wit I am told they borrowed from one Tindall'.[3] The club would have been further attracted by Tindal's apparent libertinism: reputedly, he was 'an egregious fornicator'.[4] Nonetheless, there was a considerable gulf between Tindal's philosophy and that of the Hellfire Club.

It is unlikely that members of the club exerted themselves to a great degree to comprehend the finer points of Enlightenment discourse. Their intellectual capabilities were sneered at: 'is there no difference between the knowledge of the Bishop of Cloyne and Peter Lens? Yes, as much in their understanding and learning, as in their virtues and worth.'[5] Furthermore, even in his more extreme attacks on institutional Christianity, Tindal did not recommend that it be lampooned through wholesale blasphemy. The Hellfire Club became notorious for such conduct, which can be seen as a sort of protest against the extraordinarily censorious social environment that prevailed in early eighteenth-century Ireland: although freethinkers such as Tindal suffered censure in England, their counterparts on the other side of the Irish Sea were subjected to greater condemnation.

The most notable Irish 'Enlightener' was the Donegal native John Toland, whose most famous work, *Christianity Not Mysterious* (1695), alleged that the clergy used the so-called mysteries of Christianity as means of exerting control over others. This resulted in the book being publicly denounced and burned in Dublin in 1697. There were calls for the same punishment to be meted out to Toland himself, and he fled to London to avoid arrest.[6] On the basis of Toland's experiences, Voltaire inferred that Irish society was more censoriousness than English: 'having been persecuted in Ireland for the most circumspect of his works, he was never bothered in England for the most audacious books'.[7] The Anglo-Irish establishment's desire to defend institutional Protestantism was unrelenting because of the perception that the spread of freethinking would pave the way for a restitution of Catholicism: 'if genuine Christians were once clearly rooted up, popery, or fanaticism, might be raised instead'.[8] Even mild expressions of dissent, such as Edward Synge's *The Case of Toleration Consider'd, with Respect both to Religion and Civil Government* (1725), were condemned.[9]

Many chafed under this repression, and having acquired a measure of confidence they embarked in the late 1720s on a vehement protest against institutional religion. Freethinkers began to make their opinions heard in Dublin's coffee houses, which were described in 1729 as 'so many divinity schools; nor is there a tavern or ale-house kitchen which escapes the noise and insults of divinity wranglers...old creeds [are] abrogated, new ones substituted, and absurd and incongruous systems of religion hourly introduced – This foul practice of argumentizing frequently prevails in parties of pleasure.'[10] A 1730 pamphlet identified a 'dissolute' group of atheists active in the country. Nor was protest against the Establishment confined to those with atheistic beliefs. There were also expressions of deliberate sacrilege, which provoked a stern reaction from the authorities. In 1729 two men were tried in Dublin for drinking 'healths to the devil and his angels, and confusion to Almighty God'.[11] The Hellfire Club was rooted in this tradition of atheistic and blasphemous expression. Lord Rosse's disdain for the clergy was an expression of his general opposition to institutional religion and the hold that the Christian churches exerted on the minds and morals of the people. The antipathy that he felt towards this state of affairs, and the pious conservatism of society in general, prompted him to engage in outrageous and provocative behaviour. Stripping naked to receive a visit from the eminent clergyman Samuel Madden was one form of protest exercised by Rosse. Convening a hellfire club that blasphemed to a hitherto unheard-of degree was another. Members of the club – or like-minded individuals – also went so far as to disrupt church services. One such incident was believed to have occurred 'in the most blasphemous and riotous manner' in the parish church of Omagh, County Tyrone, in 1737 or 1738.[12] Yet of all the club's activities, the one that caused the greatest uproar was its inauguration of a campaign of systematic and outrageous blasphemy. The principal agent of this development was Peter Lens.

Born in 1714 or 1715, Peter Lens was the son of Bernard Lens, an English painter who became miniaturist in ordinary to George I. Peter followed his father's trade and achieved some success as a miniaturist. Described by the engraver George Vertue as 'an ingenious youth', he attracted notoriety through his 'vile, athe[i]stical conversations and behaviour, publickly practised'.[13] Following his arrival in Dublin, where he counted both Worsdale and Matthew Pilkington among his acquaintances, he quickly earned the reputation of 'a rude fellow', unconstrained by notions of propriety. On one occasion in late 1737 he actually broke into Pilkington's bedchamber while he and his mistress 'were administering Christian Consolation to each other'.[14] Worsdale probably drew Lens into the ambit of the Hellfire Club. Although the miniaturist was of lower social standing than most of his club-mates, particularly Rosse and Santry, they may have found his atheistic and blasphemous outbursts amusing. He possibly acted as a sort of impious court jester to the Hellfire Club, coining new oaths and outrageous profanities that expressed the club's disdain for institutional religion and its practitioners. He may also have suggested that the club change its name to the 'Blasters', an obvious pun on 'blasphemers'.

Blasphemy and Devil Worship

By early 1738, the Blasters or Hellfire Club was outraging 'all serious Christians' by publicly articulating a range of newly invented blasphemous expressions. George Berkeley, the Bishop of Cloyne, was scandalized. His reaction reflected the outrage felt by many moralists and defenders of religious orthodoxy: 'It is no common blasphemy I speak of: It is not simple cursing and swearing; It is not the effect either of habit or surprize; but a train of studied deliberate indignities against the Divine Majesty; and those, of so black and hellish a kind, as the tongues alone which uttered them, can duly characterize and express.'[15] More detail on the nature of these 'indignities' was provided in the report of the Committee for Religion. Lens had described himself as 'a votary of the Devil . . . offered up prayers to him, and publickly drank to the Devil's health'.[16]

Were the members of the Dublin Hellfire Club, then, actually devil worshippers? There appeared to be some basis for asserting that they were: the very name 'Hellfire Club' invoked the sense of occult diabolism that had been attributed to its London predecessor almost twenty years earlier. Moreover, Lens's expressions of devotion to the Devil seemed like outright worship of the powers of darkness. The club's reputation for diabolism seems to have been furthered by its use of items that featured diabolic devices and ornamentation. The Irish Chippendale furniture of the early eighteenth century, made of dark mahogany and decorated with grotesque faces and carved lion's feet, seemed appropriate for use in nefarious rituals. A Chippendale table believed to have been used by the club resurfaced in 1904. It was described as having 'an unmistakeable carved resemblance on one side of his Satanic Majesty, and . . . four supporters, which terminate in what look uncommonly like cloven hoofs'.[17] Other Hellfire Club relics that surfaced in later years included several gold medals 'bearing infamous devices, believed to have been the badges of the association',[18] and a carved oblong snuffbox thought to have been fashioned from a table used by the club. On its exterior was a representation of the Devil escorting a robed figure to 'the eternal furnaces', while a couple of lines of verse were engraved on the inside of the lid: 'Prime your nose well, I'd have you be civil; / This box was in hell, And was made of the Devil.'[19]

Parties external to the club were also disposed to exaggerate and amplify its supposed diabolism. Innuendos and half-truths concerning its activities circulated in Dublin's social circles, with some proclaiming that the Earl of Rosse 'dealt avec le diable'.[20] Such rumours provided abundant fuel for the popular press. The *Dublin Evening Post* published a scathing octet that equated the club with the legion of demons exorcized by Christ in the country of the Gadarenes.[21] Meanwhile, *An Ample Discovery* characterized the club as a 'damnable cabal' in which 'subterranean, diabolical divertis[s]ements' took place, in the company of 'Luciferannean muses'. Allegedly, initiates were required to abjure the strictures of Christianity and 'all that is called good, by silly priest-rid fools, entirely to abandon'. The text hinted at human sacrifice: the reference to 'the sacrificing [of] a maid' could be taken literally, and the purported letter was signed 'Moloch', the name of a Canaanite idol associated with the ritualistic slaying of children.[22]

Notwithstanding the rhetoric and symbolism that the Hellfire Club employed, the ever-grinding rumour mill and the exaggeration of the popular press, it is unlikely that its members actually engaged in devil worship. Throughout history different parties have, for manifold reasons, massively overstated the actual extent of devil worship. The intense witch-hunts that occurred intermittently in early modern Europe, when there were very few actual witches, were perhaps the most palpable manifestations of such attitudes.[23] It is unlikely that any of the putative diabolic artefacts or other diabolic trappings that were associated with the club were products of a firm belief in hell or the powers of darkness. The whimsical nature of items such as the snuffbox reflects the club's attitudes to diabolism: references to the Devil and eternal damnation were not taken seriously – rather, they were treated as something of a joke, and put about to heighten the aura of allure and mystique that surrounded the club. Peter Lens was an atheist who did not believe in the Devil any more than he did in God or an afterlife. He and his club-mates engaged in blasphemous conduct and flaunted the trappings of diabolism in order to provoke and outrage a society that was, they believed, sunk in a dull mire of conservatism and religious orthodoxy. What Lens did not anticipate was that his behaviour would be regarded as so offensive that the authorities would initiate a legal prosecution. In Bishop Berkeley he had made a formidable enemy.

One of the leading intellectuals of his day, Berkeley ardently defended religious orthodoxy against the attacks of freethinkers such as Toland. Now he was faced with the Blasters, who in his view posed a serious challenge not only to established religion, but also to the very foundations of civil society. This was not a new idea. The anti-blasphemy statute that had been passed in England in 1698 'reflected the belief among *ancien régimes* that religion and the state were mutually supportive entities'.[24] In Berkeley's *Discourse Addressed to Magistrates and Men in Authority*, published partly in response to reports of the Blasters' activities, he contended that fear and awe of God formed the central basis of society. If this was diminished, the way would be left open for evil and lawlessness.[25] The club's members probably intended no such outcome – they were heavily dependent on the existing political order for the maintenance of their privileged social status and property. However,

Berkeley did not believe that their actions could be overlooked, and he hastened to bring the Blasters and their activities to the attention of the House of Lords. On 17 February 1738, the House ordered the Committee for Religion to investigate the 'present notorious immorality and profaneness' that had been occasioned, or at least exacerbated, by the Blasters. Soon afterwards *The Irish Blasters, or the Votaries of Bacchus*, a partial translation of the thirty-ninth book of Livy's *History of Rome*, was published. Its preface, probably authored by Berkeley, enjoined Christian magistrates to defend God from blasphemous attacks, and urged that 'the infamous society of men, known by the title of BLASTERS, may as successfully be punished as the Roman Bacchanalians'.[26]

The adverse publicity that this generated caused a furore. On 9 March Jonathan Swift, who had evidently read *The Irish Blasters*, referred disparagingly to the club as 'a brace of monsters called Blasters, or blasphemers, or bacchanalians (as they are here called in print) whereof Worsdail the painter and one Lints [i.e. Lens], (a painter too, as I hear) are the leaders'.[27] The following day the Lords' Committee for Religion presented its report. The Blasters and Lens's blasphemous rhetoric and diabolism were condemned, and the report urged the judiciary to order magistrates 'to put the laws in execution against immorality, and profane cursing and swearing, and gaming', and to investigate blasphemous clubs generally. It also recommended that a proclamation be issued offering a reward for the apprehension of Lens.[28] The acceptance of this recommendation by the Lord Lieutenant and Council of Ireland, which issued a proclamation for Lens's arrest on 24 March (see Plate 10), demonstrated just how seriously the authorities took the matter.[29] Three Dublin constables were dispatched to take Lens into custody. He fled the city, making his way to County Westmeath and from there to Longford.[30] Somehow evading his pursuers, he eventually made his way back to his native city of London.

While proceedings were underway against Lens, the other members of the club went unnamed and unmolested. This was due not only to the fact that Lens was the most notorious blasphemer in the club and, for this reason, the most likely candidate to be made an example of, but also because he did not possess either the elite status or political connections that protected his club-mates. Despite being identified by Swift as a leader of the Blasters, Worsdale was not subjected to the same proceedings as Lens, thanks no doubt to his association with Edward Walpole. In the same week as the warrant was issued for Lens's arrest, Worsdale visited Dublin Castle to paint the portrait of the Lord Lieutenant, the Duke of Devonshire. It appears that Simon Luttrell was also on good terms with Devonshire, who had gone to Luttrellstown on a shooting excursion a couple of months earlier.[31] Each of the club's military members enjoyed close contacts with Dublin Castle: Colonel Ponsonby's brother, Lord Duncannon, was a close personal friend of the Lord Lieutenant, while Clements and St George were, respectively, the brother and friend of the powerful official Nathaniel Clements.[32] As for Rosse and Santry, given their status as peers of the realm and members of the House of Lords it was no surprise that they were exempted from prosecution.

Therefore, the Lens affair did not precipitate the dissolution of the Blasters or Hellfire Club. They were still active over two months later, judging by the appearance in the *Dublin Evening Post* of 'The Blasters', a satirical octet authored by a Mr Frankland:

> TH' ejected Devils, by Sufferance Divine,
> Among the Gadarenes enter'd into Swine.
> The Fiend still fond of Swine, in ev'ry Region
> Actuates the Blasters; and his Name is Legion,
> Both stung by Hell, with Madness drive away.
> These sink in Vice, they perish'd in the Sea;
> They o'er the Steeps into the Ocean fell,
> But these shoot headlong to the Depths of Hell.[33]

No explanatory text accompanied the poem, which suggests that the club was now of such notoriety that none was required. It exemplifies the continuing public disdain for its members, who were 'sink[ing] in vice' and destined for 'the depths of hell'. Indeed, they may have been unnerved by its appearance, given that prominent figures often feared being satirized in verse.[34] Perhaps there was a growing feeling within the club that it had provided an interesting diversion, and that it was time to move on. Indeed, its demise was imminent; it was hastened by the actions of its most notorious member.

The Trial of Lord Santry

Lord Santry had escaped the wrath of the authorities on several occasions, and avoided becoming embroiled in the scandal surrounding the attempted arrest of Lens. However, his 'train of evils', as it was later described,[35] had continued unabated, and was about to culminate in another murder. On 9 August 1738, he and several companions, whose number may have included other members of the Hellfire Club, attended Palmerstown Fair, an annual gathering with a reputation for violence and disorder. The previous year had seen a riot in which a man died after having his leg partially severed, and the events of the 1738 fair were to prove equally fatal.[36] Santry and his friends went to Patrick Corrigan's tavern and began drinking. As the baron became intoxicated his mood soured and he quarrelled violently with a man named Humphreys. Enraged, Santry left the room only to find his passage impeded by a porter named Laughlin Murphy. Shoving the porter into the tavern kitchen, Santry swore that he would kill the next man that spoke. When Murphy unwisely tried to utter a conciliatory word Santry drew his sword and stabbed him. He would later protest that his actions were not due to premeditated malice, but to his being 'utterly deprived of his reason and understanding'.[37] As Murphy collapsed on the kitchen floor, bleeding heavily, the full implications of his action appeared to dawn on Santry. Distraught, he paid the landlord a four-pound piece, mounted his horse and galloped away from the scene.[38]

Murphy did not die immediately. Santry sent a surgeon from Dublin to treat his wound, and a coach to take him home. The patient lingered between life and death for several weeks, during which time he attempted variously to prosecute or obtain money from Santry. For his part, the baron appeared unperturbed, going about his business as normal. On 23 August one of his horses won the Great Plate at the Carlow Races.[39] Santry's apparent unconcern is not surprising; he had previously committed a number of crimes for which he had escaped scot-free, including the murder of a defenceless chairman. In addition, a whole range of factors, including political and familial influence and judicial favouritism, frequently impeded the successful conviction and sentencing of offending members of the upper classes.[40] However, matters became more serious when Murphy died on 25 September. His widow applied to the Lords Justices to have Santry indicted for murder. The authorities could not afford to ignore this latest outrage and a warrant was issued for Santry's arrest. He turned himself in and was imprisoned in Newgate.[41]

After some deliberation, the arrangements for Santry's trial were decided upon: he was to be tried by his peers in the newly constructed Parliament House on College Green (see Plate 11).[42] His situation attracted enormous public interest, and in the weeks before the trial Dublin was abuzz with rumour and excitement. 'The tryal of Lord Santry makes a great noise here', one commentator wrote, as scaffolding was erected in the House of Commons to accommodate the huge crowds that were expected.[43] Proceedings got underway on 27 April 1739 following extensive ceremonials. Santry had a good case: the wound he had inflicted was small, and Murphy had taken over six weeks to die. However, his defence team were incompetent, and their witnesses performed poorly. Will Bradford, the surgeon who had attended the deceased, failed to convince with his argument that Murphy had died from 'an impostom' in the lung caused by cold.[44] Even though Bradford's medical incompetence appeared to have contributed to Murphy's death as much as the original wound, the defence failed to exploit this fact or to counter the strong case put forward by the prosecution. The jury returned a verdict of guilty. Santry was sentenced to death, and the execution was scheduled for 'a long day', 23 June 1739.[45]

In a remarkable volte-face, public opinion now turned in favour of the condemned man. Thomas Rundle, the Bishop of Derry, reported that 'the whole town, who were once inveterate against him, now are as solicitous to have him pardoned... Even the poor in the streets weep for him.'[46] There was also sympathy for his plight among the jury, which consisted of twenty-three Irish peers. Santry would have been personally known by many of these men, and the knowledge that a nobleman could actually be sentenced to death caused them considerable agitation, particularly when they considered the manner in which the sentence would be carried out. In killing another of the king's subjects Santry had committed treason, and he was to undergo a traitor's death – hanging and quartering.[47] The jury sent a representation to the Lords Justices and General Governor recommending that mercy be shown to the condemned. Santry also issued his own petition, pleading for 'compassion and mercy', and referring to his father's zeal in the service of the Protestant interest.[48] Powerful representations were mounted in his favour, and when Santry's uncle, Sir Compton Domvile, along with several members of the jury, travelled to England on 4 May to petition George II on his nephew's behalf he succeeded in obtaining a reprieve.[49] The news was greeted enthusiastically in Dublin, and celebratory bonfires were lit and bells rung throughout the city. Despite this display of public goodwill, Santry's reputation was damaged beyond repair. Having been all but disowned by Domvile and abandoned by his former friends, he was induced to go into exile in Nottingham 'to tye him up from further extravagancies',[50] and his estates and title were declared forfeit.

Ultimately, the forfeiture was a temporary arrangement. However, the Santry estates were indebted to the tune of £13,000, partly as a result of mismanagement and partly, no doubt, owing to the extravagance of the baron's lifestyle. During the period of forfeiture Sir Compton Domvile and Richard Wingfield, later Viscount Powerscourt, held the estates in trust for payment of the debts and 'several other uses'.[51] Santry, for his part, did not expect to remain in exile indefinitely and he spent much of his time attempting to re-establish a relationship with his uncle and smooth the way for a return to his homeland. However, Domvile was not interested in a rapprochement. He and Santry's agent, Edward

Madden, were in close communication as to how to deal with the man that Madden disparagingly referred to as 'your unhappy ward'. Madden was confident that Domvile, by 'prudent management of him' would 'be able to effect everything you propose'.[52] Their principal objective was to dissuade Santry from returning to Ireland. When Santry wrote to his uncle in 1743 expressing a desire to return, the latter indicated that it would be best to wait until the Duke of Devonshire's viceroyalty had concluded, and that in the interim Santry should amuse himself by touring around England.[53] In fact, Domvile was merely putting his nephew off: he did not want him to return during Devonshire's or any subsequent viceroyalty. It was probably to dissuade him that Domvile and Madden visited the baron in Nottingham towards the end of the summer of 1743. Santry was soon apprised of their earnest opposition to his mooted return. As Madden recalled the following year,

> Upon yr. Lordship's mentioning your going to Ireland I took the liberty to put yr. Lo[rdshi]pp. in mind of some of the many mortifications you must necessarily meet with when ever your Lordship came here, when after a good deal of discourse upon that disagreeable subject your Lordship concluded the whole with these remarkable words – well by God I will go Ireland but God damn me if ever I stay there.

Domvile was prepared to look after the Santry estates, to settle the debts that were attached to them, and even to return the property to his nephew's management, which he did in 1744. He was not, however, willing to run the risk of Santry embarking on another career of extravagance and violence in his native city. Madden enjoined him 'to consider well with yourself... whether you can have resolution and conduct sufficient constantly & carefully to avoid all those train of evils which has cost you your hon[ou]r., a great part of yr. estate and had like & but for the great love & friendship of the best of friends & uncles... most certainly cost you your life'.[54]

Such 'love & friendship' notwithstanding, Domvile appears to have cut off direct communication with his nephew following his visit to Nottingham in 1743. Two years later, having received no reply to his various communications to Domvile, Santry complained bitterly that 'I am intirely ignorant how I have offended.' The following year he tried again to revive the relationship by sending Domvile a present of a gun. Yet his uncle remained aloof, with Santry complaining again in 1749 that he had never received an answer to his letters.[55] Only gradually did he come to accept that he would never return to Ireland. His first wife had died in 1742, leaving him childless, and although he eventually remarried (to Elizabeth Shore, at Nottingham, on 7 November 1750), he did not produce an heir.[56] Meanwhile, his health deteriorated. At different times he complained of being stricken by bad colds, and so crippled by gout that he could 'hardly creep down stairs'.[57] On another occasion he was laid low for three months with 'a violent cold and sore throat succeeded by the rheumat[is]m' and another attack of gout 'of which I am confined so that I dont write this letter with the greatest glee'.[58] Following Santry's eventual death in Nottingham on 18 March 1751, his mansion and estates passed into the ownership of the Domvile family. By the twentieth century the great house in north County Dublin had fallen into disuse and ruin, a hollow reminder of the opulent lifestyle of the last lord to occupy it. It was finally demolished in the 1940s.[59]

The Dissolution of the Hellfire Club

The scandal caused by Santry's killing of Murphy and his subsequent indictment and trial hastened the demise of the Hellfire Club. Having already been shaken by the Lens affair, it was in no position to weather this even greater scandal. As for Lens himself, his narrow escape from arrest and prosecution did not encourage him to moderate his provocative tendencies following his return to London. On one occasion, while seated opposite a clergyman in an Ivy Lane eatery, Lens proclaimed that 'of all fun whatever, nothing is so great to me as roasting a parson'. However, he reckoned without the quick riposte of the clergyman, who said 'that he would take the roasting with that decency and temper, which it became one of his cloth to receive the taunts and sneers of such who thought parsons fair game' and proceeded to help himself to the dish of mackerel and gooseberry sauce that had been set before Lens. The miniaturist was so taken aback by this and the accompanying roar of laughter from the assembled company that he got up, paid for his meal and left. The story was soon doing the rounds 'and whenever a mackerel was mentioned in Lens'[s] company, he was always knocked down as flat as a flounder'.[60] Despite such blows to his self-esteem, the miniaturist was not short of resourceful stratagems for attracting business. One of these was to have one of his friends show a picture to another in a packed theatre. On being asked who did it, the first would reply, 'Mr Lens.' On then being asked where he lived, he would profess ignorance, and then address all present in the house: 'if any person here can tell. pray speak out. that we may know where to find such an ingenious man'. Assisted by such methods, Lens maintained his artistic career in London in the 1740s and 1750s. The date of his death is not known, but may have been sometime after 1754.[61]

The departure from Ireland of Santry and Lens was followed by the slow decline of the Earl of Rosse. Long years of dissipation had reduced him to physical and financial ruin, and his son was later obliged to sell off land to the value of £43,657 to settle the massive debts he and his father had incurred.[62] Despite such difficulties, the earl's renowned wit did not desert him. His reputed quip that 'it was not his principle to pay the interest, nor his interest to pay the principal' exhibited his nonchalant attitude towards creditors.[63] Yet this belied an uncomfortable reality: Rosse desperately needed funds and around 1740 he was involved in a number of lawsuits in which he sought to secure property and effects to which he felt he was entitled.[64] Meanwhile, news of the death at sea of his second son, James, in 1739 must have caused him deep distress.[65] The extraordinary climatic shock experienced by Ireland during the winter of 1740–41 may also have played a part in the earl's declining health. Hard frosts and deep snowfalls ensured that no work could be done in the fields, driving the price of provisions to excessive heights and leading to widespread starvation.[66] By June 1741 the Earl of Rosse was also at death's door.

Despite Rosse's long-standing disdain for the clergy, they had not given up all hopes of reforming him. On at least two separate occasions in the days before his death the earl was approached by a clergyman hoping to reconcile him to his Maker. One called in person to see him, ending 'an eloquent appeal by adjuring him to call on the Lord. The Earl found strength enough to reply, with awful flippancy, "I doubt, Reverend Sir, if I be going that way, but if I chance to find myself in his neighbourhood, I will make sure of calling on his Lordship"'.[67] More famously, Rosse's neighbour John Madden, the Dean of Kilmore and a younger brother of Samuel Madden, sent him a letter urging him to repent his sinful life of 'whoring, gaming, drinking, rioting, turning day into night, blaspheming his maker, and, in short, all manner of wickedness'. Noting that the letter was simply addressed, 'My Lord', Rosse had it sealed up and sent on to Robert Fitzgerald, the Earl of Kildare, instructing the bearer to say that it had come from Dean Madden. The intent could scarcely have been more mischievous, for Kildare was one of the country's most devout noblemen, possessing a character that was the direct antithesis of Rosse's:

> L–d K–e [Lord Kildare] was an effeminate, puny, little man, extremely formal and delicate, insomuch, that when he was married to Lady M–y O–n [Mary O'Brien], one of the most shining beauties then in the world, he would not take his wedding gloves off when he went to bed. From this single instance may be judged, with what surprize and indignation he read over the Dean's letter, containing so many accusations for crimes he knew himself entirely innocent of.

Outraged, Kildare showed the letter to the Archbishop of Dublin, John Hoadly, who in turn confronted Dean Madden, demanding that he explain why he had used 'so many careless invectives against the most unblemished nobleman in Europe'. Madden, believing him to be

referring to Rosse, insisted that he had only done his duty. Although
threatened with prosecution in an ecclesiastical court, the dean refused
to retract his words. The indignant Kildare prepared to initiate proceedings of his own against Madden, which he surely would have done had
not the ruse been discovered. Rosse, meanwhile, had died. He gained
considerable posthumous notoriety from the repetition of this
anecdote.[68] It was no accident that John Madden, like his brother
Samuel, who also suffered embarrassment at Rosse's hands, was not
only a clergyman but also an active member of the Dublin Society.[69]
This group, with its moralistic agenda of improvement and industri-
ousness, was anathema to the dissipated Rosse and antithetical to the
Hellfire Club that he had helped to create.

Other Hellfire Club members enjoyed less controversial later careers.
The army officers Clements, Ponsonby and St George had never been
the most visible or vocal members of the Hellfire Club. Their association
with Lens and Santry did not harm their prospects for advancement, and
Clements's career enjoyed a meteoric rise following the club's demise. In
1741 he became an aide-de-camp to the Lord Lieutenant, doubtless as a
result of the representations of his influential brother Nathaniel, and in
1744 he achieved promotion to lieutenant-colonel.[70] Colonel Ponsonby,
meanwhile, had the honour of having his regiment, the 37th Foot,
personally reviewed by George II in June 1742. The regiment also saw
action both at home and abroad during the early 1740s. The food short-
ages of 1741 prompted some instances of local unrest, and in April 1741
five men were killed when the 37th fired on a mob that had attempted
to seize a shipment of provisions at Carrick-on-Suir.[71] With the outbreak
of the War of the Austrian Succession, domestic duties were superseded
by large-scale military operations on the Continent. In June 1743
Clements and Ponsonby both saw action at the Battle of Dettingen.
During the battle, Clements's regiment, Johnson's Infantry, came under
heavy fire from the French artillery. It was then charged by the French
Cavalry of the Guard but held firm. As one of those present noted,
'Johnson's Infantry. . . received them without retiring an inch, and made
great havock amongst them, and took of 'em 2 standards and many

prisoners.' Ponsonby, likewise, must have fought bravely at Dettingen as he was promoted to major-general following the battle. However, he was rapidly losing his taste for military life. In October 1744 he complained that 'age and infirmities grow on me apace' and expressed a desire to spend the remainder of his days at home with his wife.[72] He was not to get his wish. He and Clements were again present at the Battle of Fontenoy (11 May 1745), where both participated in the British infantry's disastrous advance against the French, whose regiments included the Irish Jacobite brigade. Ponsonby, who was in command of the first line of infantry, entrusted his watch and ring to his son Chambré with instructions to give them to his wife should he be killed. On reaching the top of the ridge overlooking Fontenoy he stopped to take a pinch of snuff. In that instant 'his head was carried off by a round shot'.[73] Meanwhile, the regiment commanded by Clements suffered severe losses. Over 300 were killed, including Clements himself. He was commemorated in a threnody that alluded both to his active social life and his military prowess: 'O! once endow'd with ev'ry pleasing pow'r, / To cheer the sad, and charm the social hour . . . The tongues of Dettingen your triumphs tell, / And weeping Tournai points where Clements fell.' Thanks in no small part to the valour of the Irish brigade, Fontenoy was a military disaster for the British Army, with Horace Walpole commenting that it had 'never lost near so many officers'.[74] Among them were two erstwhile members of the Hellfire Club.

Those who had anticipated that the hand of divine vengeance would fall upon the club must have observed the fates of its members with interest. By 1745 three of them were dead and a further two had been driven from the country. Indeed, the oldest member of the club, Richard St George, managed to outlive most of his club-mates. Over the course of the 1740s he was confirmed in his status as one of the country's most eminent military men, achieving successive promotions as brigadier-general (1743), major-general (1744) and lieutenant-general (1747). He lived out his last years at a handsome new residence in Henrietta Street, eventually dying in 1755.[75]

While nothing is known about Simon Luttrell's involvement in the

Hellfire Club other than the fact of his membership, he enjoyed the longest and most controversial career of all of its erstwhile members. Luttrell returned to England in the 1740s, probably in order to take possession of the estates that his wife had inherited there. In 1755, he purchased Four Oaks, a stately home in Warwickshire.[76] With the assistance of powerful allies such as the Duke of Newcastle, Luttrell pursued an active political career, successively becoming MP for St Michael (1755–61), Wigan (1761–68), Weobley (1768–74) and Stockbridge (1774–80).[77] His unscrupulous political dealings left him open to polemical attacks that made much of his allegedly dubious family origins. Mindful perhaps of his Hellfire Club connections, his detractors also sought to identify him with the Devil.[78] This may have been further occasioned by a dalliance with the infamous Medmenham Monks. The assertion that Luttrell was a member of this club[79] may not be without foundation, as its president was his old Dilettante acquaintance Sir Francis Dashwood. In 1768 Luttrell attained the title of Baron Irnham (see Plate 12), an Irish peerage that allowed him to retain his seat in the English House of Commons. The following year, he was caught up in the furore that erupted over the Middlesex election, in which his eldest son, Lieutenant-Colonel Henry Lawes Luttrell, stood against John Wilkes. Although Wilkes won the election by 1,143 votes to 296, his candidacy was declared invalid and Lieutenant-Colonel Luttrell was declared elected.[80] Irnham was believed to have orchestrated this outcome, and from around this time a number of increasingly bitter attacks on his character appeared in print. A 1769 sketch of his life denounced the name of Luttrell as a synonym for 'traitor, villain, bastard, coward and profligate, and every thing that can be conceived odi[o]us and horrible'. Lord Irnham was also accused of ruining a young man by encouraging him to marry a prostitute. He had allegedly performed the office of father to the bride, sleeping with her himself on the night following the marriage. Some years later, William Combe characterized Irnham as the successful applicant for the throne of Satan in his satirical poem *The Diaboliad*.[81] Though it was later stated that these various attacks were the unjust works of character assassins, 'the mere fabrications of party',[82] there seems little doubt that Irnham's behaviour was questionable on both personal and political levels.

The activities of Irnham's offspring – he had four sons and four daughters – caused him no small inconvenience.[83] When his daughter Anne Luttrell actually married a member of the royal family, the Duke of Cumberland, in 1771, the union precipitated uproar because of the Luttrell family's notorious reputation. However, it was his hostile relationship with Henry Lawes Luttrell that attracted the most attention. The dispute between father and son originated from the sale by Irnham of lands to which Luttrell had been entitled under his father's marriage settlement. In 1769, the two parties reached an agreement whereby the son was given an annuity of £600 along with possession of the house and demesne of Luttrellstown under a seven-year lease, which he described bitterly as the consideration 'for which Lord Irnham made me convey to him my birthright'.[84] Luttrell's refusal to surrender possession of the estate on the expiry of the seven years resulted in a legal battle in the Court of Chancery. Irnham complained that apart from continuing to occupy the estate, his son 'had cut down and disposed of a great quantity of timber in the woods upon the demesne, to the value of 4000l. and upwards; and also had pulled down part of the said mansion-house... appearing determined to strip the estate'.[85] Over the course of the proceedings, the relationship between the two men deteriorated to the point of outright hostility. On one occasion, when Irnham sent a messenger to Luttrell with a subpoena ordering him to pay costs he had incurred as a result of the case, Luttrell flew into a rage and struck the messenger on the jaw, causing 'a great effusion of blood'.[86] The case was decided in favour of Irnham, and Luttrell was forced to relinquish Luttrellstown. However, before he did so he denuded the house of all moveable objects. When Irnham took up residence there he found that all of his family portraits and furniture had been removed, such that he had not even a spit for roasting meat, finding it necessary to use a string instead. Not satisfied with thus discomfiting his father, Luttrell mobilized a gang of ruffians to terrorize him. Irnham complained of being menaced by a 'lawless banditti armed with clubs, bludgeons, etc,...headed by Colonel Luttrell with his sabre'.[87] It was in the context of such events that he was alleged to have challenged his son to a duel, with the latter declining on the grounds that his father was no gentleman.[88]

Despite the antagonism shown towards him by his son and his political enemies, Irnham's loyalty to the Whig Party ensured his progression in the ranks of the peerage. He was created Viscount Carhampton of Castlehaven in 1781 and became 1st Earl of Carhampton in 1785. His enjoyment of his new title was short-lived, as he died in Dublin in January 1787 at the age of 73.[89] Henry Lawes Luttrell succeeded as 2nd Earl of Carhampton and pursued a controversial military career during the 1790s, earning opprobrium by rounding up over 1,000 suspected rebels in Connacht and sending them to serve in the Royal Navy. It may have been in protest at such activities that his grandfather Henry Luttrell's grave at Clonsilla, County Dublin, was desecrated in 1798.[90] Equally, this could have been an act of vengeance aimed at the Luttrell family as a whole, which had earned itself an infamy that persisted even after the line became extinct in the nineteenth century.

While the different members of the Dublin Hellfire Club enjoyed varying fortunes in their later careers, they were united in at least one respect. The fact that no reference to the club can be found in the extant personal correspondence of any member suggests that, at least latterly, they may have regarded it as an embarrassment, something they would have preferred be forgotten rather than celebrated or revived. If this was so, they were not to get their wish. The club had cast a long shadow on the psyche of the Protestant Ascendancy and it would not be hastily forgotten, either by contemporaries or future generations. Its short-term influence can be most readily seen in the establishment of a number of imitative groups elsewhere in the country. The first of these was a contemporaneous, sister hellfire club that was founded in the Limerick area. One of those involved was the resourceful artist who had thus far eluded any negative consequences for his hellfire activities – James Worsdale.

1. The ruined hunting lodge on Mountpelier Hill in south County Dublin. Although the building has been known as the 'Hellfire Club' since at least the late nineteenth century, there is no documented evidence that a hellfire club met there.

2. Richard Parsons, later 1st Earl of Rosse, as a boy. Rosse's youthful and innocent appearance in this portrait belies his later reputation as a notorious libertine and founder of the Dublin Hellfire Club.

3. *W Domville and Friends at the Hellfire Club*. Probably painted in the early 1720s, this conversation piece by James Worsdale appears to depict William Domvile of Loughlinstown, County Dublin, socializing with members of the London Hellfire Club. Domvile is seated on the right. The identities of the other two sitters are unknown.

4. Sketch of William Domvile. Note the resemblance to the figure seated on the right in the *W. Domville and Friends* portrait.

5. *The Hellfire Club, Dublin*, by James Worsdale. Lord Santry is the figure seated on the extreme left, raising his hand to present his club-mates, who are identified as Colonel St George, Colonel Ponsonby, Colonel Clements and Mr Luttrell.

6. Hellfire Club wine glass. Engraved with the words 'The Hell Fire Club' and 'James Worsdale Master of the Revels', this glass goblet is similar in shape to those depicted in the Dublin Hellfire Club group portrait.

7. *An Ample Discovery of the Damnable Cabal, Commonly Known by the Name of the Hell-fire Club.* This undated broadsheet describes the salacious activities that allegedly took place at meetings of the Dublin Hellfire Club.

[115]

AN AMPLE

DISCOVERY

Of the Damnable Cabal, commonly known by the Name of the *Hell-fire CLUB*, kept in this City, since the 17th of *March* last, 'till the Detection of several Members thereof; in a persuasive Letter to a young Gentleman.

Dear JACK,

THE Pleasure I daily receive in being a Member of the never to be too much commended Society of *Gayest Modern Libertines*, is still imperfect without enjoying the Happiness of your promis'd Admission and Concession to our Company; as an Inducement to which, I here send you a short Sketch of our Lives and Behaviour in general, being fully assur'd a Man of your concise Taste can form a more just Idea (than I can at present in Words) of the many Benefits and subterranean, diabolical Divertisements, of which we are at present Participators; as an Introduction to which I am first obliged (*Emphasis Gratia*) to introduce that inimitable Patron and profess'd Libertine, the celebrated *Don John*, of immortal Memory, as the first Founder, and likewise (under *Lucifer*) our Patron, so lively express'd in an exact Imitator, that it appears whenever we perform any memorable Act, such as the sacrificing a Maid, introducing a *Molly*, &c. you'd really think he descended from his Throne, to share in our inexpressible Pastimes; besides, at the Election of a new Member, our Entertainments are so deliciously great, that *Pluto*, who is at present Grand Master of the Lodge, in an excellent Representative, constantly assists at the Performance of that grand Ceremony, displaying his bounteous Donations to the whole Assembly, tho' more particularly to the new admitted Devotee, who before he is confirm'd, makes the following Declaration.

Pluto, I am thine! Quick, quick receive me, by thy powerful Charms, and crown my Wishes with Excess of Pleasure——! No more shall Virtue in my Bosom reign: I, by thy efficacious, mighty Self do swear, from this auspicious Day, and glorious Æra to succeeding Passion, all that is called good, by silly Priest-rid Fools, entirely to abandon, and let Nothing share the least Part of my Favour, but what is solely urg'd by my most vicious and libidinous Desires.

At the Confirmation of which, he is enrol'd a Denizon, having immediately at Command all his boundless Wishes can desire; Performance waits his Will, and when he bids, 'tis done! 'Tis here, and only here, where brightest Nymphs do constantly abound, to satiate our constant craving Appetites; nor do we meet but when our Lusts run high, and Nature rallying gives new Force to Love.

Having a vast many Things more to say, I shall make bold to trouble you with another Epistle when Opportunity serves, in which I shall more clearly display the many Advantages accruing one's being elected a Member of our honourable Society, likewise a List of the Names by which we are known here. An Account of our different Dresses. The Rules of our Society, and also for the Benefit of your Female Acquaintance, the most private and proper Methods for their being introduc'd among our Luciferannean Muses. There being no possibility entirely of stopping Nature here, which is forcing o'ts Passage at this very Juncture, wherefore I must immediately retire to my subterranean Seraglio, and conclude,

Dear JACK,
Your Categorical Friend,
MOLOCH.

Printed for G. F. in Warborows Street.

8. Laetitia Pilkington, poet and adventuress. Her family home was situated not far from the Earl of Rosse's residence on Molesworth Street, Dublin. Following her separation from her husband in 1737, Laetitia was besieged in her lodgings by Rosse and 'several other persons of distinction'.

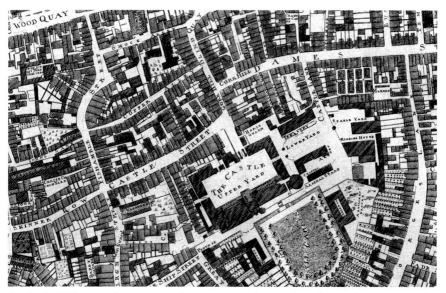

9. Cork Hill and the surrounding area in the mid-eighteenth century. The Eagle Tavern was situated to the rear of the lord chief baron's yard, the open court facing onto the north side of Cork Hill.

BY THE
LORD LIEUTENANT *and* COUNCIL
OF
IRELAND,
A
PROCLAMATION,
Promising a Reward for Apprehending *Peter Lens*, late of *Dublin*, Painter.

DEVONSHIRE.

WHEREAS the Lords Spiritual and Temporal in Parliament Assembled, Did, by their Resolution of the Tenth of this Month, Resolve, That an humble Address be Presented to His Grace the Lord Lieutenant, that He would please to Order, that a Proclamation may Issue, with a Reward, for Apprehending *Peter Lens*.

And whereas it appears by several Examinations taken upon Oath, before the Lord Mayor of this City, That the said *Peter Lens*, Painter, lately come into this Kingdom, is Charged with having several Times Uttered Profane and Blasphemous Expressions.

We therefore, having a just Abhorrence of such Impieties, and being Determined, strictly to put the Laws in Execution against Immorality and Profaneness; Do, by this Our Proclamation, Publish and Declare, That We will give the Necessary Orders for the Payment of the Sum of One Hundred Pounds, to such Person or Persons, as shall Take and Secure the said *Peter Lens*, on or before the Twenty Fourth Day of *June* next, so as he may be Proceeded against according to Law for such his Offence.

And We do hereby Charge and Command, all Mayors, Sheriffs, Justices of the Peace, and other Magistrates and Officers Civil and Military, in this Kingdom, and all other His Majesty's Loving Subjects, to use their utmost Diligence, in Taking and Securing the said *Peter Lens*, as they shall answer the Contrary at their Peril.

Given at the Council-Chamber in *Dublin*, the Twenty Fourth Day of *March*, 1737.

Hu. Armach, Wyndham, C. John Dublin, Theo: Cashel, Meath, Cavan, Molesworth, Duncannon, Ar: Meath, C: Kildare, Hen: Boyle, Tho: Carter, Ja: Reynolds, Henry King, Edw: Webster, Fra: Burton, Hen: Bingham, Lu: Gardiner, Tho: Pearce.

God Save the King.

DUBLIN: Printed by *George Grierson*, Printer to the King's Most Excellent Majesty, at the King's-Arms and Two Bibles in *Essex-Street*: 1737.

10. Proclamation promising a reward for the apprehension of Peter Lens, 24 March 1738 (Old Style 1737). The fact that the authorities offered a reward of £100 for Lens's apprehension indicates how seriously they took his blasphemous outbursts and proclamations of fidelity to the Devil.

A view of the Principal Front of the Parliament House, and part of the College in Dublin: design'd and drawn by S.ʳ Ed. Pearce

11. The Parliament House on College Green, Dublin. The trial of Lord Santry was held here in 1739. Note the dome of the House of Commons chamber (destroyed by fire in the 1790s) and the sedan chairs passing outside.

N.º XI.

L—d Iron_ham.

12. Simon Luttrell, 1st Baron Irnham, later 1st Earl of Carhampton. Irnham's political double-dealing in England made him the subject of a number of polemics, some of which emphasized his alleged diabolic connections.

13. *Hell Fire Club, Co. Limerick*, by James Worsdale. Edward Croker (1706–80), who commissioned the painting, is probably the figure seated at the centre of the table, raising his arm to present the assembled company. The white-wigged figure on the far left may be Worsdale himself.

14. James Worsdale. The portrait from which this engraving is taken was probably painted around 1752, when Worsdale was performing on the London stage in Samuel Foote's comedy *Taste*. Note the easel and the copy of *Taste* protruding from Worsdale's coat pocket.

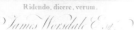

Ridendo, dicere, verum.

James Worsdale Esq.

15. Folly tower, Doonass, County Clare. Known locally as the 'Turret', this ruined tower overlooks the River Shannon opposite Castleconnell, County Limerick. Constructed in the late eighteenth century, probably by Sir Hugh Dillon Massy, Bart (c.1740–1807), it is reputed to have been the meeting place of a hellfire club.

Chapter four

Regional Hellfire Clubs

At least three regional hellfire clubs were established in Ireland between the 1730s and 1770s, in counties Limerick (probably Askeaton) and Kildare (Grangemellon) and at an unspecified location in the midlands. The fact that these groups emerged in rural, provincial settings proved that hellfire club activity did not require an urban dynamic to sustain it. The participants were generally country squires, and their motivations were largely similar to those of the Dublin Hellfire Club – a desire to engage in convivial entertainment, with a dash of diabolism thrown in for good measure. The degree to which the latter was present depended on how determined the clubs were to goad those members of the gentry and clergy who were concerned to promote industry, sobriety and moral behaviour. While none of the regional hellfire clubs attained the same degree of notoriety as their Dublin predecessor, each made a significant impact in the locality in which it operated. The activities of the Limerick and Kildare clubs inspired a number of enduring folkloric traditions, while the midlands club, known as the Holy Fathers, provoked widespread condemnation from both lay moralists and the clergy. In addition, hellfire club mythos made a notable impact on the artistic design of the period.

The ubiquitous James Worsdale was at least partly responsible for the diffusion of hellfire club ideology to the provinces. During the second half of 1738 he undertook a tour of Munster, probably financed by the thirty guineas he had received in July for painting the Lord Lieutenant's portrait.[1] He visited Mallow, County Cork, where he again demonstrated an uncanny ability to ingratiate himself with the local gentry.[2] This was due in no small part to his association with Laetitia Pilkington. Anxious to cultivate a reputation as a poet, he had offered to pay her to supply him with verse that he would then pass off as his own. Mrs Pilkington had been in straitened financial circumstances since her separation from her husband, and she accepted this 'easy and honourable method of getting a subsistence'. Having secured her services, Worsdale proceeded to use 'his' literary talents to further his relationships with the opposite sex, enhance his onstage productions and establish a reputation as a skilled poet. Mallow was then a popular spa town, heavily frequented by the nobility and gentry, for whose diversion balls, ridottos and musical entertainments of various kinds were offered.[3] Worsdale hoped to avail himself of the moneymaking opportunities that this social milieu offered, and before long he had succeeded in getting himself chosen as poet laureate to the local 'Honourable Society of Ladies and Gentlemen'. Mrs Pilkington continued to send him poems – over fifty in total – to confirm him in his new status. Worsdale was making a tidy profit from the poetry and he wrote to his supplier demanding a further 100 ballads 'by the return of the post' as he had already begun taking subscriptions for them. When she refused on the basis that she could not write that quickly, he replied that she should be damned if she didn't forward the poems, humorously exaggerating his status: 'the eyes of all Europe are on me, and damn me, if you don't send me the ballads, but I'll despise, and defy you forever'. In an amusing postscript he indicated that his standing in Mallow might have slipped a little as a result of his lascivious antics: 'by God, I can't stir out, for my landlady has beat me through the town with a hot shoulder of mutton, which she snatch'd from the fire, spit and all, only for catching me a little familiar with her daughter'.[4] Such incidents may have induced him to move on to fresh pastures. He visited County Limerick, where he fraternized with another, more controversial, society.

The Limerick Hellfire Club

Although there is almost nothing in the way of documentary evidence on the Limerick Hellfire Club, it is the best known of the regional hell-fire clubs. This is due to the fact that Worsdale depicted its members in a conversation piece that he may have envisaged as a companion piece to the Dublin club portrait. It depicts a group of jovial country squires drinking and smoking merrily around a table (see Plate 13). A total of eleven men, one woman and a boy are featured, eight of whom are identified on an accompanying tablet: Edward Croker of Ballynagarde, his son John Croker, Windham Quin of Adare, 'Royce of Nantenan', 'Bayley of Debsborough', Henry Prittie of Dunalley Castle, Pierce Creagh of Dangan and 'Blennerhasset of Riddlestown'.[5]

Edward Croker (1706–80), who commissioned the painting, may be the figure seated at the centre of the table, raising his arm to present the assembled company. The boy blowing the hunting horn on the far right is probably his son John Croker (1730–95). The Crokers, who resided at Ballynagarde some six miles south-east of Limerick city, were one of the county's most prominent gentry families. Edward's father was MP for Kilmallock between 1723 and 1727, while he himself was high sheriff of the county in 1735. He was married to Elizabeth, sister of Henry Prittie. Their son John would go on to become MP for Fethard, County Tipperary (1768–76).[6] Windham Quin (1717–89) came from an equally influential background. He was the son of the wealthy landowner Valentine Quin, whose estates at Adare and Kildimo covered thousands of acres in the 1730s. A young man of around 21 when the painting was completed, Windham later sat as MP for Kilmallock (1768–76). His son Valentine Richard would become 1st Earl of Dunraven.[7] 'Royce of Nantenan' refers to the Reverend Thomas Royse, rector of Nantenan, County Limerick.[8] He may be the white-wigged figure seated to the right of the table, garbed in clerical black. Royse's presence in the group is an enigma: what was a clergy-man doing consorting with a hellfire club? Did he share the deistic and atheistic ideals that characterized groups of this kind? Or was the

Limerick club a hellfire club in name only, exhibiting such a respectable sociability that even a clergyman did not baulk at attending its meetings?

Equally puzzling is the reference to 'Bayley of Debsborough'. John Bayly (b. 1691) of Debsborough, County Tipperary, married Deborah Neale in 1720. Deborah was a widow when she married Henry Prittie (1708–68) of Dunalley Castle, County Tipperary, in 1736; Prittie is also identified as a sitter in the painting.[9] Therefore, Bayly cannot have been present if the painting was executed in 1738, when Worsdale is known to have been in Munster. The accompanying tablet was attached to the frame at a later date and it is possible that one of the sitters was misidentified as Bayly. Henry Prittie's involvement in the club seems paradoxical, as he was a founding member of the Dublin Society, members of which deeply disapproved of the dissolution and irreligion of the hellfire clubs. Prittie may have wearied of the Dublin Society's pious attitudes and joined the Limerick Hellfire Club for convivial purposes. He later sat as MP for County Tipperary (1761–8). Pierce or Pierse Creagh of Dangan, County Clare, is either the man who in February 1739 married Windham Quin's sister, 'a very agreeable young lady' who brought with her a fortune of £6,000, or his father, Pierse Creagh Senior, who died in 1753.[10] Finally, 'Blennerhasset of Riddlestown' may be either the MP and judge Arthur Blennerhassett, who constructed Riddlestown Park, County Limerick, in 1730, or his cousin Arthur Blennerhassett, who inherited the house and died in a boating accident in Killarney in 1775.[11] Of the two, the latter is the more likely; his wife, Margaret 'Celinda' Blennerhassett is said to be the woman portrayed on the right-hand side of the painting.

While the names of the remaining individuals are unknown, several candidates have been proposed, including Richard FitzGerald, brother of the Knight of Glin. A keen duellist, FitzGerald (d. 1775) reputedly 'gave adversaries the embarrassing choice of either pistols at twenty paces or the short sword in a ten-foot ring'. A full-length portrait at Glin Castle shows him being handed a challenge to a duel with a Spaniard. He became the 22nd Knight of Glin following the death of his older brother Edmund in 1763.[12] Others who have been proposed for sitters include the poet Daniel Hayes, Nash of Ballycullen, O'Brien of Moyvane, a Mr White and a Mr Griffin. The figure on the far left, beckoning to the lady, may be Worsdale himself.[13]

While the Protestant gentry of north Munster were often at odds with one another over matters of property and politics, this particular group was fairly closely bound together by shared interests and kinship ties.[14] The painting tells us much about the nature of their club. The group is assembled around a large oval hunt table and this, combined with the boy blowing the horn and the slumbering dog in the foreground, gives the impression that those present are entertaining themselves after a day on the chase. This highlights the rural setting of the club, in contrast to the urban poise evident in the painting of the Dublin Hellfire Club. Yet this did not denote rustic boorishness, for the Limerick Club was highly sophisticated: 'The company is engaged neither in war nor sport, but in conviviality and conversation. Smart adjuncts of sociability are displayed. The sitters wear fashionable waistcoats, surcoats, cravats and wigs. They pose around a table, with elaborate chairs, decanters, glasses, punch bowl and wine cooler, all of which announce their power and style as consumers.'[15] The copious amounts of alcohol on display affirm that the club was first and foremost a drinking society. The huge punchbowl is filled almost to the brim, and the club-mates are shown imbibing and refilling their glasses enthusiastically. Three bottles of wine are in use on the table and the wine cooler in the foreground, decorated with grotesque masks and carved lion's-paw feet in the Irish Chippendale style, contains several more. Daniel Hayes's verse celebrating the drinking exploits of Croker and his companions is thought to have been inspired by the club:

> But if in endless Drinking you delight,
> C[roke]r will ply you till you sink outright;
> C[roke]r for swilling Floods of Wine renown'd,
> Whose matchless Board with various Plenty's crown'd;
> Eternal Scenes of Riot, Mirth and Noise,

> With all the Thunder of the Nenagh Boys,
> We laugh, we roar, the ceaseless Bumpers fly,
> 'Till the Sun purples o'er the Morning Sky... [16]

Clearly, drinking and rowdy carousing was just as important to the Limerick Hellfire Club as it was to its Dublin counterpart. Two centuries later, tales of the prodigious quantities of alcohol that initiates supposedly had to imbibe were still current (see below, p.72).

Yet as Hayes suggests, the members were equally concerned to satisfy their 'unruly passions'. This is indicated by the presence of Margaret Blennerhassett (or another young woman) surrounded by two men, one whom holds her possessively to his chest. As is confirmed by a portrait of her at Glin Castle, Mrs Blennerhassett was a renowned beauty. In Hayes's estimation, she had the ability to reduce men to a state of lustful awe:

> Serene in Majesty Celinda shone,
> Above her Sex and made us all her own,
> Form'd with each gentle, soft and moving Art,
> To melt the Soul, and pierce the flutt'ring heart;
> Sense, Virtue, Beauty o'er her Face diffuse,
> Seraphic Sweetness, mild as morning Dews;
> What Man beholds her swelling snowy Breast,
> But burns and raves and dies to *feel* the rest.
> Her ev'ry Glance wou'd fire declining Age,
> Or awe the Libertine's licentious Rage... [17]

Worsdale (if it is Worsdale) beckons suggestively to her, a gesture entirely in keeping with the character of a man whose amorous pursuits had caused him to be chased through Mallow by an irate landlady.

In terms of a comparison with the Dublin Hellfire Club, some general points can be made. Firstly, the Limerick Club was not as elite a group as its Dublin counterpart. It had more members – thirteen people are depicted in the painting, and there may have been others – and they were provincial squires rather than peers or high-ranking army officers. It is also possible that Catholics were admitted to the club; Richard FitzGerald, who is thought to have been a member, did not conform to the Established Church until 1740.[18] Secondly, the Limerick Club was not as controversial or confrontational as the Dublin Club. There is no evidence that its members engaged in concerted blasphemy in the vein of Peter Lens, and none are known to have possessed destructive and sociopathic tendencies of the kind exhibited by Lord Santry. The presence of individuals such as the clergyman Thomas Royse and the Dublin Society founding member Henry Prittie suggests that the club was regarded as a respectable institution. As Toby Barnard observes, a 'segment of Limerick's notables met together regularly and thought of themselves as enough of a group to merit the collective portrait',[19] and it is possible that they acquired the title 'Hellfire Club' by happenstance. Worsdale himself could have suggested it when he undertook to paint the portrait. It may have been a sister society to the Dublin club in name only, and, other than Worsdale's portraiture, there do not appear to have been any formal links between the two.

Nonetheless, the existence of traditions of raucous behaviour by the Limerick Hellfire Club indicate that it was not necessarily a model of civility. Its meeting place is traditionally believed to have been a building in Askeaton, County Limerick, a brick-and-stone edifice adjoining Desmond Castle and overlooking the River Deel. Architectural features such as the remains of a bow window (which once faced another such window at the opposite end of the building) suggest that the building was constructed in the 1730s–40s, which is consistent with its use by the Limerick club. The architect may have been John Aheron, designer of the gazebo at Dromoland Castle in County Clare.[20] Although the building is now open to the sky, it was not so when Lady Georgiana Chatterton visited it in 1838 and noted its 'irregular sloping roofs and melancholy aspect'. In her estimation, the building's interior was crude and unattractive: 'I was struck with the unfinished, ugly look of everything belonging to that old house: it is stamped with that reckless character which characterized the Irish in the last century.' As a convenient centre for the club to meet and engage in activities away from the prying eyes of wives and families, the Askeaton building was well situated. Several members resided nearby at places such as Nantenan (three miles south), Ballycullen (about two miles south-west), Riddlestown (four miles south-west) and Adare (ten miles south-east). It was probably the scene of much unruly revelry. One tradition, mentioned by Chatterton, has it that a member was thrown from one of the windows into the Deel in the course of a 'drunken frolic'.[21] It may be that such an event took place, given its persistence in local folklore. A century later the alleged incident was placed in the context of a test of admission: 'Intending members had to show their prowess by drinking a bottle of wine, bottle of brandy, bottle of whiskey and a bottle of rum. Then he should walk along a straight line some twenty yards in length. Failure to comply with the conditions led to the applicant being pushed through a window into the Deal.'[22] While this is far-fetched, it is worth noting that certain eighteenth-century groups, such as the Cherokee Club of the 1790s, placed great importance on prospective members' capacities for alcohol consumption (see Chapter 6). Such tales helped the Askeaton building to attain a 'hellfire' reputation second only to that of its counterpart in the Dublin Mountains. In a nineteenth-century story it was asserted that a mysterious stranger 'got a room fitted-up in the ould house, in the castle yard, where the Hell-fire Club used to hould their meetins long ago... dickens a one, rich or poor, barrin' himself, would put a foot in that same house, for Damer's estate'.[23]

Despite such traditions, there is a decided paucity of documentary evidence on the Limerick Hellfire Club. The earliest printed reference to it that has been discovered dates from 1811. It states that a hellfire club 'really existed some years ago in the county of Limerick; and the members actually roasted a man, to see how far he could endure the torments of hell. – A gentleman is now living in Limerick who was a member of that club; and to this day, at the mention of it, he falls into fits.'[24] Like many such accounts, this throws up more questions than it answers. The portrait of the Limerick club was painted around 1738, and it is likely that all of its members were dead by 1811. Was the club then revived at a later stage? As for the reference to the roasting alive of a man, this is a motif of hellfire club folklore that is more commonly attributed to the Dublin club (see Chapter 7). Hellfire clubs were nebulous by nature, the Limerick club more so than most. It is safe to assume that the whole truth about it will never be known.

Worsdale's Last Years

Worsdale's sojourn with the Limerick Hellfire Club was probably a brief one. He returned to Dublin, where he pursued a successful theatrical career for several years, writing plays and operas. On occasion he took to the stage himself, such as at Smock Alley Theatre in 1740 where he played Lady Scandal in *The Assembly*, a farce he had authored. The following year he was appointed deputy master of revels to the viceregal court, a position that gave him some authority over theatrical affairs in the city.[25] By this time he was heavily involved in the Dublin opera scene, both as a writer and a performer. One of his last performances in the city was in the role of Gubbins in Lampe's *The Dragon of Wantley* in January 1744.[26] Not long afterwards he returned to England, probably in order to take up an appointment as master painter to the Board of Ordnance. This was a valuable position that afforded him a regular income and lucrative commissions, notably a full-length portrait of George II.[27] Yet he also completed a portrait of Charles Edward Stuart, who landed in Scotland in the summer of 1745 to raise a rebellion. This flirtation with Jacobitism at the time of its brief resurgence was typical of Worsdale's opportunistic tendencies. However, his artistic endeavours failed to sustain him and he was unable to avoid falling into debt. Pursued by his creditors, he only managed to evade arrest by securing the protection of the Bavarian envoy Josef Franz Xaver von Haszlang. Worsdale also re-encountered Laetitia Pilkington, who had moved to London in an attempt to build a career as a writer.

He again induced her to compose literary works for him, placing her under virtual house arrest while she did so. These included, allegedly, an opera, which Laetitia lamented she did not have, as 'Worsdale was too cunning for me, and seiz'd it, sheet by sheet, as fast as I wrote it.'[28]

Worsdale continued to enjoy the friendship of Edward Walpole, who had been influential in procuring for him the position with the Board of Ordnance. A few years later, he had an opportunity to repay his friend by helping to clear him of a charge of sodomy. In April 1750, an Irish footman named John Cather issued a bill of indictment against Walpole, accusing him of assaulting him with intent to commit buggery. Cather belonged to a gang of blackmailers who seemingly concocted the charges in order to extort money. Walpole confided in Worsdale, asking him to use his talents to unmask the gang. Having discovered the drinking haunts of the ringleaders, Worsdale made their acquaintance and ingratiated himself with them. He proceeded to engineer their arrest and the exposure of the plot in court, with the result that Walpole was exonerated.[29] Worsdale continued to ride the wave of Georgian artistic life over the ensuing years. Reputedly, he was the inspiration for Samuel Foote's comedy *Taste* (1752), which followed the fortunes of a down-at-heel artist who progresses from painting shop signs to counterfeiting works by old masters. Worsdale himself acted in the play in the role of Lady Pentweazel, which is considered to be his finest stage performance.[30] It was probably around this time that he had his portrait painted by Robert Edge Pine. It shows a debonair Worsdale gesturing at a beehive, perhaps to denote artistic industry. His easel is close at hand and a copy of *Taste* protrudes from his coat pocket, hinting at his possible co-authorship of the work (see Plate 14).[31]

One of Worsdale's last known dramatic productions was *Gascanado the Great* (1759). He died in his lodgings in Kent in June 1767 and was buried at St Paul's, Covent Garden, having outlived all but one of his Dublin Hellfire Club cohorts. His self-composed epitaph alluded, not without foundation, to his generosity: 'Eager to get, but not to keep, the pelf, / A friend to all mankind except himself.'[32] However, posterity would have to balance this assessment with those of George Vertue, who condemned Worsdale's 'barefac[e]d mountebank lyes', and Laetitia Pilkington, who described him as a 'profest libertine' and a servant of the Devil. Nonetheless, he was defended as 'good-natur'd to a fault' by Laetitia's son Jack.[33] A truer estimation of Worsdale's character probably lies somewhere in between condemnation and approbation. What no one could deny was that he was a born survivor. In the unforgiving social environment of the early eighteenth century, he raised himself from obscure origins to a position of prominence in which he rubbed shoulders with some of the leading aristocratic, literary and artistic figures of the period. In this, he was assisted by his artistic talents and his undoubted verbal abilities: a gift for mimicry and affable and witty conversation. He has left us an invaluable visual record of two of the most prominent Irish hellfire clubs, to which his name will forever be attached. Little, however, is known about the extent of Worsdale's involvement in either of these groups. He did not suffer any ill effects from the scandal that attended the proceedings against Peter Lens, even when Jonathan Swift fingered him as a leader of the Blasters. Nonetheless, there was always a whiff of controversy around Worsdale's name, and this has proved to be the case almost up to the present day. In 2007 his portrait of Elihu Yale, the founder of Yale University, was removed from the university's prestigious Corporation Room on the grounds that it wrongly depicted Yale as a slave-owner.[34]

John St Leger and the Grangemellon Hellfire Club

Both of the hellfire clubs with which Worsdale was involved had probably disbanded by the time of his departure from Ireland in the 1740s. There is little documented evidence to suggest that any similar clubs were active in the country during the 1740s or 1750s, apart from Edmund Burke's reference to a group of Dublin freethinkers who met in 1748.[35] However, it is possible that there were clubs of which no trace has survived in the written or pictorial record. For instance, a hellfire club is believed to have met in a late eighteenth-century folly tower that overlooks the Shannon at Doonass, County Clare (see Plate 15).[36] Like the Askeaton building, this impressive structure is made of brick and stone. Although it is now surrounded by trees and swamped by undergrowth, it was probably once elegantly appointed: the remains of plasterwork and a fireplace can still be discerned, and it is adjoined by a turret that once housed a spiral staircase. The building was probably constructed in the 1760s or 1770s by Sir Hugh Dillon Massey of Doonass for use as a summerhouse. It was identified as such by the traveller and cartographer Daniel Augustus Beaufort when he visited Doonass in August 1788. The falls at Doonass were then regarded as one of the region's finest beauty spots and Beaufort noted that the tower, situated 'on a projecting rock just over the cataract & opposite Castle Connel', was 'most delectably placed'. He did not, however, make any reference to a hellfire club or any sinister goings-on there. Given that the Massey family papers were destroyed at Lismullen House in 1922, it is unlikely that much further information about the building and its uses will be uncovered.[37]

A more detailed picture emerges in relation to a hellfire club that was active in County Kildare in the 1760s. The principal figure connected with this group was John or Jack St Leger (1726–68), the eldest son of Sir John St Leger of Grangemellon, County Kildare, 2nd Baron of the Court of the Exchequer. Although St Leger's name has been consistently associated with the Dublin Hellfire Club, this is erroneous: he was at school in England when it flourished in the late 1730s. Nonetheless, as a noted duellist, womanizer and gambler, he possessed all the normal hellfire credentials. St Leger was educated and spent much of his youth in England. After attending Westminster School he entered Christ Church College, Oxford, on 12 July 1743. Four years later he embarked on the Grand Tour. Over the course of an extended sojourn in Italy (1747–49) he became notorious for his boorish treatment of women and his willingness to fight duels. During this time he was a principal in at least two affairs of honour, the first of which occurred in Milan in February 1748. Although he was wounded in the encounter, this did not prevent him from quarrelling with a Roman knight the following year, an affair in which he was 'well satisfied'. At Rome, St Leger hosted wild dinner parties. Improbably, his mother asserted that he and the Pope became drinking companions, often sharing a bottle and making crude and vulgar toasts to the Church and the cardinals.[38] He also became known for his foppish attire and character, which prompted Horace Walpole to describe him as 'a romping greyhound puppy'. It was an assessment with which the actress and socialite George Anne Bellamy, who encountered St Leger in London on his return from his travels, would have concurred:

> With a good understanding, a fine figure, and a handsome face, he had in his manner a good deal of the *coxcomb*, which had received no little addition from his having made the grand tour... [he was] accoutred as the complete fine gentleman. He had on a white surtout, with a crimson cape, a French waistcoat, his hair *en papillote*, a feather in his hat, a *couteau de chasse* by his side, with a small cane hanging to his button, and attended by two Italian greyhounds.

While in London St Leger became embroiled in a number of confrontations, displaying the same readiness to duel as he had in Italy.[39] He also joined one of the city's most exclusive clubs, White's, at which he became known for his extravagant dining habits and his 'dashing veracity and absurdity'.[40] Not long afterwards he returned to Ireland, where he quarrelled with Jack Hill over an old gambling debt. In the ensuing duel, fought at the Curragh in December 1753, Hill was shot in the chest and killed.[41] St Leger's fiery temper may have been quelled somewhat by his marriage to Mary Butler in 1754. She was the daughter of Colonel Thomas Butler, the Governor of Limerick, and the niece of Humphrey Butler, Viscount Lanesborough, and brought with her a massive fortune of £40,000. St Leger and his bride settled at the residence he had inherited from his father, Grangemellon Castle, situated some three miles south of Athy on the banks of the river Barrow. As the antiquarian Austin Cooper noted in 1782, it was an impressive building consisting of 'two octagon towers with a heavy pediment & cornice between, & the entrance to it, is thro' a gate way which is exactly like the house, or rather a miniature representation of it...The whole is situated in a vale on the side of the Barrow & surrounded with fine lofty trees and long avenues'. The grounds contained fish-ponds, a stone well, pleasure gardens and fruit gardens.[42]

St Leger's existence at Grangemellon seems to have been an indo-lent one. As was later observed, he 'possessed all the wit and pleasantry of his father the judge, but, following no profession, he lived upon his estates...which were very considerable'.[43] St Leger clearly possessed both time and money in considerable quantities. According to a late nineteenth-century account, he chose to spend it on the convivial entertainments and diversions of a hellfire club. This claim deserves more credence than most retrospective assertions regarding hellfire clubs as its author, Sir Anthony Weldon, was a member of a prominent Queen's County family whose residence, Kilmorony, overlooked Grangemellon from an eminence on the opposite side of the Barrow. Following the demolition of the castle at the end of the eighteenth century, the lands of Grangemellon came into the ownership of the Weldon family. According to Sir Anthony, some of the other members of the hellfire club that met there were Henry Dixon of Kilkea Castle, James McRoberts of Castleroe and Robert Hartpole of Shrule Castle, Queen's County.[44] These men were all prominent local gentry and all lived within a short distance of Grangemellon. Kilkea Castle, situated roughly six miles south-east of Athy, had been the property of the Earls of Kildare for many generations. Henry Dixon (c. 1740–97) resided at the castle under a lease he had inherited from his father or grandfather. James McRoberts (c. 1718–68) lived not far off at Castleroe House, which he rented from James Fitzgerald, 20th Earl of Kildare and (from 1766) 1st Duke of Leinster. Following a dispute with his landlord over the property, McRoberts reputedly swore that he would not be parted from Castleroe alive or dead, leaving instructions that he should be buried in a rath situated to the east of the house.[45] Robert Hartpole's residence, Shrule Castle, was located a few miles south of

Grangemellon on the western banks of the Barrow. Born in 1743, he was the son of George Hartpole, MP for Portarlington, 1761–63.[46] The Grangemellon club was said to have had several other members; however, only one other name is remembered: George Bagenal of Dunleckney, County Carlow.[47] As there was no George Bagenal resident at Dunleckney during the period in question, it may be that Beauchamp Bagenal (c. 1735–1802) is meant instead.

Each of these men, with the possible exception of McRoberts, was well known for dissolute conduct. St Leger's exploits on the duelling field had earned him a reputation as 'the fighting St Leger'. He complemented this rakish image by drinking and gambling heavily, on one occasion losing £1,300 at hazard in a single sitting.[48] Henry Dixon led 'a wild and dissipated life', while Robert Hartpole, in the tradition of his forefathers, spent his time 'merrily enjoying the convivialities of the world, principally in the night-time'.[49] Beauchamp Bagenal, for his part, was a habitual duellist who outraged local society through his womanizing, drinking and general misconduct. According to Jonah Barrington, Bagenal had engaged in a series of scarcely credible adventures while on the Grand Tour: 'He had fought a prince – jilted a princess – intoxicated the doge of Venice – carried off a duchess from Madrid – scaled the walls of a convent in Italy – narrowly escaped the Inquisition at Lisbon; [and] concluded his exploits by a celebrated fencing match at Paris.'[50] He and the others were exactly the sort of men who would have been attracted by the prospect of founding a hellfire club.

Judging by its members' circumstances, the Grangemellon club was probably active during the mid- to late 1760s: Robert Hartpole did not come of age until 1764, and James McRoberts and John St Leger died in 1768 and 1769 respectively. Like its Limerick predecessor, the club was a gathering of country squires who met in order to indulge their shared interests, principally drinking and gambling, while cultivating the trappings of a hellfire club in order to foster a sense of allure and mystery. It was remembered as a 'scandalous institution', the uniform of which consisted of a red coat, waistcoat and breeches, and white stockings.[51] This was an innovation: judging from the group portraits, neither the Limerick club nor the Dublin Hellfire Club wore uniforms. This predilection for standard attire may have influenced later groups such as the Cherokees (see Chapter 6). If the tastes exhibited by St Leger during his days at White's Club are in any way indicative of his inclinations at Grangemellon, he and his companions would have dined extravagantly on exotic dishes and fine champagne. More ominously, the club was believed to have held orgies during which a seat was kept vacant 'in case His Satanic Majesty chose to join them in person'.[52] This is another generic motif in hellfire club folklore, and there is reason to doubt the veracity of its attribution to the Grangemellon club.

Despite their reputations as incorrigible wastrels, both Beauchamp Bagenal and St Leger showed remorse for their dissolute ways. The Quaker Mary Leadbeater, who was born in Ballitore, County Kildare, in 1758, recalled how her mother Elizabeth Shackleton once confronted Bagenal regarding his drunken misconduct. He 'acknowledged the truth of her remarks, and lamented his inability to keep those good resolutions which he had often made'. Mrs Shackleton was also moved to intervene in the case of St Leger, who, like the Earl of Rosse before him, 'was reduced by his vices to a languishing condition' at a relatively early age. According to Leadbeater,

> no one about him had the courage to tell him of his danger. My mother was greatly concerned to hear this, and she imparted to him by letter her feelings on his account, urging him to review his past life, and to prepare for the life to come. I was told he was much affected by this letter; that he caused it to be read to him several times as he lay on his death-bed; and recommended it to be sent to another gentleman, who, he said, wanted such advice as much as he did.[53]

If true, this story indicates a contriteness quite at odds with the cavalier demeanour that Rosse exhibited on his deathbed. Not all adherents of hellfire clubs were as obstinate as the earl and, despite their vaunted anticlericalism and blasphemy, some found it hard to dismiss the doctrines of Christianity when confronted with their own imminent demise.[54] St Leger died in March 1769 at the age of 42 and was buried in the family vault at Kilkea. James McRoberts had expired suddenly the previous June 'after a fortnight's confinement from a slight contusion of his right leg'. In line with his wishes, he was buried in the rath near Castleroe House.[55]

The activities of the Grangemellon hellfire club were sufficiently controversial to inspire a number of ghostly tales in the locality. In 1854, an Athy resident alluded to the spectral reputation that St Leger enjoyed as a result of his hellfire credentials: 'the peasantry here believe that he often drives in a coach and four; the coachman and footmen are headless, and also the horses; some of the parties have even seen this cavalcade, and will not pass by Grangemellon after dark'.[56] It was also believed that James McRoberts's favourite horse and two hounds were interred with him in the rath, and that he and his trio of animals were afterwards seen on the road nearby.[57] While such tales are obviously apocryphal, folklore does not emerge in a vacuum and these stories may have been grounded upon the notorious reputations that St Leger and his cohorts enjoyed during their lifetimes.

The existence of a hellfire club at Grangemellon suggests that the ideology that inspired such groups remained a reckonable force in the Ireland of the 1760s. Certain gentlemen continued to be willing to provoke the conservative and moralizing elements of society by establishing such groups. For their part, moralists and clergymen continued to condemn these clubs in the harshest possible terms. Increasingly, these moralists were of a Catholic persuasion. The Irish Catholic Church was beginning to assume a more confident stance in the second half of the eighteenth century. It was re-emerging as a formidable force for orthodoxy and virtue, and it did not hesitate to attack those clubs that were particularly associated with blasphemous utterance. This was most apparent in the controversy that surrounded the emergence of a group that called themselves the Holy Fathers.

The Holy Fathers

When the Dublin Hellfire Club or Blasters publicly invoked the Devil and coined blasphemous oaths in the 1730s, their principal critics were representatives of the Established Church such as George Berkeley and Jonathan Swift. Unsurprisingly, the Catholic Church found blasphemy just as objectionable. While Catholic ecclesiastics were hardly in a position to denounce upper-class Protestants in the early eighteenth century, Irish Catholicism began to undergo some revival in the latter half of the century. It was supported by a prosperous, urban, Catholic middle class, and its growing confidence and assertiveness were reflected in the establishment of confraternities dedicated to the promotion of Catholic doctrine. Two such societies were established in Dublin in the late 1740s, the Confraternity of the Holy Name and the Sodality of the Name of Jesus.[58] These groups, which made it their business to venerate the name of God and combat blasphemy, were antithetical to the hellfire clubs that made swearing their particular business. When, in the early 1770s, a group of young gentlemen calling themselves the Holy Fathers revived the Hellfire Club's blasphemous practices, one of its fiercest critics was a Catholic clergyman and confraternity member.

Flaunting a name that evinced a sardonic disdain for the Catholic clergy and hierarchy, the Holy Fathers emerged in the midlands, 'not far from the Shannon, as if to spread [their] baneful influence more rapidly to every part of the nation'. The identities of the members are not known; doubtless the fear of infringing libel laws prevented their detractors from naming them publicly. However, most were young gentlemen with good fortunes and some were married with children. At least one held a prominent position at the Custom House.[59] The club made its first public appearance at a race meeting in the west in the early autumn of 1770, where they outraged the other attendees by engaging in conversation that was described as 'a medley of obscenity, nonsense and profaneness'. The Holy Fathers framed such toasts and sentiments, after dinner, that many decent persons quitted their company immediately. One hero began the infernal carouse, with giving a bumper to his own toast, 'the Devil;' and this before drunkenness could extenuate the offence: and after a multitude of intermediate toasts of the same stamp, a brother-blood concluded the banquet with a horrible ejaculation, 'd[amnatio]n to us all'.

Observers were in little doubt that the club was a revival of 'that accursed society, called, the Hell-fire Club'.[60] Indeed, anyone familiar with the activities and rhetoric of Peter Lens and his cohorts over thirty years earlier would have noted distinct similarities in the Holy Fathers' conduct. As it is not known whether the Limerick or Grangemellon clubs undertook to blaspheme deliberately and publicly, the Holy Fathers are the first club known to have deliberately imitated the blasphemous campaign of the Dublin Hellfire Club or Blasters.

Following this initial provocative assault on public morals, the Holy Fathers continued to engage in objectionable conduct over the ensuing months, provoking a number of condemnations in the popular press. In March 1771 a correspondent of the *Freeman's Journal* sought the newspaper's assistance in orchestrating a boycott of the club, which he described as 'a kind of pestilence, or evil spirit'. The correspondent, 'Socrates', elaborated on the divine punishments that awaited those who dared to blaspheme and entreat damnation. He went on to address the members of the club directly, urging them to a realization that their lives might be suddenly cut short by the effects of dissipation, a duel or mischance, and that they would then stand 'before the eternal judgment seat, whose vengeance they have been denying and provoking'.[61] 'Socrates' may have been Father John O'Connor, a Dominican of Bridge Street Convent in Dublin. Described by a contemporary as 'expert in the handling of affairs, eloquent in speech and of high moral character', he later came close to being appointed Bishop of Ossory. Along with his confrère, Father Laurence Richardson, O'Connor was an advocate of a sodality that was dedicated to the veneration of the name of Jesus.[62] As such, he had more reason than most to take offence at the blasphemy and diabolic invocations of the Holy Fathers.

In 1772 O'Connor published *An Essay on the Rosary and Sodality of the Most Holy Name of Jesus*, in which he denounced cursing, swearing and blasphemy.[63] He attacked the Holy Fathers for using 'such vile oaths, imprecations and blasphemies, as would foul, if possible, even hell itself', expressing astonishment that they did so 'meerly for the sake of propagating those vices'. Enjoining them to remember that there was an abyss – hell – on whose brink they were 'madly sporting', he acknowledged the essential unbelief of their stance: 'I know these geniuses have struck out an expeditious method to rid themselves at once of all fears and apprehensions, *viz.* to deny peremptorily "that there is an hell".'[64] Like Peter Lens and the Blasters, the Holy Fathers invoked the Devil and damnation not because they believed in them, but because they did not. While the threat of eternal damnation may have been no dissuasive to the club, O'Connor was hopeful that temporal sanctions could be brought to bear against them. He believed that, like the Blasters, the Holy Fathers had incurred contempt in the eyes of all rational and polite people, and he was confident that they would be ostracized. The tone, language and content of this condemnation closely resembles that of 'Socrates' in the *Freeman's Journal*, indicating that O'Connor either penned the earlier account, or that he relied heavily on it for his knowledge of the Holy Fathers.

The adherents of the Established Church also condemned the club. In April 1771 the Holy Fathers were attacked by Meade Swift, a Protestant moralist resident at Mullingar. In an apparent conflation with their predecessors, he referred to them as the Blasters and echoed Bishop Berkeley's call for the official suppression of those who blasphemed. Using the same logic as Berkeley, Swift equated blasphemy and anticlericalism with treason against the civil authorities:

> The influence that religion has upon our lives and conversation is the best security the king has for the loyalty of his subjects, and was that same religion to be exterminated (as these men would

wish) the subjects could have no confidence in one another; the consequence of all which would be anarchy and confusion in both church and state.

He also alluded to 'a gentleman of large property in this country, and advanced in years' who oscillated between blasphemy and scepticism, at one point 'ridicul[ing] our holy religion, and rail[ing] at its founder and his apostles', and at another 'endeavour[ing] to maintain, that there never was such a person as Jesus Christ'.[65] It is unclear if this individual belonged to the Holy Fathers. Crucially, however, he was an atheist rather than a devil worshipper. He did not believe in Jesus Christ and chose to express his disenchantment with religious orthodoxy through blasphemy.

The Holy Fathers also displayed a strong penchant for violence. The aggression inherent in their activities was evidenced by the fact that one of the members came close to being killed in an unspecified incident at one of their meetings. They were also keen duellists, 'appealing upon every frivolous occasion to powder and ball, which they generally carry about and exhibit in company, to prove their courage'. This was anathema to those who deplored duelling as a destructive and dangerous phenomenon.[66] However, for at least one of the Holy Fathers, described as 'the hero of the gang', the code of honour had a strong practical function. Finding himself indebted to a number of tradesmen and gentlemen, he surrounded himself with a band of 'desperadoes' and undertook extreme measures to avoid paying his creditors. Anyone who came looking for repayment of a debt faced intimidation by the chief ruffian, 'a most remarkable lawless and wicked fellow, and capable of any bad action'. If any gentleman persevered in attempting to recover what was owed, he was insulted or challenged to a duel.[67] Such conduct is reminiscent of that engaged in by George Robert Fitzgerald, the most notorious duellist of the period. Fitzgerald was given to provoking affairs of honour in order to avoid paying debts, and at one point he assembled a band of ruffians to serve 'as his personal Volunteer corps'. It is unlikely that he and the 'hero' of the

Holy Fathers were the same individual, as Fitzgerald was living in Paris in the early 1770s.[68] Yet the congruity in their actions identifies them as men of the same stamp, and exemplifies the tolerance of interpersonal violence in Ireland during the 'era of the Fire-Eaters', when the numbers of duels between gentlemen attained unprecedented levels.

Little else is known about the Holy Fathers. Like most hellfire clubs, they were an ephemeral group, and it seems unlikely that they continued in existence for long after 1771. The controversy that they engendered was indicative of the ongoing battle between the forces of morality and decorum and those who flouted these principles and conventional religious mores. Yet those who chose to propagate a hellfire club ethos did not need to blaspheme overtly, or even form a society, in order to do so. The incorporation of hellfire club motifs in the architectural and artistic design of the period is intriguing.

Architectural and Artistic Design

As mentioned in Chapter 3, the Dublin Hellfire Club sought to heighten its mystique by surrounding itself with items that seemed to incorporate diabolic symbols. A few years after the club's demise, symbolism of this kind was again in evidence in a project undertaken at Birr Castle by the 1st Earl of Rosse's cousin, Sir Laurence Parsons (1708–56), and his associate, the artist and architect Samuel Chearnley (1717–47). In the 1740s, Parsons and Chearnley collaborated on an album of unusual architectural designs entitled *Miscelanea Structura Curiosa*. While none of these designs were realized as physical structures, a number of them were clearly inspired by the burlesque and anticlerical spirit that was associated with hellfire clubs.[69] The most intriguing was a sketch of a 'grotto', intended as the entrance to a convivial setting. The appearance, however, is anything but convivial. The elevation depicts a walled approach to a cave-like entrance, culminating in two stone pillars, each surmounted by a weird trollish head. The accompanying text outlined its purpose:

This properly might be intended at ye extremity of an exten[sive] improvement where after the strang[er] has seen a variety of delightful objects he at last is brought to a frightful wilderness proper for this horrible place which ent[e]ring with terror through many windings – is at last surpriz[e]d in a delightful banqueting room – from whence an extensive prospect sho[ul]d be as answerable as ye front at ye entering confined.

Such a structure might well be regarded as a suitable setting for a hellfire club, and the mention of an 'extensive prospect' calls to mind the panoramic view commanded by the Dublin Hellfire Club's supposed country retreat in the Dublin Mountains (see Chapter 7). Another design, depicting a statue of a kneeling monk in frivolous aspect, overlooked by a row of comic masks, was redolent of an anticlericalism of which Rosse and others would have approved.[70] While it is not known if Chearnley or Parsons was actively involved in a hellfire club, in preparing *Miscelanea Structura Curiosa* they certainly drew inspiration from the occultism and anticlericalism of such clubs. They probably did so in order to mock the orthodox and conservative values that were advocated by sections of the Irish gentry and clergy. As Barnard notes, Parsons 'may not have had much sympathy with the earnest clergymen and worthy squires of the Dublin Society and Physico-Historical Society. The parodic elements in Chearnley's designs have long been recognized.'[71] These designs also anticipated the garden monuments and imitation temples that Sir Francis Dashwood later laid out in the grounds of his residence at West Wycombe, Buckinghamshire.[72]

Hellfire club symbolism was also evident in another item dating from the 1740s. This was a 'Hell-Fire Club clock-case' that is depicted in the *Georgian Society Records*, an early twentieth-century work which chronicles architectural and decorative features from Georgian Ireland.[73] Recalling the monstrous heads on the pillars in Chearnley's design, this illustration depicts a longcase clock decorated with demonic faces (see Plate 16). No documentation on the purpose and use of this curious piece has been located. It bears the date 1749, too late for it to have belonged to either the Dublin or the Limerick Hellfire Club. However, it is laden with hellfire club symbolism and its design was doubtless inspired by the same ideology that motivated *Miscelanea Structura Curiosa*. The burning wine glass on the trunk of the clock-case denotes both drink and the flames of hell, while the coat of arms incorporating a hand of cards signifies the importance of gambling. The carved faces clearly represent devils. The clock-case probably belonged to a group that regarded themselves as a hellfire club. According to Edmund Burke, at least one group of freethinkers was active in Dublin in the late 1740s: 'a set of men ... who tho' they allow of morality, cry down reveal'd religion, yet in their practice, they make them equal, neglecting both'. Burke hinted that these men were given to dissipated conduct, and that (like the hellfire clubs that preceded them) they justified this by reference to an Enlightenment-inspired 'system of morality'.[74] It is possible that this or a similar club had the clock-case designed and constructed for their use.

The period between the 1730s and 1770s saw the emergence of a series of regional hellfire clubs which, to varying degrees, engaged in dissolute revelry and, in the case of the Holy Fathers at least, blasphemous and aggressive behaviour. The existence of these regional groups could be taken as evidence of a single organization constituted on a countrywide basis, with a 'metropolitan' branch in Dublin and regional branches elsewhere.[75] However, it is improbable that the hellfire clubs operated according to a countrywide or coordinated structure. There were significant intervals between each group's emergence, and each appears to have been constituted on an independent basis. At the same time, the character and demeanour of these clubs was inspired by a general 'hellfire' ethos. The blasphemous conduct of the Holy Fathers derived from their antipathy towards the 'superstitious' doctrines and rituals of conventional Christianity, provoking vehement condemnation from Protestant and Catholic moralists and ecclesiastics. It is probable that the Limerick and Grangemellon hellfire clubs shared the

Holy Fathers' sentiments; certainly the folklore that emerged in relation to them in later years – that the former roasted a man alive to see
if he could endure hellfire, while the latter left a vacant seat for the
Devil during 'orgies' – indicates that they did. There were also clubs
such as the Trinity or Holy Ghost Boys, about whom nothing is known
other than that they were said to award prizes 'to the fabricators of the
most blasphemous sentiments'.[76] The 'hellfire' ethos that these groups
shared can be viewed as a counter-statement against the culture of
politeness, morality and piety that other societies and individuals
promoted. The latter found the 'hellfire' ethos deeply unsettling. Not
only did the hellfire clubs disregard civility and conscientiousness, they
also utilized rhetoric and imagery that played on deep-rooted fears of
the Devil, hell and damnation. Samuel Chearnley's designs, and objects
such as the Hell Fire Club clock-case, would have appeared bizarre and
unnerving to those who viewed them. The advocates of hellfire ideology had opened a dark window in the upper-class psyche.

At the same time, blasphemy and diabolism were tangential to the
hellfire clubs' main activities, which were hedonistic, sensual and often
aggressive, involving the maltreatment of servants, women and others.
As mentioned previously, the last three decades of the eighteenth
century saw the emergence of a number of rakish clubs that eschewed
the philosophical pretensions of the hellfire clubs, while maintaining
their more visceral practices. Dublin's Pinkindindies caused major
controversy through their drunken acts of vandalism and their nocturnal attacks on unsuspecting passers-by, prostitutes and watchmen. Their
successors, the Cherokee Club, undertook similar activities, though to
a lesser degree. Neither group showed much interest in theological
issues and there is little sign that they were influenced by deistic or
atheistic thought. They did not engage in deliberate and public displays
of blasphemy, nor did they accoutre themselves with diabolic symbols.
Nonetheless, they were sufficiently similar to the hellfire clubs to
induce contemporaries to bracket them together. Andrew O'Reilly
believed that the Cherokee Club, at least one member of which he was
personally acquainted with, was the successor to the Dublin Hellfire

Club 'in notoriety and profligacy',[77] while Lady Sydney Morgan (c. 1780–1854) placed both the Cherokee Club and the Pinkindindies in the same category as the Hellfire Club.[78] Nor did later commentators scruple to distinguish between rakish and hellfire clubs. For writers such as William O'Neill Daunt, John Edward Walsh, John T. Gilbert and James J. Gaskin, the Dublin Hellfire Club, Pinkindindies and Cherokees were clubs or gangs of 'bucks' that epitomized all that was wild, provocative, unrestrained and repulsive about the Georgian era.[79]

Possibly the most turbulent decades of this era were the 1770s and 1780s, when levels of duelling and interpersonal violence among the gentry attained unprecedented levels.[80] The growing ubiquity of duelling as an accepted means of dispute resolution was already observable in the Holy Fathers' willingness to engage in affairs of honour. Such developments may have dovetailed with a general culture of upper-class violence. This is strongly observable in the conduct of the most notorious rakish club, the Pinkindindies.

Chapter five

The Pinkindindies

On 19 January 1785, a gentleman named Richard Crosbie ascended from Ranelagh Gardens near Dublin in a hydrogen balloon. Watched by a crowd estimated to be in the tens of thousands, the balloon and balloonist were carried north-east by the wind, traversing the fringes of the eighteenth-century capital. As he approached the sea, Crosbie realized he was unprepared for an extended voyage. Releasing some of the gas from his apparatus, he managed to effect a landing on the strand near Clontarf Island.[1] This was not the first manned balloon ascent to take place; that had been initiated by the Montgolfier brothers at the Château de la Muette near Paris in November 1783. However, it was the first such feat to be accomplished by an Irishman, and, in recognition of his achievement, Crosbie was feted by the Lord Lieutenant, the Duke of Rutland, and presented with a cheque for £200. He was also the subject of plaudits and glowing tributes such as Samuel Whyte's panegyric, 'The Balloon'. It was Crosbie's intention to become the first man to cross the Irish Sea by air. Despite a series of further attempts, he failed to achieve this ambition and his name faded into obscurity over the ensuing years. In more recent times, however, there has been a major revival of interest in the man and his achievement. In 1985, a commemorative postage stamp was issued to mark the bicentenary of Crosbie's ascent. Further recognition followed in the 2000s, when a local campaign sourced funding to commission a statue of the intrepid balloonist. The statue was unveiled in Ranelagh Gardens in September 2008 amid considerable popular and media interest. Rory Breslin's stylistic bronze piece depicts Crosbie as an inquisitive youth accoutred with aeronautical devices, including a boomerang, a paper plane and a rotor. The organizers of the Ranelagh Arts Festival described him as 'the great Richard Crosbie' and the *Irish Times* referred to him as a 'heroic daredevil', while to the *Irish Independent* he was a 'flight of fantasy aviator'.[2]

Significantly, none of these commentators mentioned the less salubrious reputation that Crosbie enjoyed in Dublin a few years prior to his aeronautical escapades. In the late 1770s he was a leader of the Pinkindindies, with whom he committed wanton acts of vandalism and aggression. The fact that these less-than-heroic feats were not remembered either at the time of Crosbie's aeronautical feat or at the unveiling of his statue over two centuries later bears witness to the degree to which eighteenth-century society was prepared to overlook nefarious conduct by members of the upper classes, while routinely sending poorer offenders to the gallows. Although the Dublin press frequently condemned the Pinkindindies and called for severe measures to be taken against them, the authorities often adopted a lenient attitude towards the members of the gang, including Crosbie, who were brought before them to answer for their crimes. This should not disguise the fact that in the late 1770s and early 1780s the Pinkindindies were a serious menace. Operating mainly at night-time, they smashed lamps and windows, robbed and wounded passers-by, attacked and abused women, wrecked brothels and engaged in furious battles with the city watch.

Superficially, there was nothing new about such conduct. Over the course of the eighteenth century, the frequency of murder, assault, brawling, robbery, abduction and rape, along with the ubiquity of the press gang, combined to create a decidedly hostile atmosphere on the streets of Dublin.[3] Moreover, the city had long been plagued by factional strife. Gangs of tradesmen such as the weavers of the Liberties and the butchers of Ormond Market (known as the Liberty boys and Ormond boys) met intermittently in public places to engage in full-scale battles that often resulted in multiple deaths. In the 1770s, considerable animosity erupted between the civilian population – particularly the Ormond butchers – and the 2,500 soldiers stationed in

Dublin.[4] While such animosity was partly motivated by resentment towards recruitment for military service in America, civilians were also outraged by the atrocities that soldiers perpetrated, such as the gang rape of a woman in Fishamble Street in 1778. Reprisals inflicted by the mob often took the form of 'houghing' or cutting the hamstrings of soldiers.[5]

Contemporaries sometimes conflated the 'houghers' with the gangs of 'chalkers' that haunted Stoneybatter and other areas peripheral to the city during the late 1760s and 1770s.[6] 'Chalking' was the name given to the practice of inflicting wounds that were calculated to maim or disfigure rather than kill, and in many cases these attacks were actuated by purely malicious motives. According to a contemporary dictionary of slang, the chalkers were 'men of wit, in Ireland, who in the night amuse themselves with cutting inoffensive passengers across the face with a knife', but this was too narrow a definition.[7] More accurately, the 'Chalking Act' that was introduced in 1773–74 to curb these practices defined a chalker as a person who 'by lying in wait or watching, or waiting for the opportunity. . . with any knife, or other sharp weapon, shall cut or stab any person or persons in the face, or in any limb or member, or in any part of the body, with intent in so doing to murder, rob, or maim, or to disable or disfigure him, her or them'. Four years later, an amendment to the Act indicated that such attacks were carried out with 'a wanton and wicked intent to disable or disfigure' and added wounding by pistols to the list of crimes for which offenders could be capitally convicted.[8]

Prior to the emergence of the Pinkindindies, then, Dublin was plagued by a variety of dangerous and aggressive gangs, ranging from tradesmen's factions to delinquent soldiers to gratuitously violent bands of chalkers. However, there was a significant social distinction between these groups and the Pinkindindies. While the former were generally drawn from the lower social strata, the latter tended to be students of Trinity College and the sons of upper-middle-class and gentry families. Benefiting from superior education and opportunities, the Pinkindindies had less excuse than their lower-class counterparts for carrying out assaults and engaging in crime. They might have claimed in their defence that they were merely pursuing a long tradition of street violence as perpetrated by groups of well-heeled young men. This tradition was most firmly established in London, which was plagued by rakish gangs in the late seventeenth and eighteenth centuries. The Scowrers of the 1680s–90s were notorious for committing unprovoked acts of aggression and vandalism in public places.[9] They were succeeded by the Mohocks, whose nocturnal attacks on pedestrians threw the city into consternation in March 1712. As previously noted, the Mohocks were manifestly upper class, counting among their number a baronet and the son of a peer. Other groups of upper-class men acted out similar scenarios over the ensuing decades. The term 'buck', which might be equated with 'rake', became a synonym for the drunken young gentleman out on the town, while the harmful and mischievous behaviour in which he engaged became known as the 'frolick'. According to the *Gentleman's Magazine* of 1755:

> the noblest exploit of a man of the town, the highest proof and utmost effort of his genius and pleasantry is the frolick. This piece of humour consists in playing the most wild and extravagant pranks that wantonness and debauchery can suggest; and is the distinguishing characteristic of the buck and blood... The present race of bucks commonly begin their frolick in a tavern, and end it in the roundhouse, and during the course of it practise several mighty pretty pleasantries. There is a great deal of humour in what is called beating the rounds, that is in plain English, taking a tour of the principal bawdy-houses; breaking of lamps, and skirmishes with watchmen are very good jests; and the insulting any dull sober fools... or a rape on a modest woman are particularly facetious.[10]

The Dublin Hellfire Club had occasionally been known to behave in such a manner, but it tended to carry on its objectionable conduct indoors, in taverns or in the quarters of unfortunate servants and isolated females. In addition, the Hellfire Club was convened for the purposes of conviviality and provocative blasphemy rather than public aggression and vandalism. The Pinkindindies, however, were conspicuously dedicated to the 'frolick', the description of which in the *Gentleman's Magazine* could have been the template for their activities. The Mohocks, rather than the Hellfire Club, were their inspiration, and the college environment in which they emerged afforded young gentlemen ample opportunity to consort.

The Collegians

For many years, the students of Trinity College, or Collegians, had drawn attention to themselves through their involvement in disturbances in Dublin. They were avid participants in factional warfare, maintaining an antagonistic relationship with the city watch and occasionally taking part in the hostilities between the Liberty and Ormond boys. Collegians also undertook incursions characterized by arbitrary vandalism and aggression, such as at Smock Alley Theatre, where a gang led by a student named Kelly wrecked the stage and the green room in 1747.[11] Jonah Barrington, who entered Trinity in 1773, engaged enthusiastically in such activities: 'we were in the habit of going about [the streets] on dark nights, in coaches, and, by flinging out half-pence, breaking the windows of all the houses we rapidly drove by, to the astonishment and terror of the proprietors'. He and his fellow students threw fireworks into china shops, delighting 'to see the terrified shop-keepers trampling on their own porcelain and cut glass, for fear of an explosion'. They smashed lamps, plunging entire streets into darkness, and invaded gambling houses, knocking out the lights and depriving the gamblers of their stakes.[12] Such 'tumults' were an ongoing cause of concern for the Trinity College authorities, who frequently censured students for participating in nocturnal disturbances in Dublin.[13]

These reprobate students were also subjected to satirical attacks. In *Walker's Hibernian Magazine*, the 'College-Buck' (see Plate 17) was characterized as a shiftless youth whose preoccupations were drinking, fighting and womanizing. He was given to 'knocking down all he meets', and his weapon of choice was a heavy room key wrapped in a handkerchief or a piece of cloth – 'a devilish good weapon in a dark night, in a street wrangle or a gutter fray'. This was not mere hyperbole. On one occasion a group of drunken students, armed with keys in their handkerchiefs, forced their way into a house on Essex Street and bludgeoned a servant so badly that he was left in a critical condition.[14] Yet anyone who attacked the Collegians in print ran the risk of incurring dire consequences, as the printer Michael Mills found when he ran a piece criticizing student misbehaviour in his newspaper, the *Hibernian Journal*. On 11 February 1775, Mills was abducted from his shop on Capel Street by around twenty sword-and-pistol-wielding students and driven in a coach to Trinity College. Having dragged him to the pump that then stood in the front square of the college, his assailants forced him to the ground and pumped water into his mouth and ears. Mills would in all likelihood have been suffocated had it not been for the intervention of a number of gentlemen.[15] The assault caused considerable public outrage, and the college authorities had little option but to take action against the perpetrators. Though the principal ringleader, Emmanuel Thompson, was censured, it appears that he and the other perpetrators escaped prosecution.[16]

For many Collegians, then, violent misconduct was part and parcel of everyday life, and gangs of students frequently involved themselves in factional warfare, the vandalism of theatres and shops, and attacks on individuals such as Mills. Yet these gangs tended to be informally constituted bodies that disbanded as soon as the deeds were done. Soon, however, a number of Collegians established an association of a more enduring character, designated by a peculiar name and code of conduct. One of its leading members was a young undergraduate named Richard Crosbie.

Richard Crosbie

Born at Crosbie Park near Baltinglass, County Wicklow, in 1755, Richard Crosbie was the second son of the baronet Sir Paul Crosbie. As a boy he exhibited an inquiring scientific mind, particularly in relation to mechanisms and their construction. Despite his father's and his schoolmasters' efforts to encourage him to focus his attention on his books, Richard availed himself of every opportunity to indulge his fascination with mechanisms. At school he avoided the sports field, locking himself away in order to work on clockwork devices and other gadgets. In 1773, aged 17, Crosbie entered Trinity College, where he continued to devote much of his time to extracurricular research into mechanisms and their construction.[17] At Trinity he became a close friend of Jonah Barrington, who described him as 'very good-tempered, exceedingly strong, and as brave as a lion, but as dogged as a mule: nothing could change a resolution of his when once made, and nothing could check or resist his perseverance to carry it into execution'.[18]

The friendship between Crosbie and Barrington was reinforced by the fact that both were earnest advocates of the code of honour. On one occasion, Barrington received a challenge from a fellow student, Richard 'Dasher' Daly, a dedicated duellist who was said to have fought sixteen encounters within the space of two years. Though puzzled as to what he might have done to offend Daly, Barrington accepted unquestioningly and asked Crosbie to act as his second. He then apprised his friend of a quandary: the duel was scheduled to take place the following morning and he had no pistols with which to fight it. Crosbie believed that they could cobble together a set from some old locks, barrels and stocks that he had in his possession. The pair set to work and by two o'clock in the morning they had assembled 'three entire pistols, which . . . struck their fire *right well*, and that was all we wanted of them'. At seven o'clock Crosbie and Barrington set out for the agreed rendezvous at Donnybrook, fortifying themselves against the cold and wintry wind with draughts of chocolate and cherry brandy. On their arrival they were confronted by the sight of Daly, dressed splendidly in silk stockings, a tasselled three-cocked hat, and a pea-green coat with a tucker bearing a large diamond brooch. On catching sight of his adversary, Daly realized that he had challenged the wrong person. Through his second, Jack Patterson, he endeavoured to have the duel called off, as 'a mistake on his part, originating through misrepresentation'. Barrington would have been content to let the matter end there, but Crosbie would have none of it:

> Crosby, without hesitation said, 'We can not do that *yet*, sir: I'll *show* you we *can't*: (taking a little manuscript book out of his breeches pocket,) there's the *rules*! – look at that, sir,' continued he, 'see No. 7: "No apology can be received *after* the parties meet, *without a fire*."' 'You see, there's the rule,' pursued Crosby, with infinite self-satisfaction; 'and a young man on his *first blood* can not break rule, particularly with a gentleman so used to the sport as Mr Daly. Come gentlemen, proceed! proceed!'

The duel went ahead. Barrington fired first. Daly was hit in the chest but saved by his diamond brooch, which stopped the ball from penetrating the flesh, though part of the brooch lodged in his breastbone. Crosbie extracted the brooch and the two parties parted, with less good will than they might have had the duel been averted.[19]

The incident illustrates Crosbie's bullish approach to life: he was fond of confrontation and did not scruple to avoid bloodshed. However, scientific experimentation with various machines and apparatuses continued to be his predominant interest. In Barrington's estimation he was 'beyond all comparison, the most ingenious mechanic I ever knew... His chambers at college were like a general workshop for all kinds of artisans.' Crosbie spent much of his time in these rooms, tinkering with automatons, clocks and watches. Yet his work was hindered by a lack of finance: 'his purse was not sufficiently stocked to support any considerable experiment, or indeed any extensive piece of mechanism'.[20] Of course, the requisite funds could be obtained through crime, and Crosbie appears to have decided to pursue this course. At some point in the late 1770s, he joined with a number of his fellow Collegians to form an armed association dedicated to nocturnal assault and robbery. They called themselves the Pinkindindies.

The Rise of the Pinkindindies

The extent to which the Pinkindindies were a formal club or society is uncertain. No rules of membership or minutes of meetings are known to have survived, and the group is probably best regarded as a loosely organized gang, albeit one which operated according to a distinct code of conduct. Crosbie, according to one contemporary, was the leader. Another prominent member was James Gillespie, a Dublin attorney's son who had enrolled in Trinity on the same day as Crosbie, 3 November 1773.[21] It is likely that Jonah Barrington also belonged to the gang, given his close association with Crosbie and his propensity for late-night vandalism. Other members were probably student acquaintances of Crosbie and Barrington, the sort of men who liked to indulge in brawls and tumults, frequently provoking the censure of the college authorities.[22] Yet membership of the gang was not exclusive to students. According to the actor and portrait painter James Dowling Herbert (c. 1762–1837), some Pinkindindies were non-Collegians, young men from well-to-do backgrounds whose parents 'permitted them to get up to man's estate in idle habits, without adequate means of support'. One such individual, Michael O'Berne, would later face execution for his part in the robbery of a gentleman.[23] Between students and others, the gang must have had a reasonably large membership. It was principally active between 1778 and 1780, when it engaged in an intermittent but ongoing campaign of crime and violence.

The name Pinkindindies was a derivation of 'pinking-dandies', the term 'pinking' denoting the pricking or stabbing of unwary passers-by with the point of a sword, the tip of whose scabbard had been cut off for the purpose.[24] Yet the name also had other connotations, which were intended to distinguish the gang from common rioters or ruffians. To be 'in the pink' was to be in the best condition or degree, and 'dindies' or 'dandies' denoted fashionable gentlemen. The members of the gang appear to have regarded themselves as a sort of gentlemanly fraternity who, though they rioted, raped, robbed and wounded, did so in fashionable attire and with a gay swagger.[25] While the Pinkindindies' victims frequently attested to their assailants' well-dressed and respectable appearance, there was little about their conduct that could be regarded as respectable. As the courtesan Margaret Leeson cuttingly observed:

> however they might be deemed gentlemen by their birth, or connexions, yet, by their actions, [they] deserved no other appellation than that of RUFFIANS...They ran drunk through the streets, knocking down whoever they met; attacked, beat and cut the watch; and with great valour, broke open the habitations of unfortunate girls, demolished the furniture of their rooms, and treated the unhappy sufferers with a barbarity and savageness, at which a gang of drunken coal-porters would have blushed.[26]

Such arbitrary and chaotic conduct was largely prompted by a perverse sense of mischief, arising from factors such as boredom, intoxication and a desire to emulate gangs such as the Mohocks. Yet the Pinkindindies also had more practical motivations.

The gang's usual stamping ground was the network of streets and alleys between Dame Street and the Liffey, an area well known today as the popular tourist haunt of Temple Bar. In the late eighteenth century it was the most densely populated part of the city, and also one of the most insalubrious. While the area's western reaches had undergone some physical reorientation in the 1750s with the opening of Parliament Street, linking Essex Bridge and Dublin Castle,[27] this had done little to improve its seedy reputation. At night-time it was an epicentre of crime, gambling and illicit sex, the resort of prostitutes, beggars and thieves. The alleys and lanes to the east of Parliament Street were crammed with brothels, including one on Temple Bar where girls aged as young as 11 and 12 were prostituted. On Essex Street, a colonnaded walk known as the 'piazzas' was frequented by some 'of the worst characters of both sexes'. There were also many gambling dens, with five situated between Parliament Street and the corner of Eustace Street alone.[28] These dens were described as 'the asylum of sharpers, midnight robbers and pinking-dindies', and indeed members of the gang were known to frequent one of them, possibly an establishment on the corner of Essex Street and Crane Lane where dice games went on every night from midnight until eight o'clock in the morning. If they were unlucky at play, all was not lost, for they could and did seek to recoup their losses in the vicinity.[29]

Although many Pinkindindies came from upper-middle-class or upper-class backgrounds, it did not always follow that they possessed means. The allowances that students received from their fathers to support them during their studies were generally not sufficient to maintain them in lives of dissipation, and such allowances could always be withdrawn if they were shown to have been misspent. The need to acquire funds was a powerful inducement for assault, robbery and extortion. As a contemporary noted, Pinkindindies subsisted largely on the proceeds of 'midnight plunder'.[30] They generally roamed the streets in groups of three or four, armed with swords and bludgeons and on the lookout for victims. James Dowling Herbert, who was personally acquainted with at least one member of the gang, described their 'plan of attack' as follows:

> Two of them, walking arm-in-arm, jostled the victim they meant for prey; then, with their swords in their scabbards, chapeless, so that the point just protruded, they pricked him in various parts, and if he did not throw down his watch and money, two others came and took it by force; whilst two more in reserve were on the watch to give alarm if any persons approached. In that case they disappeared, and had their hiding-places adjacent, doors open; so, that if the punctured man was willing to pursue, he knew not where to go, but was glad to get away, bleeding and terrified.[31]

The Pinkindindies' activities were rarely as well coordinated as this, however. While their assaults were generally attended with considerable violence, this as often took the form of cutting or bludgeoning as 'pinking'. In July 1778 James Gillespie led a heavily armed group of Pinkindindies in a vicious assault on a Mr Dea. Having knocked Dea to the ground, Gillespie wounded him in the thigh with his sword and broke three of his ribs. This was no isolated incident. Gillespie, described as 'one of the ringleaders' of the gang, perpetrated a number of vicious assaults over the course of 1778. On the night of 7 October he assaulted a gentleman in Crampton Court, but was chased from the scene. After being discovered hiding in a bagnio on Essex Quay he was apprehended and lodged in gaol.[32] Other Pinkindindies were not deterred, however. In the early hours of the morning of 4 June 1779, three Pinkindindies rampaged through Parliament Street, Essex Street and Sycamore Alley, insulting, striking and wounding all whom they encountered. They cornered and severely beat a countryman, robbing him of nineteen shillings.[33] The fact that the Pinkindindies did not look like criminals gave them an added element of surprise. On 4 July, a Mr Lloyd of Trinity College was waylaid between Dublin and Clontarf by 'four well dressed ruffians' who knocked him off his horse and divested him of four guineas, his watch and his hat. Having 'inhumanly abused' their victim, the four men made off in the direction of Donnycarney, 'huzzaing for the pink-in-dindies'. The following January, a Mr Mahony of Dominick Street was attacked on Essex Bridge by three men who cried out 'Hie! for the Pink-in-dindies!' On seeing that his assailants were well dressed, Mahony attempted to remonstrate with them. He was insulted and beaten for his pains and robbed of a gold watch, a gold-headed cane and his hat.[34]

Violence against Women

While isolated gentlemen had much to fear from the Pinkindindies, they were not the only sufferers of the gang's depredations. The women who worked in the sex trade of eighteenth-century Dublin led danger-ous and uncertain lives. Although prostitutes were characterized as 'alluring wantons' who laid 'snares' for youthful and susceptible males, they were themselves particularly vulnerable to exploitation by unscrupulous parties.[35] The Pinkindindies earned the nickname 'rent gatherers' as a result of their extortion of money from prostitutes, and they frequently visited brothels in order to exact 'from unfortunate girls . . . their share of what they deemed booty; and for this boon each had his wife, as he called her'.[36] Payment of such levies did not guarantee protection from the gang's excesses, as the Pinkindindies sometimes went so far as to break the windows or destroy the interiors of brothels. Indeed, students had a long-standing reputation for undertaking such forays, which they justified by the pretence that they were punishing vice: 'if we jolly bucks did not sometimes lend a reforming hand, these houses would swarm about us – and do a great deal of mischief'.[37]

The Pinkindindies possibly used this skewed logic to excuse one of their most serious outrages, an attack on Margaret Leeson's brothel on Drogheda Street early in 1779.[38] Mrs Leeson, who was popularly known by her maiden name, Peg Plunket, was then one of Dublin's most sought-after courtesans (see Plate 19). The many rich and powerful clients she entertained over the course of her career included the Duke of Rutland, Lord Lieutenant between 1784 and 1787, and David La Touche, the governor of the Bank of Ireland. She also occasionally entertained students, and may have been on familiar terms with some of the Pinkindindies, as is hinted at in a whimsical play of the period entitled *Peg Plunket, or the Dublin Courtezans*. The play features a street battle between watchmen and Pinkindindies, after which one of the latter takes refuge in Mrs Leeson's house.[39] However, if there was at one point a civil relationship between the courtesan and the gang, it was not long before it turned decidedly hostile. At around eleven o'clock on the night of 22 February 1779, Richard Crosbie arrived at the brothel at the head of a large party of heavily armed Pinkindindies and demanded admittance. When Mrs Leeson refused, they broke the windows and the hall door 'and entered through the shattered pannels'. Crosbie was a huge man, heavily built and over six feet three inches tall, and the brothel's inhabitants were in no position to withstand his and his companions' assault.[40] The invaders destroyed the furniture in the parlours, with Crosbie taking care to smash a portrait of Mrs Leeson to pieces. They proceeded to roam through the house with drawn weapons searching for her companion, John Lawless, whose head they swore they would cut off and carry away on their sword points. Luckily for Lawless, he was not present and the assailants turned their attention to the females, who were kicked, dragged and robbed of 'those sweet ornaments which fashion had heaped upon their heads'. A prominent courtesan named Katherine Netterville (popularly known as 'Kitty Cut-a-dash') managed to make her escape by climbing through a rear window. Mrs Leeson was not so lucky. She was injured and suffered a seizure, causing her to lose the child with which she was then pregnant. Her young daughter, who was also present, later died as a result of the trauma she suffered during the raid. The arrival of the watch resulted in a full-scale battle, with many injuries received on both sides. Only the eventual appearance of two sheriffs and a party of soldiers caused the Pinkindindies to take flight.[41]

The exact reasons why the gang chose to invade and vandalize the brothel are unclear. They may have been motivated by a desire to exact vengeance on Katherine Netterville, at whose house a gentleman named Mr St— had shot himself some weeks earlier. This had provoked an explosion of outrage in the press, which blamed the courtesan for driving St— to suicide.[42] It is also possible that the women who operated out of the Drogheda Street brothel had defaulted on the payment of a protection levy to the gang. In Mrs Leeson's estimation, however, the raid was actuated solely by a perverse sense of fun, and this may indeed have been the principal motivation. A band of rowdy, drunken Pinkindindies, out on the town in search of mischief, would have seen the brothel as a soft target: prostitutes were regarded as fair game, and those who mistreated them did not expect to incur punishment for their actions. However, they had underestimated Mrs Leeson's capacity for revenge. She instituted proceedings against seven of her assailants, offering large rewards for their apprehension. Though the 'minor ruffians' fled the city to avoid prosecution, Mrs Leeson's principal target was their leader, whom she was determined to prosecute for the murder of her unborn child. According to her memoirs, when Crosbie heard that she had begun proceedings against him, 'he swore he would shoot me, and I on my part, openly declared I would keep a case of pistols in my pocket, and blow his brains out if he approached me'. Crosbie remained in Dublin, evidently in the belief that his familial connections would enable him to weather the storm. Though several students called at Mrs Leeson's house to threaten her, she refused to be intimidated and succeeded in having Crosbie arrested and imprisoned in Newgate. The Pinkindindy leader's situation was a grave one: a successful prosecution for murder would have resulted in a capital conviction. His brother, Sir Edward Crosbie, and a number of sheriffs made representations on his behalf, with the result that Mrs Leeson was persuaded to abandon the charge of murder. However, she continued with a prosecution for destruction of her property.[43]

Crosbie was tried for this offence at the Court of King's Bench on 7 July 1779. The proceedings took place amid quasi-theatrical scenes as Mrs Leeson, Katherine Netterville and two other courtesans arrived in the court to give evidence: 'the ladies were dressed in the extremity of the *ton*, and claimed uncommon attention'. Mrs Leeson, who at one point addressed one of the judges as 'my dear', delivered her testimony with the flair of a consummate performer:

> after Peg had recited most of the depredations, she closed with a remarkable climax: 'My Lord (quoth this nurse of fruition) all that he [Crosbie] had done availed but little, compared to his last barbarous act, regardless of my sex's delicacy – regardless of the charming object – the inhuman man lifted his hand in violence – and broke to pieces – my own beautiful picture!'

Katherine Netterville, determined not to be outdone, next took the stand and immediately 'fainted away at the sight of so many men'. She revived sufficiently to corroborate her colleague's testimony. The next two witnesses, Sarah Hayes and Elizabeth Townley, behaved so coquettishly towards the judges on the bench 'that by the barometer of my

Lord M—r's countenance, they raised the mercury higher than was consistent with its natural gravity'. Further evidence for the prosecution was provided by a number of sheriffs and aldermen who, it was alleged, were later entertained in Drogheda Street out of gratitude for their support.[44] On the strength of this well-ordered prosecution, Crosbie was convicted of having broken Mrs. Leeson's windows and destroyed a quantity of her furniture. He was fined £50, sentenced to one month's imprisonment and ordered to give security for good behaviour for three years.[45] However, proving the old adage of 'hell hath no fury', Mrs Leeson was not prepared to let the matter rest there. Following his release, she had Crosbie arrested and prosecuted again, this time for damages. He was again found guilty and imprisoned in Newgate. However, her later claim that her prosecutions resulted in Crosbie spending a year in prison seems to be an exaggeration.[46]

The incarceration of their leader and the decampment of several other members did little to discourage the remaining Pinkindindies, who continued to commit depredations over the ensuing months. Prostitutes were not the only women to suffer at their hands, for females in general constituted a particularly vulnerable group in eighteenth-century society. Those who ventured unaccompanied onto the streets ran a considerable risk of being attacked and raped, while unmarried heiresses were sometimes abducted and forced to marry their kidnappers. As one historian puts it, 'most men took little cognizance of female feeling'.[47] This is certainly borne out by the conduct of the Pinkindindies, who enjoyed 'pinking' unfortunate females, often divesting them of their clothes and property.[48] Many such assaults terminated in rape or attempted rape. On the night of 20 June 1779, four members of the gang seized two young gentlewomen in Drogheda Street 'with a design to drag them to an infamous receptacle in that neighbourhood' – clearly the proceedings that were underway against Crosbie had not succeeded in deterring other Pinkindindies from visiting Mrs Leeson's establishment. The appearance of several gentlemen prevented them from carrying out their plan and they settled for robbing one of the ladies of her cloak, with which they

made off. Other women were less fortunate. On 27 September a
servant girl was overpowered in Essex Street by three Pinkindindies
and 'most grossly abused'.[49] The early summer of 1780 saw the
Pinkindindies carry out several further audacious assaults on females. In
late May or early June they visited the residence of a lady on the
Glasnevin road, from whom, 'after using her in the most barbarous
manner', they stole a quantity of clothes. Around four weeks later
several Pinkindindies attacked a Mrs Marston of Fleet Street. Her
screams alerted a number of people in a nearby public house, who
intervened to save her from further violence.[50] Given that many
Pinkindindies were young men without any ready income, they may
also have attempted to abduct women of fortune. A week before the
attack on Mrs Marston, a 'Miss H-w-rd' of Queen Street was seized by
several members of the gang near the Old Bridge and bundled into a
chaise. It is possible that she was an heiress who was kidnapped with a
view to inducing her to marry. Luckily for her the chaise was over-
turned before her abductors could make their escape, and some passing
gentlemen rescued her.[51]

The crimes detailed above are those for which the Pinkindindies
were positively identified as the assailants. The gang may also have
committed many of the other assaults that were recorded in the press
around this time, but for which no definite identification of the perpetrators was made. In February 1780 an army captain and two students,
who may or may not have been Pinkindindies, accosted a female and
dragged her inside the railings of the Parliament House, where they
attempted to rape her. When her father and brother tried to succour
her they were attacked and grievously wounded, the father fatally. The
following September an elderly woman was robbed and beaten in St
Stephen's Green by four 'genteel dressed' men.[52] Similarly, a number of
violent incidents that occurred in the days following the Drogheda
Street raid bore the hallmarks of rampaging Pinkindindies. On 23
February 1779 several armed men assaulted the patrons of a Temple Bar
public house, critically wounding the owner. A few nights later, 'six or
seven of those rioters who seem lately associated to commit crimes of

the blackest hue' beat a watchmaker named Talman in Capel Street 'in a cruel manner'. Immediately afterwards they seized a man on Essex Bridge and flung him into the Liffey.[53] Such a sustained campaign of violence by a street gang was extraordinary even by the standards of late eighteenth-century Dublin. It was clear that a resolute policing effort would be needed in order to curb the Pinkindindies. The problem was that the force responsible for handling such crimes, the city watch, was hopelessly inadequate.

The Pinkindindies and the Watch

Prior to the establishment of a dedicated police force in 1786, the watch was the principal agent of law enforcement in Dublin. Each parish had its own dedicated body of watchmen, appointed by the Lord Mayor and aldermen, whose responsibility it was to ensure that the city streets were kept safe at all hours of the night. Watchmen occupied watch houses, in which wrongdoers could be temporarily confined, and stands, small booths from which they were supposed to maintain vigilance. They could also be seen patrolling the streets crying the hour and the weather, as depicted in a contemporary representation captioned 'Nine o'clock! Nine o'clock! Past nine o'clock, and a dark cloudy night' (see Plate 20). Here a capable-looking watchman does his rounds carrying a bill (a halberd with a hook for catching fleeing miscreants) and a lantern.[54] Despite this representation of efficiency, the watch was not equal to the realities of nocturnal crime in Dublin; indeed, it had long been accused of negligence and incompetence. Watchmen were frequently drunk or absent from their stands. On one occasion, several of the watch of St Andrew's parish were discovered drinking in a night-house on College Green when they should have been at their posts. When the Independent Dublin Volunteers patrolled the parishes of St Thomas's, St Paul's, St Michan's and St Mary's on the night of 23 December 1780, they found that each parish watch was undermanned. Of the watchmen that were present, several were drunk and unable to perform their duties, and by four o'clock in the morning most had abandoned their stands.[55] Following a Pinkindindy rampage in the Essex Street area in June 1779, it was observed that 'there was not a watchman to be seen at the hour mentioned', three o'clock in the morning.[56] Even when watchmen were at their posts, their apathy in the face of criminal activity was a frequent cause of complaint.[57] Such apathy may occasionally have been motivated by complicity in the crimes in question. According to one observer, 'the watchmen who are generally employed are ... usually connected with street robbers and house-breakers'.[58] Indeed, the number of times that passers-by intervened on behalf of victims in instances of assault and robbery bespeaks a society where ordinary people looked to assist one another, in the full realization that little could be hoped for in the way of law enforcement.[59]

There was a long tradition of hostility between students and the watch, and the intermittent encounters between the two bodies sometimes resulted in fatalities. In June 1775, a student named William Donaldson was killed by two watchmen of St Andrew's parish, one of whom held his arm while the other struck him on the head with his bill. The college authorities were particularly concerned by the murder, which they claimed had been perpetrated 'without any offence or provocation whatever'.[60] Incidents such as this embittered relations between students and watchmen. The feud between the two bodies gained new impetus with the emergence of the Pinkindindies who, like the Mohocks before them,[61] were disposed to challenge the watch when assembled in sufficient numbers. The guardians of law and order generally came off the worst in these encounters.[62]

Between 1778 and 1780, there were a number of nocturnal clashes between the watch and the Pinkindindies, most famously on the occasion of the Drogheda Street raid, during which 'many cuts and hurts were received on both sides'. In September 1778 a Pinkindindy named Patrick Reilly and a number of associates attacked and injured three watchmen, one of whom had his skull fractured.[63] On 28 January 1780 a gang of Pinkindindies confronted several watchmen in Parliament Street, driving them from their stands and 'knocking down, beating, or cutting' anyone who came in their way.[64] Other incidents, in which the Pinkindindies were not specifically identified but may have been involved, include attacks by groups of armed men on the watch of St Andrew's parish in May 1779 and January 1780. Four watchmen were critically wounded in the latter affray.[65] It is also possible that the Pinkindindies orchestrated the riotous scenes of 9 May 1780, in which over twenty armed students rampaged through the city, 'abusing, wounding and ill-treating such unfortunate watchmen and others as came in their way'. They captured several watchmen's poles and lanterns, which they carried away triumphantly. Not long afterwards, a watchman killed a student named Richard Lockwood in what was probably a reprisal attack.[66] A few weeks later, a member of the St Bridget's parish watch was attacked by a number of men who took his pole from him and struck him on the head, fracturing his skull.[67] The modus operandi of these assaults argues strongly for Pinkindindy involvement. The twenty-odd Collegians who were responsible for the disturbances of May 1780 could have been Pinkindindies; certainly they are likely to have been inspired by or acting in imitation of them. It is also notable that there is no reference to robbery in any of these assaults, apart from the triumphal carrying away of poles and lanterns. They appear to have been perpetrated simply for the sake of attacking watchmen and anyone else who was unfortunate enough to be in the vicinity.

Proceedings against the Pinkindindies

Lacking an effective police force, the authorities seemed largely impotent in the face of Pinkindindy activity. Though some offenders were brought to trial, it was often difficult to secure convictions. On 21 February 1780 two men were tried and acquitted of the murder of a St Andrew's watchman, probably one of those who had been critically wounded in the previous month's clash. On 29 May, four gentlemen were tried for the murder of a watchman on Inn's Quay; again, they were acquitted.[68] Individual prosecutions by victims resulted in some Pinkindindies being found guilty, but even then they tended to escape with moderate sentences. It was only thanks to Mrs Leeson's tenacious efforts that Richard Crosbie was convicted of the destruction of her property. Although this resulted in him facing a hefty fine and incarceration, his punishment was relatively light in the circumstances. Similarly, when James Gillespie was convicted in October 1778 of a vicious assault that left his victim with three broken ribs and a deep wound in the thigh, he received a fine of three marks and one month's imprisonment. Gillespie was back in court the following December, when he was indicted for assaulting and wounding Michael Shiel, Joseph Waters and James Prendergast.[69] Although Prendergast had initiated the prosecution, he was unable to attend the proceedings as Gillespie's assault had left him with a fractured skull. He was reported to be 'in a remote part of the country, and from the abuse given him by the prisoner... unable to attend'. As a result, the trial was postponed and Gillespie was granted bail.[70]

The sentences received by Crosbie and Gillespie appear lenient when compared to the capital convictions that other persons suffered for relatively minor offences such as petty theft. Yet if the courts can be accused of bias, the distinction they made was not between Pinkindindies and non-Pinkindindies, but rather between people of higher and lower social standing. This was an enduring characteristic of the eighteenth-century legal process: a similar situation had obtained during legal proceedings against the Mohocks in 1712: 'The court, at the same session in which it was meting out penalties of a day in the pillory and whipping at the tail of a cart to women and men who had committed petty property offences, fined Cole, Reading, Squibb and Jones three shillings and four pence each for the assault and riot.' It is significant that when lower-class criminals began to permeate the ranks of the Pinkindindies in the early 1780s, they were subjected to an altogether harsher form of justice. In July 1780 a Pinkindindy named Henry Hand was sentenced to seven years' hard labour for his part in the theft of a candlestick and two goblets (see below).[71]

With the watch clearly unequal to the task, the Trinity College authorities made a belated effort to curb the Pinkindindies. The provost and fellows of the college regularly censured students for rioting and disturbing the peace in Dublin; however, it was only belatedly that they realized that an armed student gang was active. On 29 November 1779, the Board of Trinity College, having received information that several students had formed an armed society, deemed this state of affairs 'contrary to the statutes of this College & subversive of discipline'. They enjoined the college tutors to do their utmost to prevent student involvement in any such group and to give them any information thereof, threatening to censure any individuals found to be implicated.[72] This action seemed overdue, as by that time the Pinkindindies had been operating in the city for well over a year. However, the college authorities enjoyed some success in curbing student excesses over the following months, so much so that when the Collegians rioted in May 1780 it was almost regarded as an exception: 'the Provost and Fellows of the University... by a most praise-worthy exertion have for a considerable time past prevented such outrages against public peace and safety'.[73]

Despite such efforts, Pinkindindy activity continued intermittently throughout 1780. In the absence of concerted opposition by the watch, there may have been some vigilante activity in response to the gang's depredations. As a Dublin newspaper observed, 'the community are greatly interested that the sword or stiletto of midnight ruffians may not be unsheathed without meeting due punishment'. The army officer and duellist Captain David 'Tiger' Roche was said to have formed a vigilante association that patrolled the city, quelling the excesses of Pinkindindies and like-minded groups. In the absence of harder evidence this claim must be treated as apocryphal, as Roche appears to have been living in London in the late 1770s (he died in Westminster on 11 September 1779).[74] Nonetheless, Pinkindindy activity declined appreciably after 1780. While this decline was in some quarters attributed to the vigilance of Dublin's sheriffs,[75] it is perhaps more likely that the gang lost impetus as its leaders and actuators moved on to other pursuits. As they did so, it also began to lose its upper-class character.

This was already evident in June 1780, as an incident in a

Mecklenburgh Street brothel illustrates. In the early morning of 16 June 1780, two Pinkindindies named Henry Hand and Gleeson, accompanied by three soldiers, pounded on the door of the establishment, run by Mary (Moll) Hall, a close friend of Mrs Leeson. Initially it seemed that a repeat of the Drogheda Street outrage was in store, as the men threatened that if Mrs Hall 'did not instantly open the door, they would not only break the windows, but afterwards pull down the house'. She complied, no doubt mindful of the havoc that had been wreaked in Mrs Leeson's premises. On this occasion, however, the antagonists' principal motivation was robbery. On pretence of searching for a deserter, Gleeson purloined a plated candlestick and two plated goblets, with which the robbers made off. Hand and two of the soldiers were later apprehended in a public house on Ormond Quay, though Gleeson evaded arrest. Mrs Hall had the miscreants prosecuted for the offence and they were tried the following month at the Court of Oyer and Terminer.[76] It is significant that neither Hand nor Gleeson were students of Trinity College. They kept company with ordinary soldiers and were probably themselves from lower-class backgrounds. The infiltration of the Pinkindindies by members of the lower orders was further evidenced by the apprehension in April 1781 of a butcher named Geary, who was 'charged with various atrocious offences, as well as being one of a desperate gang of vagabonds, called Pink-in-dindies or Chalkers'.[77] This conflation of the Pinkindindies with lower-class gangs such as the Chalkers may indicate that it was losing its identity as an upper-class group. There was a further spate of Pinkindindy activity in the autumn of 1782, when members of the gang attacked and vandalized the house of a Marlborough Street surgeon. Some weeks after this incident a Pinkindindy named Kelly was arrested for an assault on a Mr Herrick, whom he cut on the face with a knife.[78] Like Geary, Kelly was probably from a lower-class background.

Over the ensuing years the Pinkindindies all but disappeared from the city streets. Although efforts seem to have been made to revive the gang in 1784, it was not as active as hitherto. The replacement in March 1786 of the parish watch system with a well-resourced and formidable police force seems to have precipitated the final dissolution of the Pinkindindies.[79] The impact of the new force was soon felt on the city streets, which became safer and better policed, a significant alteration to the conditions that had allowed the gang to operate with relative impunity. Yet the police force was not set up solely in response to the Pinkindindies' depredations. In the early 1780s, Dublin was beset by all manner of agitation, unrest and riot, as companies of Volunteers agitated for free trade and parliamentary reform, while the Dublin mob rioted sporadically against food prices and the importation of foreign fabrics. The establishment of the police was Dublin Castle's attempt to regain control of an urban situation that appeared increasingly disturbed and subversive.[80] In 1788 the *Freeman's Journal* saw fit to congratulate the police on quelling the 'midnight broils, riots and disturbances' that had been occasioned by 'different sets of pinkindindies and drunken buckeens'.[81] Admittedly, the *Freeman*, which was then owned by the pro-government 'sham squire' Francis Higgins, was more an organ of official propaganda than of accurate reportage. It was, however, elsewhere acknowledged that 'these watchful guardians of liberty [i.e. the police] are so much more formidable than your old watch'.[82]

Nonetheless, certain ex-Pinkindindies chose to continue to pursue criminal activities. In 1786, a man named James Gillespie was committed to Newgate for robbery.[83] If this was the same man as the Pinkindindy who had twice been indicted for assaults in 1778, he had clearly chosen to continue to pursue long-term criminal activities. Another former Pinkindindy, Michael O'Berne, was indicted in Dublin in July 1794 for assaulting and robbing Francis Bennet near the entrance to Bennet's house on Fleet Street. Then aged around 40, O'Berne was well known in the city. He was described at his trial as wearing 'about him the wreck of an handsome, athletic person, and too universally known in Dublin to require further description'. He was found guilty and sentenced to be hanged, but reprieved several times on the basis of representations made by well-connected friends. In 1795 he was pardoned on the condition that he emigrate to America, a circumstance that demonstrates, again, that one law obtained for the rich and another for the poor.[84] The experiences of Gillespie and O'Berne show that having become inured to crime, it was difficult for some ex-Pinkindindies to pursue an honest living. However, at least one erstwhile member of the gang did manage to leave his questionable past behind. This was Richard Crosbie, who made a name for himself as Ireland's first aeronaut.

'Balloon' Crosbie

Crosbie suffered no lasting stigma from his involvement in the attack on Mrs Leeson's brothel or his ensuing trial and imprisonment in Newgate. There is no record of his being censured by the Trinity College authorities; indeed he was offered the grace of the house to undertake his Bachelor of Arts degree only days after his trial in July 1779. Facing a month's imprisonment, Crosbie was not in a position to undertake the degree and beside his name in the college register the registrar simply wrote the words 'did not commence'.[85] Following his eventual release after two spells in Newgate, Crosbie turned his back on criminality. In December 1780 he married Charlotte Margaret Armstrong, daughter of Archibald Armstrong of Barnagrotty in the King's County, at St Peter's Church in Dublin. The couple would go on to have a son and a daughter. By 1781 he was 'settled in life', and apart from a brief period during which he took command of a provincial regiment, he spent his time pursuing his chief interest, scientific and technological research.[86]

At Trinity College, Crosbie had demonstrated a strong interest in 'the practicability of flying', and on learning of the aeronautical feats of the Montgolfier brothers, he determined to construct a balloon of his own. His scientific competence was subjected to some denigration, most notably by the Scottish lecturer James Dinwiddie, who expressed scepticism as to the technological merits of the 'aeronautic chariot' that Crosbie designed in 1784.[87] Unfazed by the criticism, Crosbie pressed on with his plan to become the first man to cross the English Channel by balloon. Poor health and limited financial resources delayed his efforts to achieve this objective, and Jean-Pierre Blanchard beat him to the post. Undaunted, Crosbie prepared to undertake a balloon ascent in Dublin, with the long-term objective of crossing the Irish Sea. He made his first attempt at Ranelagh Gardens on 4 January 1785, but was foiled by heavy rainfall. Two weeks later he tried again at the same location. The splendid attire that Crosbie donned for the occasion recalled the Pinkindindies' foppish tendencies: he was 'resplendently dressed in white quilted satin lined with fur, an oiled silk loose-coat, lined with the same, red Morocco leather boots and a superb cap of leopard skin' (see Plate 21). Margaret Leeson was among the huge crowd that turned up to watch the spectacle, and she had no qualms about wishing Crosbie well: 'as I thought no less than that he would be drowned, I heartily forgave, and shook hands with him'.[88] A shrewd social operator, she was no doubt equally motivated by a desire to be seen by the large numbers of nobility and gentry that were present. Crosbie's initial effort to ascend was hindered by rainfall and insufficient inflation. He added extra gas to the balloon and tried again, with the result that a 'most beautiful, solemn and wonderful sight now took place'. To the delighted applause of the assembled dignitaries and the tens of thousands of people who had thronged the surrounding fields, the 'balloon ascended with its courageous master, slow, perpendicular and majestic; but soon encreasing its velocity, rose above the clouds and was out of sight in three minutes and half'.[89]

As the first Irishman to make a balloon ascent, Crosbie attained a celebrity that eclipsed his Pinkindindy notoriety, becoming known as 'Balloon' Crosbie.[90] He later made a number of efforts to cross the Irish Sea, each of which proved abortive. On 12 May 1785 he was involved in an adventure that the aeronautical historian L.T.C. Rolt describes as 'pure farce'. Attempting to ascend from the Palatine Square in the Barracks before a large crowd that included the Lord Lieutenant, Crosbie found that his weight overpowered the balloon. It rose 'as high as the roof of the Barracks, [when] it came down with such velocity, as not a little to alarm the spectators for the safety of the aerial traveller'. A young army officer named Richard McGwire then took Crosbie's place and this time the balloon began a steady ascent. A strong wind drove it north-eastwards beyond Howth and out once over the Irish Sea. It went no further than nine miles over the water before it plummeted rapidly, depositing its occupant into the sea where he managed to remain afloat for some three-quarters of an hour. Fortunately for McGwire, a number of gentlemen had followed the balloon on horseback as far as Howth, where they hired a boat to rescue the aeronaut.[91] McGwire received a knighthood in recognition of his efforts, and Crosbie, his ego no doubt somewhat ruffled as a result, made a further attempt to traverse the Irish Sea on 19 July, this time ascending from Leinster Lawn (see Plate 22). On this occasion he may have gone as far as midway across the channel before the balloon again plunged into the water. Crosbie managed to keep afloat with the assistance of a cork waistcoat and several specially designed bladders that he had affixed to the balloon's 'car' before being picked up by a barge that had been dispatched for his rescue. Despite the again farcical nature of the adventure, he was feted by the Lord Lieutenant for his achievements.[92] The following year witnessed little abatement of Crosbie's aeronautical adventuring. On 27 April he ascended from the square of the House of Industry in Limerick, coming to ground at Ballygirreen, County Clare. This gave rise to 'great terror' among the local peasantry 'who fled with affright from the supposed supernatural visitant'. He had not, however, abandoned his plan to traverse the Irish Sea, and his attempts to raise funds to attempt a crossing from Belfast provoked his friend the Earl of Charlemont to remark that he was possessed of a ' "ballo[o]n manie," which he will never get rid of till he has crossed the channel or drowned himself'.[93]

As it turned out, Crosbie achieved neither of these fates. Driven to near-destitution as a result of his various ballooning projects, he emigrated to America around 1792, probably in order to escape imprisonment for non-payment of debt. Bryan MacMahon has unearthed some fascinating information about this later phase of Crosbie's life. Initially he attempted to pursue an acting career in New York, but suffered criticism for his inept performances. This seems to have induced him to return to aeronautical activities, and on 27 October 1800 he oversaw the release of a number of unmanned balloons from New York's Mount Vernon Garden. He also made plans to undertake another manned ascent, but apparently failed to raise the necessary finance. Although little is known about Crosbie's experiences over the ensuing two decades, in 1819 he was 'discovered' living in Baltimore, Maryland, by a local resident, George H. Stuart. By this time, Crosbie had been reduced to penury, living in a makeshift shelter in the eastern part of the city. Thanks to the charity of a local blacksmith he was able to continue to indulge his interest in scientific mechanisms, and when Stuart encountered him he was working on a hydrostatic device with which he hoped to realize the principle of perpetual motion. The encounter provided the basis for a vivid description of the aged Crosbie: 'a fine looking man, who evidently had seen better days. He was over six feet in height, large in proportion, with a grand head, nearly bald, his snow-white hair falling on his neck... His bearing was that of a dignified gentleman, too proud to tell his needs, and yet gracious in acknowledging kindness... but the practised eye soon found a mind falling into ruin.'[94] On learning of Crosbie's past career as an aeronaut, Stuart contacted a 'Lord C' in Dublin (possibly the 2nd Earl of Charlemont, whose father's patronage Crosbie had enjoyed in the 1780s) who arranged for him to return to Ireland in 1820. Reunited with his friends and family, he lived out his final years in comfort in Dublin. He died in his townhouse on North Cumberland Street in 1824.[95]

In some respects, Crosbie's career parallels that of Lord Santry: both led violent and dissipated lives in their youth, both were arrested and tried for criminal activities, and both lived much of the latter period of their lives in exile, abandoned by former friends. Like Santry's misdeeds and atrocities, Crosbie's activities as a Pinkindindy leader should not be ignored or forgotten: the assault on Mrs Leeson's brothel was only one instance of the brutality and destruction that he and his cohorts visited on the weaker and more vulnerable members of society. However, it would be unfair to place Crosbie too firmly in the same bracket as the most notorious member of the Dublin Hellfire Club. Unlike Santry, he managed to leave his unsavoury youth behind and undertake an aeronautical career that was as remarkable for its historical significance as for the colour and spectacle it offered spectators of every social background. Today, Santry is remembered as the violent young peer who murdered a servant in an unprovoked attack and escaped punishment for the crime. Crosbie, on the other hand, enjoys a more elevated reputation as the first Irishman to achieve flight.

In many ways, the Pinkindindies were no different from the other gangs of rowdy and destructive young men that have emerged to plague urban areas at different times in history. Their violent and destructive antics were largely motivated by youthful exuberance, excessive drinking and a desire for ready cash, factors which are common to most eras and societies. Yet it is also true that the Pinkindindies were a product of the fractious social environment of late eighteenth-century Ireland. Dublin was a woefully under-policed city that allowed such groups to operate with a large degree of impunity. The force responsible for maintaining law and order – the watch – was undermanned, incompetent and unequal to its task, with the result that many crimes went unpunished. The Pinkindindies took full advantage of this state of affairs. It was only when they were actually apprehended following their crimes, or resolutely prosecuted by their victims, that they were brought to account for their actions. Even then, they rarely faced the full rigours of the law. This was partly because eighteenth-century society afforded young gentlemen a tacit licence to misbehave. In certain circles, the drunken, irresponsible and aggressive young rake or 'buck' was an acceptable social type, and violent conduct was even celebrated when it was conducted within the boundaries of the code of honour. As Crosbie's career highlights, a gentleman could be brought to public scrutiny as the leader of a notorious and destructive gang and yet escape any lasting stigma for his actions. For two reasons, then (the inefficacy of law enforcement and the peculiar latitude they were given), the Pinkindindies were suffered to continue largely unmolested for a period of several years in the late 1770s and early 1780s.

As indicated previously, the Pinkindindies are to be regarded as rakes or 'bucks' rather than libertines. They were not a true hellfire club, as they did not pursue a campaign of blasphemy or surround themselves with a veneer of diabolic mystique. Nor were they an eminently elite group; they did not count any peers among their members, and their personal resources were far more limited than those that were available to people such as Lord Rosse, Lord Santry and John St Leger. Nonetheless, insofar as the Pinkindindies were a group of swaggering, upper-class men who engaged in behaviour that was antisocial and deliberately provocative, they acted in imitation of the Dublin Hellfire Club and the Holy Fathers. Nineteenth-century writers recognized as much, placing the Pinkindindies firmly in the hellfire tradition.[96] Yet, by the 1780s and 1790s it was becoming more difficult for groups of rakes to operate with impunity. Despite the leeway that had hitherto been afforded them, many were becoming less inclined to tolerate their drunken and destructive ways. However, the Pinkindindies were not the last rakish club. That dubious honour belonged to the more aristocratic order that succeeded them – the Cherokee Club.

16. Hellfire Club clock-case. The carved demonic faces, flaming wine glass and hand of cards denote the 'hellfire' traditions of diabolism, drinking and gambling.

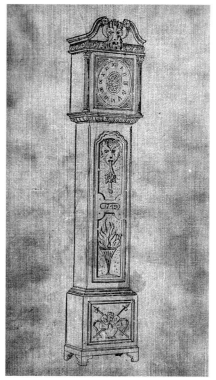

The College Buck.

17. The 'College-Buck'. Note the ponderous metal key dangling from the handkerchief, a favourite weapon of the rowdy student out on the town.

18. Jonah Barrington. An enthusiastic duellist, Barrington befriended Richard Crosbie when the two were at Trinity College Dublin in the 1770s. He may also have been a member of the Pinkindindies, the vicious gang of rakes led by Crosbie.

M. Hoare pinx. Miss Plunkett *J. Watson fec.*
Printed for John Bowles at the Black Horse Cornhill.

19. Margaret Leeson. This celebrated courtesan was subjected to particularly brutal treatment by the Pinkindindies, who wrecked her Drogheda Street brothel in February 1779.

NINE o'Clock! Nine o'Clock! paſt Nine o'Clock, and a dark cloudy Night.

20. A Dublin night watchman carrying a bill (a halberd with a hook for catching fleeing miscreants) and a lantern. Despite this representation of efficiency, watchmen were not equal to the realities of nocturnal crime in Dublin and were frequently bested in battles with the Pinkindindies.

RICHARD CROSBIE Eſq.ʳ
The Celebrated Irish Aeronaut

21. Richard Crosbie at the time of his aeronautical triumph. Crosbie's successful balloon ascent from Ranelagh Gardens on 19 January 1785 drew much favourable comment from the Dublin press, which chose to ignore his dubious past as a Pinkindindy leader.

22. Richard Crosbie ascends from Leinster Lawn, 19 July 1785. This was one of Crosbie's many ill-fated efforts to cross the Irish Sea by balloon.

23. Thomas 'Buck' Whaley as a youth. This portrait was probably painted around the time the 16-year-old Whaley left for France, where it was intended he should complete his education. Instead, he embarked on a number of ill-fated liaisons and squandered thousands at the gaming tables.

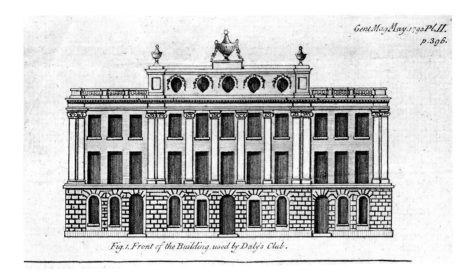

Gent Mag May 1790 Pl II.
p.396.

Fig.1. Front of the Building used by Daly's Club.

24. Front elevation of the newly completed Daly's Club-House on College Green, Dublin, described as 'the most superb gambling house in the world'.

25. The Lying-In Hospital on Rutland Square (now Parnell Square), Dublin. The round room of the Rotunda can be seen to the right of the main building.

An IRISH CHEROKEE.

26. An 'Irish Cherokee' as depicted in *Walker's Hibernian Magazine*. The apparent physical resemblance to Lord Thurles induced him to threaten legal action against the publishers, which elicited a scornful response from the Dublin press.

27. William Conolly, Speaker of the Irish House of Commons. Conolly purchased the Rathfarnham estate, including the hill of Mountpelier, from the Duke of Wharton in 1723. He probably constructed the hunting lodge on the hill around 1725.

28. This late-nineteenth-century sketch purports to show the lodge on Mountpelier as it was in 1776. Note the cut-stone steps leading to the main entrance on the first floor and the semicircular wall enclosing the front courtyard.

North View of Old House on Mount Pelier
and Cairn that formerly Stood there

29. Rear view of hunting lodge and cairn on Mountpelier. Note the chimneys, long since fallen away, which served the fireplaces on the ground and first floors.

Co Dublin
Hill of Mt. Pelier. 24 May 1841.

30. Sketch of ruined hunting lodge on Mountpelier, 1841, showing a remnant of the front semicircular wall.

Chapter six

Daly's Club, 'Buck' Whaley and the Cherokees

By the 1790s the Pinkindindies had vanished from Dublin's streets and the Hellfire Club was but a distant, if disconcerting, memory. The early months of 1792 witnessed the emergence of a club that sought to. emulate the drunken misconduct of the former, while evoking the aristocratic swagger of the latter. Although the Cherokee Club was not quite as controversial as some of the rakish and hellfire clubs that had preceded it, its members' nocturnal diversions caused outrage in Dublin society. At least one individual associated with the Cherokees was long remembered in the capital. This was the extraordinary Thomas 'Buck' Whaley (see Plate 23), whose amorous exploits, catastrophic losses at cards and wager-driven journey to Jerusalem combined to ensure his enduring notoriety. He was even believed to have revived the most notorious of all Irish clubs. For the name of the Hellfire Club had not been forgotten. Indeed, in the context of the mounting agitation of the 1780s, when a range of parties campaigned for economic and political reform, it came to be used as a weapon of vilification.

On 17 June 1784 the *Freeman's Journal* published a letter authored by 'Quinbus Flestrin' attacking 'a club, instituted about four months since in this city, under a veil of profound secrecy, and which is christened, after the one formerly established in London, by the title of the

HELL-FIRE CLUB'. Purported extracts from the club's minutes were set forth, describing its members as men who, being unable to obtain fortunes by inheritance or industry, had resorted to 'a scramble' to further themselves. To this end, they were engaged in fomenting public unrest and heaping abuse upon the administration, particularly the new Lord Lieutenant, the Duke of Rutland. This 'Hell-fire Club' aimed to stir up further dissent by urging Catholics to pursue concessions additional to what they had obtained under the Catholic Relief Acts of 1778 and 1782. 'Quinbus Flestrin' then revealed what he alleged to be the club's true objectives: to exacerbate the distresses of the lower classes, to provoke hostilities between Britain and Ireland, and to nominate their own king. The leading members were identified, including 'J— N— T—dy' (James Napper Tandy), 'J—n B—ns' (John Binns) and 'George Robert F—d' (George Robert Fitzgerald). A few days later, 'Quinbus Flestrin', in a second letter, alleged that the club had been convened immediately after the appointment of the Lord Lieutenant in February 1784. The club had denigrated the Lord Lieutenant's charitable donations, including a gift of £1,000 to the poor manufacturers of Dublin, as having been 'done with the base design of corrupting their hearts'. The ultimate objective of the club's president, 'Quinbus Flestrin' revealed, was to make himself Lord Lieutenant, 'nay, KING' of Ireland.[1]

The satirical nature of these published missives was apparent. This was merely the latest in a number of attacks by the *Freeman's Journal* on the movement for political reform then being orchestrated by the radical politicians James Napper Tandy and John Binns. A long-standing campaigner for free trade and constitutional reform, Tandy had been at the forefront of popular protests against the defeat of bills for the reform of Parliament and protecting duties in the House of Commons earlier that year. On 5 April, he had invaded the House at the head of a crowd of protestors.[2] Binns, a silk merchant, was closely allied with Tandy in this campaign. At an aggregate meeting in Dublin on 7 June they had gone so far as to form a resolution calling for franchise to be extended to Catholics.[3] Rhetoric of this kind, coming on the heels of the previous April's agitation, infuriated the government and its supporters. The *Freeman's* proprietor, the government-allied Francis Higgins, possibly authored the 'Quinbus Flestrin' pieces. Probably he hoped to malign Tandy and Binns by identifying them as confederates of the odious George Robert Fitzgerald, who was well known for his hostile demeanour and conduct, and members of a notorious hellfire club.[4] Whatever their association with Fitzgerald, Tandy and Binns did belong to the radical Block and Axe Club, whose members were regarded as 'seditious wretches, who aped the abominable glory of being thought king-killers'.[5] Despite this controversial image, the Block and Axe Club had, from the perspective of many, a legitimate political agenda. To be thought to belong to a hellfire club would be much worse, and 'Quinbus Flestrin' hoped to denigrate Tandy and Binns by associating them with the sense of nefarious conduct and repugnance that the term evoked. It is also possible that he was inspired to do so by the fact that a hellfire club *had* recently emerged in Dublin.

Lord Drogheda and Daly's Club

While there is little to indicate that a group known as the Hellfire Club existed in the capital in the 1780s, family traditions concerning Charles Moore (1730–1822), 6th Earl of Drogheda, suggest that such a belief is not entirely groundless. Like Whaley, Drogheda was an inept gambler who incurred heavy losses at the card tables. According to one of his descendants,

> [he] devoted (especially latterly) a great deal of his time to cards, being a member of the Dublin 'Hell-fire Club,' where the play was notoriously high, and where some of the players, after having gambled all their available money, used to bring down the title-deeds of the townlands of their estates, and play for them as the stakes...Drogheda frequently lost at cards, and by degrees the property became more and more diminished.[6]

As Drogheda was a minor when the original Dublin Hellfire Club was active, the group with which he was involved must have been a later incarnation. The term 'especially latterly' suggests that this involvement occurred during the later period of his life, possibly in 1784, when he was reported to be 'ruining his health and fortune by drink and play'.[7] However, Drogheda is not believed to have harboured any of the irreligious sentiments that motivated men such as Lord Rosse and Peter Lens, and this revived Hellfire Club, if it existed, probably concerned itself with gambling rather than blasphemy and diabolism. It is also possible that it was a sort of subgroup of gamblers operating within the celebrated Daly's Club.

Daly's was probably established sometime in the 1770s at the chocolate house of that name on Dame Street. Much frequented by Members of Parliament, the club boasted a large membership whose principal pursuits were drinking, dining and gambling.[8] These were activities in which Thomas Whaley, who was MP for Newcastle, County Dublin, from 1785 to 1790, would have avidly participated. In 1789 the members arranged for the erection of a purpose-built clubhouse on College Green between Foster Place and Anglesea Street (see Plate 24). Little expense was spared on decor and furnishings. When the new premises were unveiled in March 1791, observers marvelled at the splendid marble chimneypieces, inlaid tables and carpets, and fine silk table coverings. One visitor to Dublin described it as 'the most superb gambling house in the world'.[9] Tales of the high play that went on behind the heavily draped windows of the new clubhouse became part of the folklore of the capital, typified by this hypothetical late nineteenth-century account:

> The noon-day sunshine streams against the windows of a handsomely decorated mansion overlooking the hawthorns of Trinity College, but, for the thick red curtains and heavy shutters, no arrow of light can penetrate within. Suddenly behind these shutters a clamour arises; passers-by glance apprehensively at the windows, through which, the hangings rent back now, the garish

light falls into a candle-lighted chamber, where, over cards, dice, and shivered glasses, 'a company with heated eyes' scuffle and struggle fiercely. With torn ruffles and disordered wigs, they drag forward a white-faced player – a marked card fluttering from his sleeve – the sash is flung open to its highest; the detected cheat still clutches at the window-sill, then drops with a sickening crash upon the paving-stones. The knot of street spectators betrays no unusual emotion, for such a scene is not rare in the Palladian-fronted building, 'where half the land in Ireland has changed hands' – Daly's Club-house, in College Green.[10]

While defenestration was a much-mooted punishment for card cheats,[11] it is not known if it ever occurred at Daly's; certainly it is unlikely to have been practised as often as is indicated above. Yet there is little doubt that prolonged gambling sessions went on there and that excessive amounts were wagered. Lord Drogheda's efforts at the card table inspired a scene in Charles Lever's novel *The Knight of Gwynne* (1847). Here, he and the fictional Knight of Gwynne attend Daly's to play a card game in which an entire estate is staked against £50,000.[12] Although Drogheda emerges as the winner in this imagined bout, in reality he continued to lose heavily at cards, such that in the closing years of his life he was reduced almost to a state of penury, subsisting on an annual allowance from his creditors. In his final years he was given to sitting in the drawing-room window of his Sackville Street townhouse wearing a yellow nightcap, 'and when George IV passed through the Street during his visit in 1821, he recognised the venerable nobleman, then in his 92nd year, and bowed to him'.[13]

Daly's Club also had a reputation for pranks and raucous conduct generally. One of the most well-known stories associated with it concerns the rake and duellist William Alexander 'Buck' English (d. 1794). According to Margaret Leeson's memoirs, English fell asleep one night at Daly's while a dice game was in progress. His companions contrived to play a prank on him by extinguishing all of the lights and then pretending to engage in a violent quarrel over a dice roll. The noise awakened English who, unable to see anything, believed he had been struck blind as divine punishment for his murderous ways. He was immediately humbled into prayer and repentence. On 'recovering' his sight and realizing that he had been the victim of a prank, he flew into a rage, threatening to take dire vengeance on those who had duped him. However, the story may be apocryphal. It derives, possibly, from an earlier account of a similar incident. This story appears in a collection of wit and humour attributed to Laetitia Pilkington, published in 1764. Here an unnamed man plays at hazard with two friends, who are shocked by his oaths and blasphemies. After he has fallen asleep, his companions extinguish the lights and then pretend to quarrel over a dice roll. When he awakes they convince him that he is blind. He repents, and his sight 'returns' in the morning.[14]

Despite such anecdotes, there must have been, as R.B. McDowell pointed out, a 'humdrum side' to the proceedings at Daly's Club. For every irresponsible and raucous MP, there was a responsible and hard-working equivalent, and some of those who frequented the club would have had serious matters to discuss.[15] However, it is unlikely that Thomas Whaley would have been counted among the latter. Although he had barely attained manhood in 1785, his excesses on the Continent had already earned him the reputation of an unrestrained profligate.

Thomas 'Buck' Whaley

Born on 15 December 1766, Thomas was the eldest son of Richard Chapel Whaley (1700–69) of Whaley Abbey, County Wicklow. When he was an infant, his father, 'a man of very large property', died, leaving in him in possession of a lump sum of over £60,000 and an estate worth £7,000 a year.[16] At the age of 16, Whaley was sent to France to complete his education under the supervision of a tutor. The pair travelled to Auch in the south of the country, where it was intended that Whaley would learn French and receive instruction in riding, fencing and dancing. Instead, however, he gave vent to a taste for the high life by embarking on a series of ill-fated dalliances and gambling sessions.

One liaison, with a young gentlewoman, resulted in a pregnancy and the birth of a daughter who died soon afterwards. Following this, Whaley abandoned his unfortunate lover in a convent. Meanwhile his extensive gambling resulted in huge losses, most spectacularly in Lyons, where two Irish gentlemen got him drunk and extracted £14,800 from him in a single evening's play. The incident induced a speedy return to Dublin, but not before the hapless Whaley was again defrauded by confidence tricksters, this time in London.[17] In Dublin he continued his career of dissipation, installing himself, along with a courtesan he had brought over from London, in a 'magnificent house' where 'I kept my midnight orgies, and saw my friends, according to the fashionable acceptation of the word.' It is not known if these 'orgies' took place in the context of club activity, but one of the 'friends' may have been Colonel John Hayes St Leger, the son of John St Leger of the Grangemellon Hellfire Club.[18]

In November 1788, Whaley embarked on his celebrated journey to Jerusalem. It is for this adventure, which resulted from a wager made over dinner at the Duke of Leinster's townhouse, that he is most remembered.[19] Whaley's account of the journey and his observations on the customs and behaviour of the different countries and inhabitants he encountered represent an interesting outsider's view of the Mediterranean and Middle East in the late eighteenth century.[20] Having succeeded in completing the trip and securing proofs of the same (including a certificate issued by the Superior of the Convent of St Mary in Nazareth), he returned to Dublin to collect his winnings, which amounted to £15,000. Once the cost of the journey was deducted, Whaley's net profit from the enterprise was £7,000. His claim that this was 'the only instance in all my life before, in which any of my projects turned out to my advantage'[21] was not inaccurate. Over the ensuing years he continued to gamble and lose heavily. Facing financial ruin, he staked £5,000 in an all-or-nothing attempt to regain his fortune, and lost. This was followed by a spell in a debtor's prison in London, after which he moved to the Isle of Man in order to write his memoirs, with the avowed intention of dissuading other young men from pursuing lives of dissipation. On 2 November 1800, Whaley died at Knutsford, Cheshire, while en route to London. Although newspaper reports attributed the death to rheumatic fever, it was rumoured that one of his mistresses had stabbed him in a jealous rage after she discovered that he had been carrying on a liaison with her sister.[22]

Whaley's posthumous reputation as one of Ireland's greatest libertines received a boost with the eventual publication of his memoirs in 1906. Even prior to that, stories circulated identifying him as a member of a hellfire club that frequented the hunting lodge on Mountpelier.[23] However, no reference to this occurs anywhere in the memoirs. Indeed, the Mountpelier lodge had fallen into a state of dereliction by 1779 and it is unlikely that any club used it after that.[24] Yet Whaley was the sort of character whose name was invoked in connection with all types of libertines and rakes' clubs, irrespective of basis. For instance, he was also named as a member of the Cherokee Club,[25] despite the fact that he was mostly absent in France when that group was active in the early 1790s. Nonetheless, the Cherokees attained a degree of notoriety that for a time rivalled even that of Whaley. For a nineteenth-century writer, they were the final ostentatious manifestation of the hellfire and rakish phenomenon: 'their whole dress, including their stockings, was of a bright flame colour, save only their coat, which, lined with flame coloured silk, was of black cloth. They were . . . the Cherokee Club, the last successors to the "Hell Fires," the "Devil's Owns," and "Pinking Dindies" of more barbarous and fierce times.'[26]

Origins of the Cherokee Club

In March 1792, the *Freeman's Journal* published what purported to be a description of the customs and characteristics of the Cherokee Indians, a group of whose chiefs had recently visited England. They were described as tall and ungainly men with pale complexions, the apparent result of heavy drinking. They hunted and gambled excessively, avoided sunlight by remaining in bed all day and, in drunken confusion, rode their horses at high speed through crowded areas. Their clothes, black with red trimmings, ribbons and buttons, called to mind 'the figures which represent the demons of hell in some of our pantomimes'. Such were their extravagant lifestyles that most were reduced to the condition of broken men by the age of 30.[27] A delegation of Cherokee and Creek chiefs had indeed spent time in London in the recent past. However, as anyone acquainted with the Dublin social scene would have recognized, they were not the real subjects of this satirical piece. It was a thinly veiled critique of a new club that had emerged in Dublin, to 'the surprize and terror of civil society'. According to the *Hibernian Magazine*, 'a set of young men, *fashionables* of fortune' had 'formed themselves into a kind of hostile corps, which they call the CHEROKEE Squadron'. Apart from womanizing, drinking and gambling, the 'Cherokees' made it their business to violently disrupt the social gatherings of the upper classes, particularly in the city's most fashionable venue, the public rooms of the Lying-In or Rotunda Hospital on Rutland Square (see Plate 25).[28] Before long, the outrages perpetrated by the Cherokees induced the closure of the venue, provoking public revulsion and an official backlash. While efforts were made to have the offending members prosecuted, it does not appear that any were brought to trial. This was due in no small part to the fact that they belonged to the very highest echelons of society. In this and other respects, the Cherokee Club was a successor to the Dublin Hellfire Club. The Cherokees' attire was described as 'an improvement on the black and yellow flame coloured uniform of the old "HELLFIRE CLUB"'.[29] While there is no evidence that the Hellfire Club had such a uniform, the indications are that the Cherokees identified with and, to a degree, sought to imitate them. Both groups consumed alcohol excessively and engaged in provocative and aggressive conduct. However, the Cherokees did not initiate overt and burlesque mockeries of institutional religion, nor did they commit serious offences of the order of homicide or blasphemy. Like the Pinkindindies, they are best seen as a society of rakes, rather than a fully fledged hellfire club.

As is the case with most groups of this nature, the exact circumstances in which the Cherokee Club emerged are uncertain. According to a nineteenth-century account, it was formed by 'the most dashing and care-driving members of Daly's and the Kildare Street clubs'.[30] Given that at least six members of the Cherokee Club were also MPs, it is tempting to regard it as an offshoot of Daly's. It may be that, at Daly's, the Cherokees engaged in conduct which the other members found objectionable, leading to their expulsion and their foundation of a separate association. However, the club probably emerged independently. Its name and some of its characteristics were peculiar to it, and these were influenced by a range of contemporary factors. By one account, the Cherokees owed their name to Joseph Leeson, 2nd Earl of Milltown. Following a masquerade at the house of Mr Latouche in County Wicklow, Milltown invited a group of young gentlemen back to his own residence, Russborough House in County Wicklow, where he entertained them with burgundy wine and champagne. The party became loud and boisterous, prompting the earl to quip that his guests were 'as clamorous as Cherokees'. The comment occasioned much laughter, 'and the name was afterwards adopted as a title of an association of these young men of fashion'.[31] The term 'Cherokee' carried considerable resonance in the early 1790s, conciding with increased popular interest in Native American tribes and their culture, as described by travellers such as John Long and William Bartram.[32] The visit to England of a delegation of Cherokee and Creek chiefs in the winter of 1790–91 attracted extensive publicity. The delegates, accompanied by a British American named William Augustus Bowles, attended a variety of social events, including plays and dinners at which they gave renditions of Cherokee songs and the battle cry known as the 'war-hoop' or war-whoop.[33]

It is likely these unusual visitors were the principal inspiration for the Cherokee Club. The young men who founded the club may have seen themselves as the 'civilized' counterparts of the Cherokee and Creek warriors, who were reputed to be handsome men in their twenties with a love for brandy and tobacco,[34] and their activities were inspired by Native American ways and customs. They were observed to practise 'the science of the bow and arrow, in order to compleat their characters', and war-whoops, attacks and ambushes allegedly featured in their disruptions of social events.[35] That there was a theatrical dimension to these activities was no accident, for several members of the club were involved in amateur dramatics.[36] Perhaps most significantly, there was a strong precedent for modelling a gentlemen's club on a Native American tribe: eighty years previously, the visit to London of a group of Iroquois chiefs had inspired the emergence of the infamous Mohocks.[37]

Membership, Appearance and Ethos of the Cherokee Club

No group portrait of the Cherokee Club is known to exist. The names of its principal members are provided in two nineteenth-century works: *The Staff Officer*, an account of an Irish recruiting officer's adventures written under the pseudonym Oliver Moore, and *Reminiscences of an Emigrant Milesian* by Andrew O'Reilly. These texts indicate that the principal members were Walter and James Wandesford Butler (later, respectively, 1st and 2nd Marquesses of Ormonde) and Francis Mathew (later 2nd Earl of Landaff) and his brother Montague. A number of other members are identified in *The Staff Officer*: Lord Conyngham, his brother Burton Conyngham, Lord Erroll, Thomas Whaley, his brother John Whaley, Frederick Falkiner, Cavendish Bradshaw and 'all the Beresfords'. O'Reilly additionally names Lord Cole, Sir Henry Parnell, Sir Wheeler Cuffe and William Palmer.[38] As these writers were contemporaries of the club (O'Reilly was personally acquainted with at least one member), their testimonies may be regarded as broadly reliable. However, they are recollections rather than contemporary accounts and are not correct in all specifics. Some of the named individuals could not have belonged to the Cherokee Club: as already noted, Thomas Whaley was absent on the Continent during the early 1790s, while Henry Brooke Parnell (1776–1842) was at school at Eton between 1791 and 1793, the time of the club's activity.[39] The exact circumstances of Sir Wheeler Cuffe and William Palmer are unknown.

There is no apparent reason to doubt that the other named individuals belonged to the Cherokee Club. Even a cursory glance at their social backgrounds indicates that it was an eminently elite association. The most high-ranking member, and leader, was Walter Butler, Lord Thurles (1770–1820), who would succeed as 18th Earl of Ormonde in 1795. His brothers John (1772–96) and James Wandesford Butler (1774–1838) also belonged to the club. The three were scions of one of the oldest and wealthiest families in the country. Their father's marriage to Lady Frances Susan Wandesford in 1769 had united the Ormonde and Wandesford estates, the combined rentals of which exceeded £16,000 per annum. As one contemporary observed, 'some German princes are obliged to support standing armies with less'.[40] Heir to a prestigious title and an enormous fortune, Walter Butler was prone to erratic behaviour from an early age. In her memoirs, Margaret Leeson recalled how she was once visited at her brothel (probably the premises on Pitt Street from which she operated during the 1780s) by a 17- or 18-year-old Butler. Faced with the lad's repeated refusal to say who he was, the courtesan told him that she did not admit strangers without proper recommendation. Butler, in a rage, threw a few guineas onto the sofa and asked her whether or not she thought he was a gentleman. Her response that she took him 'for some English flashman' caused her visitor to become 'like a madman. He gave me half a score hearty curses, calling me every opprobrious name he could recollect, and picking up his guineas went away swearing he would never enter the house again.'[41] This was conduct suggestive of an unstable personality, and the young man would prove particularly susceptible to the pitfalls of high living. In 1791, on his father being confirmed as 17th Earl of Ormonde by the House of Lords, Butler was styled Viscount Thurles. Now grown into a tall and handsome man, contemporaries remarked upon his 'brilliant but dissipated' character. In the words of his close friend Jonah Barrington, he 'was whirled at an early age into the vortex of fashionable life and dissipation … many of his naturally fine qualities were absorbed in the licentious influence of a fashionable female connexion; and thus became lost to himself and to many of those friends who had most truly valued him'.[42]

Though not quite on a social par with the Butlers, the Mathew brothers, Francis and Montague, were the sons of Francis Mathew, Baron Landaff of Thomastown. They were well known in fashionable circles and, at 'upwards of six feet high respectively', physically 'finer men' than the Butlers. Francis Mathew (1768–1833) was educated at Harrow and at Corpus Christi College, Oxford, after which he was commissioned a lieutenant. Despite the fact that his election in 1790 as MP for County Tipperary was contested, he represented the constituency for the next two years. He was regarded as the more supercilious of the brothers.[43] Montague (1773–1819) or 'Mounty' was known for his 'princely, manly [and] frank' demeanour. He became a cornet in the 18th Dragoons in 1792 and went on to enjoy a significant military and political career.[44] The remaining Cherokees occupied similarly elevated places on the social ladder. Henry, Viscount Conyngham of Mount Charles (1766–1832), another professional soldier, possessed large estates in Ireland and on the Isle of Thanet. He was described as 'warm and spirited' in manner, 'but too much marked with the remains of soldier-like importance and military insolence'. His twin brother Francis Nathaniel Burton Conyngham (1766–1832) served as MP for County Clare in the 1790s and was later Lieutenant Governor of Lower Canada.[45] John Willoughby Cole (1768–1840), styled Viscount Cole, was obliquely described as a 'very good sort of young man – but very Irish'.[46] He would succeed as 2nd Earl of Enniskillen in 1803. George Hay, 16th Earl of Erroll (1767–98), joined the Cherokee Club during an extended sojourn in Dublin in the late 1780s and early 1790s.[47] Frederick Falkiner (1768–1824), MP for Athy, had trained as a lawyer at Trinity College. The considerable fortune that he possessed allowed him to decline the 'drudgery' of the bar to focus on social amusements and amateur dramatics. Augustus Cavendish-Bradshaw (1768–1832), son of the baronet Sir Henry Cavendish, was MP for Carlow between 1790 and 1796.[48] Little is known about the career of John Whaley (d. 1847), younger brother of Thomas Whaley. He entered Trinity College on 19 October 1782 but failed to graduate. Though he was a regular visitor to Margaret Leeson's brothel, he was rarely in a position to pay for her services, probably because his brother was busy squandering the bulk of the family fortune.[49] Finally, it is possible that the three elder sons of the powerful politician John Beresford (1738–1805) belonged to the Cherokee Club: Marcus (1764–97), George de la Poer (1765–1841) and John Claudius Beresford (1766–1846). All three were MPs at the time the club was active. Marcus was married to Frances Arabella Leeson, daughter of the Earl of Milltown, who supposedly christened the club. Although George de la Poer Beresford later became Bishop of Kilmore and Ardagh, he was known for disreputable conduct in his youth, and his membership of the club is not improbable. John Claudius Beresford later became notorious for his harsh treatment of insurgents during the 1798 rebellion.[50]

The Cherokee Club was, first and foremost, a society of fashion, and contemporaries agreed that its members placed great importance on being well turned-out in public. Their devotion to Native American culture did not extend to their uniform, which was a lavish outfit, 'rather too good for the attire of a ferocious tribe'. It was variously described as 'scarlet lined with yellow, and edged with black', 'black faced with red...designed with taste [and] ornamented with brilliant buttons', and 'black from head to foot [with] scarlet silk covered buttons, and bunches of the same coloured riband at the knees of the breeches and in the shoes'.[51] The attire of some Cherokees was extravagant even when they were not in uniform, as is clear from Andrew O'Reilly's description of the Mathew brothers:

> The dress of the Mathews was, and remained nearly to the day of their deaths, as striking and singular as their personal qualities...consisting of a blue or green coat, double-breasted white waistcoat, and nankeen shorts or tights, with silk stockings...their linen trimmed, including a copious *jabot*, or

frill. Their hair was powdered, flowing over their shoulders, but confined carelessly, as it were, near the ends with ribbon.[52]

While some perceived foppery in such displays – Montague Mathew's ostentatious dress and bearing made him the subject of at least two drawings by the famous caricaturist James Gillray[53] – it did not follow that the Cherokees were effeminate or could be insulted with impunity. In O'Reilly's estimation, 'two braver men never stepped than the Mathews'.[54]

Certainly, the Cherokees wished to be perceived as men who were not only brave but also skilled in the use of arms. In a satirical exposé published in the *Hibernian Magazine*, a list of putative qualifications for membership was set out. It was stated that prospective members had to be experienced duellists as well as extraordinarily proficient marksmen and fencers, and capable of astonishing feats of drinking, womanizing and gambling:

> In order to become a member of the CHEROKEE CLUB of Dublin, it is first necessary that the candidate should have carried off and debauched a MAID, a WIFE, and a WIDOW, or an indefinite number of each.
>
> Secondly, that he should have fought three duels; in one of which, at least, he must either have wounded, or have been wounded, by his antagonist.
>
> Thirdly, he must at some one time of his life have drank six bottles of Claret after dinner, in half pint bumpers, and given a new Cyprian toast with each bumper.
>
> Fourthly, to arrive at the honour of the President's chair, it is absolutely requisite that the member should have killed, at least; one man in a duel, or a waiter in a violent passion.
>
> Fifthly, that no religious distinctions should disturb the tranquillity of the several meetings, it is absolutely necessary that the members in general should disavow every theological knowledge.

Sixthly, each candidate must be so good a marksman, as to split a bullet discharged from an ordinary pistol on the edge of a case knife, three times in five, at the distance of nine feet.

Seventhly, each candidate must be an expert fencer.

Eighthly, each candidate must either have won or lost the sum of one thousand pounds, at one sitting, at the game of hazard.

Ninthly, each candidate must be proposed by a brother in a full meeting, and proper evidence given of his qualifications. And,

Tenthly, he must take an oath before admission, to support the interests of the society by every possible means, and at risk of his life and fortune.[55]

Despite the heavily satirical nature of this piece, it did to a degree reflect the club's principles and behaviour. While not all of the Cherokees were experienced duellists, they were earnest advocates of the code of honour, and several would later involve themselves in confrontations. Lord Cole tried to duel with Thomas Russell in 1793. Seven years later, Walter Butler, who by then had succeeded as 18th Earl of Ormonde, exchanged pistol fire with an army officer. Only an intervention by the Speaker of the House of Commons prevented Montague Mathew from duelling with his fellow MP William Fitzgerald in 1813.[56] The stipulation that each candidate should disavow religious knowledge concurs with the attestation that the Cherokees were, at least ostensibly, freethinkers.[57] As regards the consumption of alcohol, there is little doubt that the Cherokees indulged to an extraordinary degree. It is elsewhere stated that under the rules of the society, any member found sober after dinner was subject to a fine of thirty pounds for a first offence, fifty for a second, and expulsion from the club for a third. On one occasion a convoy of thirty cars, loaded with fine wines, was observed leaving Dublin for the country residence of a member of the club.[58]

The Cherokees and Dublin Society

The Cherokees were men of fashion and one of Dublin's most fashionable quarters was the area around Rutland Square. Its streets were lined with elegant terraced houses and striking mansions, the residences of some of the wealthiest and most prominent people in the capital.[59] Several of the Cherokees could claim residence on Rutland Square itself (Lord Thurles and his brothers at their father's house on Cavendish Row and Lord Cole on Granby Row). One of the city's most prestigious venues was also situated on the square: the grounds and round hall of the Rotunda Hospital. The entertainments and musical events that took place there attracted large numbers of attendees, strutting gentlemen and ladies of the kind depicted in an illustration in the July 1790 issue of the *Hibernian Magazine*. In the 1780s the premises were extended, with the construction of new public rooms adjoining the round hall.[60] The public rooms were constituted on a charitable basis, with proceeds from the events that were held there going towards the maintenance of the hospital.[61] Keen to maximize their profits, the hospital's governors published an advertisement in February 1792 enjoining 'persons of fashion' to avoid having private parties on any of the nights on which entertainments were scheduled for the public rooms, hoping thereby to attract the largest possible number of potential customers.[62] Concerts, masquerades and promenades were held at the venue. According to the French traveller De Latocnaye, promenades were a form of entertainment that was peculiar to Dublin:

> The visitors walk in a circular hall called the Rotunda, and while there is somewhat more freedom than that which obtains at private entertainments, people only mix with, and speak to members of their own circle. After a certain time a bell sounded, and the company hurried through a door just opened, and groups of friends settled round tea-tables … everywhere there reigned a kind of quiet enjoyment which gave me much more pleasure than I had expected to find.[63]

Promenades at the Rotunda were popular events. One held on 12 February 1792 attracted 1,204 upper-class attendees.[64] Yet the 'quiet enjoyment' of these occasions was rudely shattered not long afterwards.

Although the *Hibernian Magazine*'s satire on the Cherokees was laced with sardonic exaggeration, it nonetheless reflected the activities that they engaged in. According to this account, the club's meetings commenced with a 'sumptuous dinner' at a well-known Dublin tavern, at which each member was required to consume four bottles of claret and a bumper of cherry brandy. They then outlined a strategy for the violent disruption of the evening's public entertainments. Having targeted an event or establishment, it was deliberated 'whether the attack shall commence with CAT CALLS, which they call the WAR-HOOP, or with whistlings, which is termed the WOOD-HOOP; or whether by direct assault or surprize'. Having checked their weapons, the Cherokees 'sall[ied] forth for action'.[65] In reality, it is unlikely than the club deliberated carefully on a strategy of disruption, but rather that they dined, drank heavily, and then proceeded to invade public gatherings. As often as not, they chose to attend the events that were held in the Rotunda's public rooms.

On 21 February 1792 five members of the club, including Lord Thurles and Lord Conyngham, attended a masquerade at the public rooms. Before the event took place, 'several disturbances' were occasioned by 'the unguarded conduct of a few'. The governors of the hospital hinted that any repetition of such behaviour might force the closure of the venue.[66] This did not deter those who went to the public rooms with mischievous intent, and a major fracas occurred at a promenade held on the evening of Sunday 8 April. Though the exact nature of what transpired is uncertain, it appears that a number of intoxicated 'young men of fashion' tried to introduce some sort of sparring contest to the proceedings, provoking a full-scale riot.[67] The culprits were identified as members of the Cherokee Club, and the *Hibernian Magazine*'s description of their conduct, though satirical, gives some idea of the kind of scene that took place: 'when they enter the play-house, or the rotunda, and set up the war hoop, the women, in general, response through terror, and nothing is to be seen or heard but screams and faintings; the candles are all knocked out, and darkness follows', under cover of which 'the ladies are found to be pinched and pricked in the most indecent manner'.[68] The disturbances of 8 April provoked a public outcry and a swift response from the hospital's governors, who announced that the promenades would be discontinued and the public rooms closed. The hospital was not supported by a permanent established fund and relied heavily on the income generated by events in the public rooms, the closure of which, it was anticipated, would result in losses of £1,500. Some feared that the hospital itself would have to be shut down.[69]

Although the governors signalled their intention of prosecuting the offenders 'with the utmost severity', it was elsewhere observed that it was unlikely that they would be brought to trial, given the reluctance of their female victims to undergo cross-examination.[70] While the governors published an advertisement on 18 April offering a reward of fifty pounds to anyone who would prosecute to conviction those who were involved in the affray, the tone was more lukewarm, with the governors not presuming 'to interfere in the conduct of individuals, respecting inebriety'. Almost as if to draw a line under the incident, they affirmed that, should the public rooms reopen at a later date and there be any further misconduct, they would support the criminal prosecution of the perpetrators.[71] It is possible that the governors were swayed by the representations of the offenders' well-connected families. Whether social or political influence was brought to bear must remain a moot point; ultimately, however, no criminal proceedings were undertaken as a result of the events of 8 April.

Meanwhile, the Cherokees were also making their presence felt on the streets. According to the *Hibernian Magazine*, 'such is the general dread of this new military corps, that the citizens actually go armed after dusk, and the whole town appears like a garrison in fear of an assault from a foreign power'. Although this is an exaggeration, there were reports of Cherokees clashing with the police[72] and carrying out assaults on females that recalled the violent misconduct of the

Pinkindindies. On 22 April, two members of the club forced their way into a brothel on Longford Street. When the procuress, Miss Groves, refused to entertain them, they struck her on the head with a knotted stick and fled. Bleeding from her wound, she pursued her assailants as far as Bride Street, where she unsuccessfully solicited the assistance of a group of soldiers in apprehending them.[73] Several months later, on Abbey Street, a party of gentlemen who were believed to be members of the Cherokee Club abused several women. One of the victims, 'a young lady of family', was treated with 'the grossest rudeness, merely because she would not lend them her under-petticoat'. Again, the Cherokees avoided any adverse consequences for their actions, with one of the ringleaders avoiding public identification as a result of the esteem in which his family was held.[74]

Instances where the identities of upper-class miscreants were withheld in the press offered the Cherokees and like-minded individuals little incentive to moderate their behaviour. Moreover, the trend whereby the courts awarded lenient sentences to gentlemen who were convicted of assault continued. On 29 March 1792 two gentlemen named Cruise and Johnson were tried for an assault on Miss Agar, a sister of the Archbishop of Cashel, whose sedan chair they stopped on Grafton Street, demanding that its occupant be surrendered to them. When the chairman attempted to resist, one of the assailants put his sword through the glass at the front of the chair. He then pulled Miss Agar out of the chair 'and abused her in a stile of epithet too gross to be repeated'. For this crime, Cruise and Johnson were fined one mark each and sentenced to one month's imprisonment. The *Hibernian Journal* reacted with disgust to this outcome, inferring that it would hardly dissuade other rakish gentlemen from acts of violence: 'Hear this, ye bucks of spirit, ye souls of fun and fire, Cherokees, &c.'[75]

The Decline of the Cherokee Club

Nonetheless, official tolerance for the activities of rakish clubs was becoming strained. Increasingly, such clubs were perceived as a threat not only to public order but also to the morals of society in general. Addressing a newly sworn grand jury at the end of April 1792, Judge Robert Day lambasted clubs such as the Cherokees for encouraging, by their bad example, the spread of immorality among the lower classes:

> If clubs, said he, shall be initiated upon the express stipulation of constant inebri[e]ty, if the peaceful citizen and his virtuous family are to be insulted with impunity in their evening's relaxation, by fashionable and titled ruffians, more savage in their manners even than in their name...no wonder that the pernicious example, like all other fashions, descended to the humble ranks of life, and tainted the whole mass of the people.

Day expressed the hope that should the jury attend at the trial of any such individual, 'they would not pass it over as a youthful frolic, nor wink at the guilt of power or title', and that the law would be applied firmly and impartially.[76] Day also urged more stringent measures against those who became involved in affairs of honour.[77] Just as he and others in authority were becoming increasingly less disposed to countenance duelling, so also were they less willing to put up with the drunken and riotous behaviour of certain clubs.

This reflected a general hardening of attitudes against how elements of the upper classes conducted themselves in society. As reports of the Cherokees' misconduct mounted, the Dublin press became increasingly critical of the club. Individual members came in for particular scorn. The *Hibernian Magazine*'s satire on the club was accompanied by an illustration of a fashionably attired 'Irish Cherokee' (see Plate 26) staggering in a state of obvious inebriation while brandishing a heavy cudgel. The apparent resemblance to Lord Thurles provoked a threat of legal proceedings from the latter, occasioning a dismissive response from the *Freeman's Journal*: 'Among the eccentricities of the day, few are more laughable, or have attracted public attention more than the anger so strikingly displayed by the NOBLE CHEROKEE on seeing his person exhibited in WALKER's MAGAZINE.'[78] Elsewhere in the press, the Cherokees were condemned more generally. *Faulkner's Dublin Journal* described them as 'a few men, who, from the accident of birth, assume a rank in society their conduct proves them unworthy to hold'. The *Dublin Evening Post*, meanwhile, execrated the Cherokees for spending 'your time, your health, your fortunes in dissipation and riot!'[79] Just as the scandals that surrounded the proceedings against Lens and Santry in 1738 contributed to the decline of the Hellfire Club, growing criticism of the Cherokee Club made the continuance of its activities more difficult. The Earl of Ormonde, who was dismayed at his son's reputation, succeeded in enticing him away from Dublin to a more settled residence at Kilkenny.[80] There is little evidence to suggest that the Cherokee Club was active after 1792. It was supposed to have disbanded when the outbreak of war with France in February 1793 offered 'more honourable employment' to its members, or at least such of them as were professional soldiers.[81]

Increasingly, the country itself was disturbed. As the 1790s progressed, secret societies such as the United Irishmen and the Defenders posed an increasingly viable threat to the Establishment, which had the support of the majority of the country's nobility and gentry. Lord Thurles became colonel of the Kilkenny militia in 1793 and succeeded as 18th Earl of Ormonde following his father's death in 1795. Despite his avowed support of government, his apparent seduction of Lady Clare, the wife of the chancellor, won him few friends in Dublin Castle.[82] Ormonde fared no better as a military commander. When he led the Kilkenny militia into battle against General Humbert's Franco-Irish army at Castlebar on 27 August 1798, disaster ensued. In the face of a French bayonet charge, the Kilkenny militia turned and fled. According to the under-secretary Edward Cooke, 'Lord Ormonde exerted himself to stop his men; he first begged and beseeched; he then upbraided and swore at them; he ran two of them through the body, and burst into tears.'[83] Such erratic conduct seemed to confirm the contemporary view of Ormonde as an unstable character. During the period following 1798 he lent his support to the Union and other government measures in the hope of achieving the restoration of the extinct title of Duke of Ormonde. While he did not succeed in this endeavour, he was created 1st Marquess of Ormonde in 1816, four years prior to his death. It appears that by this stage he had deteriorated into a state of near mental incapability. Barrington's summation of Ormonde's life, even allowing for his customary exaggeration, gives a sense of a life and advantages squandered in the well-established traditions of an eighteenth-century rake:

> never have I remarked, through the course of a long, observing life, any progress more complete from the natural levities of youth to confirmed habits of dissipation, from the first order of early talent to the humblest state of premature imbecility than that of the late Marquess of Ormonde, who had, at one period of our intimacy, as engaging a person, as many noble, manly qualities, and to the full as much intellectual promise, as any young man of his country.[84]

Ormonde was not the only member of the Cherokee Club whose dissolute ways caused him difficulties later in life. Frederick John Falkiner, who was noted for his steadfast opposition to the Union, indulged 'extravagant habits [that] led to his circumstances becoming embarrassed'. When he received a baronetcy in 1812 he could not pay the twenty or thirty pound fee that would ensure its reversion to his nephew. He later resided in Paris and Naples, where he killed himself in 1824.[85] Montague Mathew went on to represent County Tipperary at Westminster, distinguishing himself by his provocative and stentorian speeches in favour of Catholic Emancipation. By 1818, however, his health was 'breaking down' and he died the following year.[86] Other erstwhile members of the club underwent various adventures and misadventures in their later careers. In October 1792, Augustus Cavendish-Bradshaw came close to death when he and his servant's horses plunged into the Liffey after being frightened by an ass on the Leixlip–Dublin road. Though his servant was drowned, Cavendish-Bradshaw managed to save himself. He went on to represent Honiton and Castle Rising at Westminster.[87] Francis Mathew succeeded as 2nd Earl of Landaff in 1806. He later resigned from the Kildare Street Club in protest at the blackballing of Montague, taking care to first address those who had voted against his brother as 'eighty-five — scoundrels'.[88] However, the Cherokee who attained the greatest prominence in later life was possibly Lord Conyngham, who was created Viscount Mount Charles and Earl Conyngham in 1797. Three years earlier he had married Elizabeth Denison, the daughter of a London banker. When Conyngham was elevated to a marquessate in 1816, it was said to have been as a result of his wife's burgeoning relationship with the prince regent. Following the latter's accession to the throne as George IV in 1820, she became his mistress, a role which she occupied until his death in 1830. Conyngham himself died two years later.[89]

The Cherokee Club had an even more short-lived existence than the Hellfire Club or the Pinkindindies. Yet in the few months that it was active, it made a distinct impression on the Dublin social scene. The club's conduct at the Rotunda public rooms was sufficiently disruptive, violent and abusive to ensure the temporary closure of the city's most prestigious venue. The Cherokees also initiated fracas in brothels and on the streets, assaulting prostitutes and other women, and sometimes fighting the police. The increasingly loud calls by media commentators and members of the judiciary for the curtailment of the offenders bespoke a society that was wearying of the culture of the rakish club, and increasingly less inclined to countenance misconduct by members of the upper classes. This was also evidenced by the growing opposition of moral reform societies to club excess. As James Kelly notes, 'The Cherokees were perceived as an affront to public decency by the still-embryonic movement for moral reform, whose most significant contemporary organizational achievement was the Association for Discountenancing Vice (founded in 1792).' By 1795 another morally minded group, the Society for Promoting Religion and Virtue, was actively monitoring events at the Rotunda and enjoining the governors to discontinue the promenades on the basis of their threat to public morals, even though there was no suggestion of a renewal of the disturbances of three years previously.[90] Additionally, the deteriorating political situation in the Ireland of the 1790s served to distract men of property from dissipated pursuits and focus their attention on the defence of the Establishment, on which their social position depended. In this increasingly circumspect climate, it became more difficult for rakish clubs to thrive.

Ultimately, however, the Cherokee Club was a less robust version of the clubs that had preceded and inspired it. The Cherokees did not conduct themselves with the same ruthlessness and brutality that had made the Pinkindindies so notorious. The attacks they perpetrated were less numerous and less violent, and they did not wreck brothels, or abduct females, or rob gentlemen. There is no evidence that they killed or seriously wounded any of their victims. Nor did the Cherokees achieve the notoriety of the Dublin Hellfire Club. Though they were believed to be freethinkers, they did not 'practise any of those profane and atrocious ceremonies which fame attributed to [their] infernal predecessor'.[91] Crucially, the Cherokees had sufficient judgement to know how far they could push social boundaries before they broke. None of the members exhibited the daring of Peter Lens in publicly invoking the Devil, or the sociopathic tendencies that led Lord Santry to carry out unprovoked and fatal attacks on servants. However, the Cherokee Club was the equal of its 'infernal predecessor' in at least one respect – its capacity for alcohol consumption. Judge Robert Day correctly identified the club as having been 'instituted upon the express stipulation of constant inebri[e]ty', and given that thirty carloads of fine wine were reputedly conveyed to a member's residence on at least one occasion, it is not hard to imagine that their drinking was extraordinary even by the standards of the period. This helped to ensure the Cherokees' notoriety well into the nineteenth century. The club made a cameo appearance in Lady Morgan's novel *The O'Briens and the O'Flahertys* (1826), where the members' near-religious devotion to alcohol is evoked in a quartet intoned by one of the protagonists: 'The bottle's the sun of our table; / Its beams are rosy wine; / We, planets that are not able / Without its light, to shine.' The boast that each member could drink six bottles of wine at a single sitting became part of the club's folklore and was reiterated well into the nineteenth century.[92] The Cherokee Club was the last noteworthy rakish club of the eighteenth century. It was a sort of coda to the hellfire phenomenon, a final fling of raucous dissipation and provocative aggression by an elite group before the nineteenth century ushered in an era of restraint and circumspection in which excesses of the kind that had characterized the eighteenth became unthinkable.

Chapter seven

The Hellfire Myth

One of the most curious things about the Irish hellfire clubs is the fact that they remain subjects of popular interest in the present day. Why should these small, exclusive groups of nobility and gentry, about which little was known even in their heyday, be the subject of attention so many years after their demise? The answer lies in the powerful aura of mystique and allure that the subject exudes and the tales of black masses, demonic cats and encounters with the Devil that continue to circulate. Such stories are part of what might be termed the 'hellfire myth', a rich body of folklore that developed in the nineteenth and twentieth centuries. It was complemented by the identification of a number of old buildings as the erstwhile meeting places of these clubs, the emergence of a range of supposed hellfire club relics, and the acquisition by the National Gallery of Ireland of the Dublin and Limerick Hellfire Club portraits.

By the early nineteenth century, the phenomenon of upper-class men gathering in hellfire and rakish clubs was a spent force. The passing of the Act of Union in 1800 had dire implications for Dublin's once-vibrant social scene. The abolition of the Irish parliament, and the departure for Westminster of the nobility and gentry who had sat in the House of Lords and House of Commons, greatly reduced the social base from which such clubs were formed. Dublin was particularly affected, as the peers and MPs who had previously crowded the precincts of College Green and Dublin Castle deserted the city. Prior to the Union, most of the 300 members of the House of Commons and over 200 members of the House of Lords had lived in Dublin on a permanent or occasional basis. By 1821 only thirty-four peers, thirteen baronets and five members of the House of Commons had fixed residences there.[1] As Dublin lost its elite, its prestige and allure declined. No longer did the vibrant round of balls and social events that had accompanied the parliamentary season enliven the capital. Even the nobility and gentry who had not been actively involved in politics found Dublin a less attractive prospect, preferring to remain on their country estates.[2] Inevitably, there was an economic corollary to this development. The departure of the peers of the House of Lords, to say nothing of their House of Commons counterparts, caused the city's merchants, shopkeepers and tradespeople an annual loss of revenue of around £624,000.[3] The change in fortunes was neatly encapsulated in Stockdale's engravings of College Green before and after the Union. The 'before' scene depicts a procession of state coaches flanked by outriders approaching the Parliament House, cheered on by crowds of well-dressed onlookers. In the 'after' scene, this once-proud epicentre of social and political life has deteriorated into a haunt of beggars. Groups of impoverished folk cluster in the foreground and the only traffic consists of a couple of modest coaches and an overcrowded jaunting car.[4] Stripped of its propertied, monied and fashionable elite, for many Dublin was reduced to the status of a provincial town, a shell of its former self.

Equally, the position of dominance that the Protestant Ascendancy enjoyed could not continue indefinitely. The Catholic Relief Acts of the late eighteenth century prefigured the rise of a Catholic middle class that would assume increasing power and importance over the course of the nineteenth century, particularly after the attainment of Catholic Emancipation in 1829.[5] In this increasingly bourgeois society there was little latitude for upper-class clubs to rampage unchecked. The doctors, lawyers and civil servants who now began to dominate society were more concerned with sober and professional endeavour than aristocratic swagger and excess. As R.B. McDowell observed, 'with a new century and a new political structure, benevolence, allied with an easy-going tolerance of anomalies and inefficiency, was rapidly falling out of fashion, and the new age of the calculator, the reformer, the economist, the philanthropist, and the systematic administrator was dawning'.[6] The period also saw increased evangelical activity, with Protestant bodies such as the Association for Discountenancing Vice and the Hibernian Sunday School Society giving a new impetus to the moral agenda. Concurrently, middle-class Catholics demonstrated their commitment to moral behaviour and discipline through their growing involvement in convents, schools, sodalities and confraternities. In this increasingly strait-laced environment, raucous behaviour or the flouting of Christian values by members of the upper classes was less likely to be tolerated. Indeed, there is evidence that even the upper classes began to adopt a middle-class mindset. As James Kelly observes, 'in the early nineteenth century a confluence of forces that include a more interventionist state, a more conservative political climate, a vigorous evangelical as well as mainstream religious sector, and a code of behaviour that extolled personal discipline lent itself to the increased acceptance of the world view of the "middling sort"'.[7]

Just as this process assisted the decline of duelling, it also sounded the death knell of the hellfire/rakish phenomenon. One commentator noted in 1821 that Dublin's inhabitants had 'become more serious and religious, and those sums formerly lavished on expensive pleasures, are now happily converted to purposes of a much more exalted nature. Club-houses and gaming-tables are nearly deserted . . . vice of every kind has visibly diminished.'[8] While it is not correct that club life had vanished from Dublin, society had certainly become less willing to tolerate the sort of upper-class misconduct and violence that had characterized hellfire and rakish clubs. Indeed, as time went on, authors found tales of the eighteenth-century 'bucks' and the outrages they had committed increasingly hard to credit. As John Edward Walsh noted in the 1840s, these 'traditionary anecdotes [are] so repugnant to the conduct that marks the character of a gentleman of the present day, that we hardly believe they could have pretensions to be considered as belonging to the same class of society'.[9] A certain prudishness was also discernible, with writers diluting colourful descriptions of eighteenth-century antics in order to avoid offending their readers' sensibilities. For instance, in his *History of the City of Dublin* (1859), John T. Gilbert altered Jack Pilkington's anecdote of Lord Rosse's deathbed prank, substituting objectionable words and phrases for less offensive alternatives: thus 'whoring' becomes 'profligacy', 'whore-monger' becomes 'profligate', and reference is made to the Earl of Kildare embracing his wife rather than going to bed with her.[10]

At the same time, nineteenth-century writers hearkened back to the excesses of the preceding century with a sort of fascinated nostalgia. Works such as Jonah Barrington's *Personal Sketches of his Own Times* (1827–32) and John Edward Walsh's *Ireland Sixty Years Ago* (1847) chronicled a turbulent era when duels and abductions were ten-a-penny and libertines, rakes and 'half-mounted' gentlemen swaggered through taverns, coffee houses and gaming dens. The hellfire and rakish clubs were an integral part of this boisterous world. As William O'Neill Daunt put it, 'then were the golden days of duelling; of drunkenness; of profligate clubs in the metropolis, "the Cherokee," "the Hellfire," "the Pinkers and Sweaters," whose orgies are still preserved in the local traditions of Dublin'.[11] These traditions also served as fertile ground for works of fiction. In *The O'Briens and the O'Flahertys*, Lady Morgan characterized the Cherokee Club as a group of rakes who take pleasure in breaking furniture, frightening old ladies in sedan chairs and 'playing H[e]ll and Tommy through the town'. One of the novel's characters, Sir Terence O'Flynn, is described as 'the chief of the Pinking Dindies': he 'pinks' his friend in a duel and kills his coachman with a tennis ball. Similarly, one of the protagonists of Gerald Griffin's *The Collegians* (1829) is an erstwhile member of a hellfire club and 'a great *sweater* and *pinker*'.[12] Hellfire clubs also feature in William Carleton's tales of rural Ireland, most notably 'Squire Warnock', in which a society of blasphemers is a haunted by the ghost of a deceased member, and 'The Castle of Aughentain', in which the preconditions for would-be members of a provincial hellfire club are set out: 'no person could join that hadn't fought three duels, and killed at least one man; and in ordher to show that they regarded neither God nor hell, they were obligated to dip one hand in blood an' the other in fire, before they could be made members of the club'.[13] Such hyperbole doubtless reflects the hellfire club traditions that were then current in rural areas.

However, it was the Dublin Hellfire Club, rather than the Cherokees, Pinkindindies or provincial groups, that most caught the imagination. As well as inspiring several works of fiction, it spawned an abundance of folklore that persists to the present day.

The Folklore of the Dublin Hellfire Club

Although the ruined hunting lodge on Mountpelier is today integral to the folklore of the Dublin Hellfire Club, many nineteenth-century accounts situated the club in Dublin city rather than the lodge. These accounts offered various assessments of the club's nature. According to some, it was an elite society of duellists that granted admission only to those who had killed their opponents in affairs of honour.[14] Such assertions had little bearing on the historical reality of the Hellfire Club and are best seen in the context of the campaign against duelling: the authors no doubt hoped to denigrate the practice by associating it with a nefarious and iniquitous group. Those who emphasized the club's reputation for blasphemy stood on surer ground, although the claim that members who were unable to coin new oaths had to pay a forfeit was probably groundless.[15] Others highlighted the club's reputation for aggressive and riotous behaviour, recalling 'its unlicensed and disgraceful orgies and brutalities, and its indulgence in riot, and every species of violence'.[16] Given the known misdeeds of the club's members, this was not an unreasonable indictment.

Unsurprisingly, however, much of the folklore of the Dublin Hellfire Club was bizarre and colourful, comprising tales of fiery destruction, occult practices and supernatural occurrences. Several core motifs are identifiable:

1. Imitation of hell – the club-mates burn themselves or set fire to their meeting place in order to prefigure the torments of hell.

2. Burning of a servant – a butler or other servant belonging to the club is burned alive.

3. The cat and the clergyman – a clergyman who is invited by the club to a banquet conducts an exorcism on their mascot, a demonic cat.

4. Scaltheen – the club-mates concoct and drink a fiery beverage known as scaltheen.

5. Burlesque activities – the members dress up and act out mock rituals and conduct black masses.

6. The cardplayers and the Devil – the club members play cards with a mysterious stranger who turns out to be the Devil.

The 'imitation of hell' motif occurs in relation to a number of different hellfire clubs. The earliest mention of it in an Irish context relates to the Limerick Hellfire Club (see Chapter 4). The motif also appears in *Hibernicus* (1828), the memoir of an expatriate Irishman, which states that Sir John St Leger (1674–1743), the father of John St Leger of Grangemellon, belonged to a hellfire club. He and his fellow members would strip themselves naked and

> 'prepare for merry hell,' by roasting themselves in front of a large fire, being attached to a spit, and turned round before it. On one of these trials of misapplied fortitude, St Leger was undergoing the torture, and finding the fire too severe, particularly on his shins, petitioned to be withdrawn, exclaiming with an oath, that he could have borne it better, if he had his boots on.[17]

This tale may have originally been associated with the Grangemellon Hellfire Club, with Sir John St Leger being confused with his son. Alternatively, Sir John may have been believed to be a member of the group that is most frequently associated with the 'imitation of hell' motif, the Dublin Hellfire Club. In a number of accounts it is stated that the club's members set fire to their meeting-room in order to ready themselves for future torments. The resultant fire causes the destruction of the building.[18] While it is difficult to discern a factual basis for these tales in Ireland, an incident of this kind did occur in Glasgow in 1793. In this instance a group of political radicals 'who designated themselves the "Hell-fire Club"...indulging in jokes against one another, as to their individual capacity to resist heat', set fire to the Laigh Kirk session house, burning it to the ground.[19] Perhaps this incident was transmuted to an Irish context; if so, it is an indicator of the flux-like nature of hellfire club folklore.

The story of the burning to death of a servant or butler, which originates from Lord Santry's murder of his sedan chairman, appears regularly in the folklore of the club. It inspired an unpublished work of fiction by the Kilkenny writer Michael Banim (1796–1874) that survives in an incomplete manuscript version in the Royal Irish Academy and a less detailed, but complete, one in the National Library of Ireland.[20] In this tale the club's rendezvous, the Eagle Tavern, is sited in Saul's Court (the probable scene of the murder of the chairman) rather than Cork Hill. The club-mates and their president, an unnamed nobleman, meet in a lavishly furnished chamber, the walls of which are adorned with 'scenes of the most undisguised and bro[a]dest licentiousness & sensuality'. Significantly, the president addresses one of those present as 'Harry', the familiar form of Henry, Lord Santry's Christian name. The company is visited by a mysterious stranger who signals his intention of 'testing the claim to preeminence of the metropolitan h[el]l fire Club over the provincial clubs'. Despite the fact that the visitor introduces himself as Lucifer, only the club's 'special attendant', Tony Reardon, appreciates his true diabolical nature. He attempts to apprise the president of this fact, but is overheard by Lucifer, who promises the servant that they shall play the game of 'h[el]ls delight' before they part. A heavy drinking session ensues, during which Lucifer recalls the immoral, violent and murderous deeds he has committed. In the meantime, Reardon has been busily refilling the drinking vessels, all the while consuming copious amounts of brandy himself. As the atmosphere of conviviality begins to wane, Lucifer takes the servant by the cuff of his coat and forces him to drink 'bumper after bumper' of brandy. Reardon collapses on the floor in drunken nausea, and Lucifer seizes his chance to play 'hell's delight':

> into the mouth of the prostrate gaping Tony he poured brandy until the gaping receptacle would hold no more[.] on his person he poured abundant libations of the same until his garments were saturated[.] he applied a lighted taper to the alcohol carrying out the sport of D[evi]ls delight to the utmost setting the unconscious victim in a blaze internally and externally the blue flames floating round him so sever[e]ly as to dazzle the eyes of the lookers on[.]

Despite the efforts of the club members to quench the flames, Reardon is burned to death. In the confusion, the mysterious stranger vanishes. Bemoaning his servant's fate, the president solemnly acknowledges that their visitor 'was the D[evi]l in proper persona'.[21]

The most striking thing about this story is the specific description of the mode of burning, which accords closely with the near-contemporary description of Santry's killing of the chairman (see Chapter 2). It seems that Banim was familiar with this crime and the manner of its execution. Later versions of the story exhibit considerable variation; however, the core element of a servant being doused in spirits and set ablaze remains. Curiously, a butler rather than a chairman is almost always mentioned as the victim of the crime. In one version, the butler is drenched in whiskey rather than brandy, and his death by burning gives the club its name. In another the butler is brought to the club's meeting place and confronted with its diabolic paraphernalia. He conducts himself so flippantly that his infuriated master throws a jug of scaltheen over him and sets him on fire. The butler runs screaming from the house and his charred body is later found 'lying in a boreen, with the flames of the burning liquid still flickering over his calcined features'. In an account recorded by the Irish Folklore Commission in the 1930s it is stated simply that 'a quarrel arose and they put the butler into the fire and burned him'.[22] Despite the increasing confusion over the details, it is clear that the atrocity committed by Santry lived on in folk memory well into the twentieth century.

The 'cat and the clergyman' motif occurs in many nineteenth- and twentieth-century accounts of the Dublin Hellfire Club. In this story, a priest or minister accepts an invitation to attend a banquet at the club's meeting place. On arrival he notices, seated at the head of the banquet table, a large black cat, which is deferred to in being served before any of the others present. When the clergyman asks why this is so he is told that it is out of respect, as the cat is older than any of the others present. The clergyman states his belief that the animal is a fiend or 'an imp of darkness', upon which the members resolve to kill him for his insolence. Allowed time to say his prayers, he hurriedly utters an exorcism. The cat transforms into a demon and flies off, tearing the roof from the building in the process and, in some versions, causing a fire that results in the destruction of the club.[23] It is not known what, if any, actual incident inspired this tale.

There are repeated references in Hellfire Club folklore to the drinking of scaltheen. Recipes for the beverage vary, though most involve heating whiskey, sugar and butter.[24] Evidently scaltheen was widely consumed in Ireland until the time of Father Theobald Mathew's temperance campaign in the 1830s; in some localities its use continued long after that. The German Prince Hermann Heinrich Ludwig von Pückler-Muskau is believed to have sampled it in Cashel, County Tipperary, in 1828.[25] According to Malachi Horan of Killenarden, County Dublin scaltheen was served at the Jobstown Inn near Tallaght, where it was 'taken red hot' and 'would make a corpse walk'. However, it was difficult to concoct, as the whiskey and butter tended to burn easily.[26] The Hellfire Club's association with the drink is first mentioned in the nineteenth-century miscellany *The Book of Days*. Here, several traditions pertaining to the club are presented as the testimony of a scaltheen-maker who 'had learned the art . . . from an old man, who had learned it in his youth from another old man, who had been scaltheen-maker in ordinary to . . . the H[ell] F[ire] club in Dublin'. A later account has it that the scaltheen-maker was actually a member of the club who went by the name of 'Brewer of the Fiery Liquid'.[27] Although there is no factual basis for this assertion, it is not impossible that scaltheen was brewed for the Hellfire Club's use. One tradition conflates the scaltheen and 'imitation of hell' motifs, implausibly stating that the members of the club 'drank burning scaltheen, standing in impious bravado before blazing fires, till, the marrow melting in their wicked bones, they fell down dead upon the floor'.[28]

Nineteenth- and early twentieth-century sources refer intermittently to the Hellfire Club's burlesque activities. *The Book of Days* has it that 'in the H.F. clubs blasphemous burlesques of the most sacred events were frequently performed; and there is a very general tradition, that a person was accidentally killed by a lance during a mocking representation of the crucifixion'. Other accounts state that the club's president attired himself as the Devil: 'he occupied a sort of throne during the sessions, and was decked out in the fancied garb of Satan, with scarlet robes, horns, wings, a forked tail and cloven hoof'. While it is possible that the Hellfire Club introduced burlesque elements to its proceedings, there is no contemporary evidence to support the above claims. As Robert Chambers speculated, it is probable that 'the recitals in question are merely imaginations arising from the extreme sensation which the H.F. system excited in the popular mind'.[29] At the same time, other eighteenth-century clubs were known for their burlesque activities.[30] It is also possible that these stories were transposed from England, as the London Hellfire Club is said to have held 'diabolical masquerades', one of which is depicted in a contemporary engraving.[31]

Finally, arguably the most enduring folkloric motif pertaining to the Hellfire Club is that of the card-players and the Devil. It is also the one that is most firmly associated with the club's alleged meeting place on the hill of Mountpelier. While it remains uncertain if there was any actual connection between the club and this building, an exploration of the history of Mountpelier may help to ascertain how it attained its reputation. A gutted, noisome pile, it stood as a testament to an earlier age of dark deeds and occult practices.

Mountpelier

Of all the locations that are associated with Irish hellfire clubs, the lodge on Mountpelier is by the far the most famous (or infamous). The place had a 'hellfire' connection even before the heyday of the Dublin Hellfire Club, as Mountpelier was part of the Duke of Wharton's Rathfarnham estate in the early 1720s.[32] After suffering catastrophic losses of over £120,000 in the South Sea Bubble, Wharton sold the Rathfarnham estate for £62,000 in 1723. The purchaser was the politician and property speculator William Conolly, Speaker of the Irish House of Commons and, reputedly, the richest man in Ireland.[33] At some point thereafter, Conolly (or his nephew) constructed a house on the summit of Mountpelier.[34] While most accounts have it that this happened around 1725, the actual date of construction is unknown. Built in the Palladian style, the lodge may have been designed by Edward Lovett Pearce (d. 1733), architect of Conolly's mansion, Castletown House in County Kildare, and the Parliament House on College Green.[35] Tradition has it that stones from an ancient burial cairn, situated to the rear of the present building, were used in the construction.[36] Not long afterwards, the original slate roof on the lodge was blown off in a furious storm, supposedly sent by the Devil in retaliation for the desecration of the cairn. According to the local historian William Domville Handcock, Conolly was not dissuaded by this misfortune and soon reroofed the building: 'He built an arched roof with large stones placed edgeways, and filled to a smooth surface with smaller stones and mortar. So well was this done, that much of it remains to the present, in spite of its exposed situation and of its never having been repaired.' Whatever the circumstances of the building's construction, the persistent claim that it was built as a hunting lodge rings true: Mountpelier was situated within a 1,000-acre, walled-in deer park that can be seen on John Rocque's 1760 map of County Dublin.[37]

The lodge in its original state was comfortable and well furnished. A set of cut-stone steps led to a fanlit main entrance on the first floor.

The principal reception rooms, consisting of a parlour and a drawing room, were situated on this floor. They were probably finely decorated; as Michael Fewer notes, 'the number and distribution of wall niches in the reception rooms suggest that the original interior finishes were more than utilitarian'. The ground-floor rooms served as the kitchen and servants' quarters. There was also a third storey, a small loft or bedroom at the top of the building.[38] Two old sketches of the front and rear of the lodge as it was when a fully functional building depict a neat and sturdy structure with windows and chimneys, a front courtyard enclosed by a semicircular wall, and the steps leading to the first floor entrance (see Plates 28 and 29).[39] It is unlikely that the lodge was inhabited on a permanent basis, being used mainly as an occasional resort for hunting parties. The statement that Charles Cobbe, the eldest son of the Archbishop of Dublin, was killed there in a duel in 1751 is erroneous.[40] The lodge's cut-granite windowsills, doorsteps and courtyard walls were probably removed in 1763 for use in the construction of Dollymount House on the lower slopes of Mountpelier.[41] The following year, the lands of Mountpelier were leased to one William Barnewell at a half-yearly rent of £70, probably as pasture.[42] By this time, the lodge was falling into ruin. When the antiquarian Austin Cooper visited it in 1779 it was 'entirely out of repair'. Cooper also noted the presence of cattle, as well as the remains of the cairn to the rear of the lodge.[43]

While Mountpelier had attractive qualities – it was and is known for its prominent location and extensive views of Dublin and Dublin Bay – by the end of the eighteenth century it had somehow attained a sinister reputation. In 1798 the area was a haunt of United Irish rebels, one of whom, Joseph Holt, spent a night on Mountpelier while on the run from Crown forces. Holt approached the lodge, which he described as 'that enchanted house', with some trepidation, but he was so fatigued that 'the name of inchantment was not able to deter me. I contemplated, "there is nothing worse than I am," and, in God's name, I said my prayers and slept soundly.'[44] Other sources also attested to the building's ominous aspect. In 1801, at the time of the purchase of

Mountpelier by the property speculator Luke White, it was referred to as 'the haunted-house'.[45] In the 1820s there were rumours that a murder had been committed there:'on the crown of this hill is a lodge falling to ruin, not having been inhabited for thirty years; it is called the *haunted house*, and the hill *Bevan's hill*: local tradition states, that, in this house, a man, named Bevan, murdered his wife'.[46] Whether the lodge attained its reputation as the result of a murder or a hellfire club connection or some other factor is uncertain. The first direct reference to a link between the lodge and a hellfire club that has been discovered occurs in Handcock's *History and Antiquities of Tallaght* (1876). Handcock referred to the 'tradition that the Hell-fire Club held some of their meetings here', indicating that such a belief had existed for some time. He also felt that it had a factual foundation:'that mysterious and iniquitous assembly existed about the time this house was built; and a member of the Club then lived not far off'.[47] While it appears that this tradition had not been widely known prior to the publication of Handcock's work, it became popular during the closing decades of the nineteenth century. The idea of a mysterious society engaging in nefarious activities in this lonely place seems to have appealed to the darker side of the Victorian imagination, and references to the club's use of the lodge began to appear in print with increasing frequency.[48] Names such as 'the enchanted house' and 'the haunted house' fell into disuse and the lodge became popularly known as the 'Hellfire Club'.

Notwithstanding this burgeoning reputation, there is no documented evidence that the Dublin Hellfire Club or any similar group used the lodge. The closest thing to such evidence is a letter dating from 1739, which references an incident that *may* have occurred on Mountpelier: 'a whole hell-fire club was actually put to flight, and chaced out of [a] house, by a goose dropped down a chimney that was on fire, within at most twenty miles of Dublin, and about that number of years [ago]'.[49] Situated within twenty miles of the then city, the lodge may be the house referred to. However, which hellfire club is in question? As it is unlikely that the Dublin Hellfire Club existed prior to

1737, there may have been an earlier version active near the city. However, in the absence of firm evidence, this will remain a matter of speculation.

The question of whether the Dublin Hellfire Club itself ever met on Mountpelier will also remain unresolved, at least until such time as definitive contemporary evidence of the same is uncovered. However, there are some intriguing congruities between the folklore of Mountpelier and actual events involving members of the club. This is particularly evident in a story collected by the Irish Folklore Commission in the 1930s:

> a party of Dublin gentry came out to a large party [at Mountpelier.] They ate and drank to excess, and a quarrel arose and they put the butler into the fire and burned him. The butler's wife, who was at home was uneasy when her husband did not return, and started investigations[.] While these were in progress, a high official of the Dublin waterworks threatened to stop the water supply if the investigations were not stopped. no more was heard of the 'alleged' murder.[50]

This account conflates two murders committed by Lord Santry, the burning of the sedan chairman and the fatal wounding of Laughlin Murphy. Significantly, it references known historical facts relating to the latter incident. Following Murphy's death, his widow applied successfully for an indictment to be issued against Santry. In addition, the baron's uncle, Sir Compton Domvile, was responsible for the maintenance of the water supply in south County Dublin (the waterworks were actually situated in the grounds of his residence, Templeogue House).[51] Although there is no evidence that Sir Compton ever threatened to cut off the supply in order to hinder proceedings against his nephew, it is clear that the murders committed by Lord Santry were associated with Mountpelier. A possible explanation for this is that the club did frequent this location, and that Santry's violent actions elsewhere came to be seen in the context of what went on at the lodge. It may be that the club adjourned to the lodge briefly in the summer of 1738 after the scandals surrounding Lens and Santry made its continued presence in Dublin untenable.

However, the most enduring folklore associated with Mountpelier concerns supernatural encounters rather than actual incidents. The most common tales involve the Devil joining the club in a card game. The Irish Folklore Commission recorded a typical version:

> many men used to go to [the] Hell Fire Club to gamble. It is said that one night they were playing cards and there was much money on the table. One man dropped a card on the floor, and when he stooped down to pick it up he noticed a man there with cow's feet, and he wore a red cloak. The men were very frightened and they made a great uproar. The man turned into a ball of fire and set the place on fire. All the men were burned in the fire. There was one man who had a bunch of medals attached to his coat, and he was the only man who escaped from the burning house.[52]

The tale of the Devil participating in a card game, being recognized by one of the players and then disappearing in a ball of flame or through the ceiling or chimney of the building is a common motif in Irish folklore. It occurs in relation to a number of other locations besides Mountpelier, principally 'big houses' such as Loftus Hall in County Wexford and Castletown House in County Kildare. Éilis Ní Anluain has identified fifty-five versions of the legend in different parts of Ireland. Such stories were cautionary tales against card playing and gambling, which would have been as common a pastime in country residences as in gentlemen's clubs. Cards were sometimes called 'the Devil's prayer book' and card-playing was said to attract the Devil.[53] Thus, it seems that one of the most enduring tales associated with the lodge on Mountpelier arose from the club's gambling proclivities.

By the early twentieth century the lodge's reputation as the supposed meeting place of the Dublin Hellfire Club was firmly established. Many of the tales relating to the club – the 'imitation of hell', the burning of a servant, the cat and the clergyman and the drinking of scaltheen – were now identified as events that had occurred on Mountpelier.[54] From time to time newspapers ran features on the club, generally focusing on the lodge.[55] By the late twentieth century it was officially known as the 'Hell Fire Club' and marked as such on Ordnance Survey maps of the area. Recent years have seen heightened interest in the building and its associated traditions, such that one Dublin tourist organization now even offers 'ghost bus' tours to the lodge in the week leading up to Halloween.

Relics and Paintings

Although the Mountpelier lodge was the most visible physical reminder of the existence of the Irish hellfire clubs, it was not the only one. In the late nineteenth and early twentieth centuries, an array of relics and paintings believed to be associated with the clubs emerged. The relics ranged from innocuous domestic items such as a corkscrew and a door-knocker to more sinister objects such as furniture carved with diabolic symbols and faces. The appearance of these items dovetailed with the growing notoriety of Mountpelier and the increasingly abundant references to hellfire clubs in books, newspapers, magazines and other publications.

The most prolific type of relic was the silver punchbowl. At least three such items, each of which was believed to have belonged to a hellfire club, made their appearance in exhibitions and auctions. In 1873 a silver Monteith punchbowl, 'formerly belonging to the Hellfire Club', was exhibited in the Loan Museum of Art Treasures at the Industrial Exhibition Palace in Dublin. Monteith punchbowls were so called because of their scalloped rims, similar in style to a cloak worn by the Scottish nobleman Lord Monteith. The design had a practical function, allowing glasses to be placed within the bowl, hanging from the depressions on the rim.[56] Manufactured in London in 1698, this punchbowl was thought to be connected with that city's hellfire club, rather than any of the Irish groups. Its then owner, 'William Domvile Esq.', was probably Sir William Domvile (1825–84), a descendant of Sir Compton Domvile. Sir Compton had inherited the estates and effects, including 'a large quantity of plate', of his cousin William Domvile of Loughlinstown following the latter's death in 1763.[57] It may be that the collection included this punchbowl; if so, it supports the idea that Domvile was involved with the London Hellfire Club. Other punch-bowls were associated with Irish hellfire clubs. One such item, made by the Dublin silversmith Joseph Walker in 1699, was purchased by the collector Kurt Ticher in 1944. This bowl had belonged to the Rowan Hamilton family of Killyleagh Castle in County Down, from whom it was purchased by the tenor Count John McCormack. It was also at one point owned by the connoisseur Henry Naylor.[58] However, the lack of any other information on its provenance prevents it from being defin-itively identified as a relic of an Irish hellfire club.

A stronger case can be made for the authenticity of a Monteith punchbowl fashioned in 1700–01 by Anthony Nelme and auctioned in Dublin in 1944 as part of the estate of Sir Compton Meade Domvile (1857–1935). Other lots in this sale included an oblong snuffbox and a wrought iron door-knocker. All three items were said to have been used by the Dublin Hellfire Club.[59] The punchbowl was previously displayed at the Irish International Exhibition in 1907, when it was stated to have once belonged to 'the last Lord Santry, figured in the orgies of the "Hell Fire Club," of which that nobleman was a promi-nent member... the bowl is represented in the portrait group of the Club now in the National Gallery, Dublin'.[60] While the latter claim is dubious – the item featured in the club portrait does not have a Monteith design – the assertion that the bowl once belonged to Lord Santry may well be accurate. Sir Compton Meade Domvile was a descendant of Santry's uncle, Sir Compton Domvile, who inherited his nephew's effects. It is possible that the bowl had originally belonged to Santry and that it was passed down through several generations of the Domvile family. In 1971 it was presented to the Wadsworth Atheneum, where it is currently held.[61]

As noted above, the snuffbox was engraved with diabolic imagery, as was an early eighteenth-century Chippendale table acquired by the National Museum in 1904 (see Chapter 3) and a 'Hell-Fire Club clock-case' that was sketched by the architect Alfred E. Jones for the *Georgian Society Records of Eighteenth-Century Domestic Architecture and Decoration in Ireland* (see Chapter 4).[62] Another supposed hellfire club relic, a silver corkscrew, was also exhibited at the International Exhibition of 1907. Its estimated date of manufacture, 1760–70, makes it unlikely that it belonged to the Dublin Hellfire Club, though it may have been associated with a regional group.[63] Apart from the Nelme punchbowl, no information has been found as to the current where-abouts of any of these items. Moreover, the only hellfire club relic whose veracity is incontrovertible is the commemorative wine glass engraved with Worsdale's name (see Chapter 2). This item was acquired by George Horace Lorimer (1867–1937), an American publisher and collector of fine glassware. In 1953 Lorimer's son bequeathed the wine glass to the Philadelphia Museum of Art, where it is currently held.[64] Although the authenticity of the other relics was open to question, their appearances in exhibitions and auctions nevertheless helped to further publicize the hellfire clubs and their notorious 'orgies'. For instance, the National Museum's acquisition of the Chippendale table in 1904 occasioned an article on the Dublin Hellfire Club in the *Weekly Irish Times*.[65]

However, in terms of sheer visual appeal even the most eye-catching relic could not match James Worsdale's conversation piece portraits. The most famous of these, *The Hell-Fire Club, Dublin* (see Plate 5), was also the first to emerge into the public arena. Having been commis-sioned by Lord Santry, this painting was housed at Santry Court for well over a century. Around 1867 it was purchased by John Wardell, whose son presented it to the National Gallery of Ireland eleven years later. Measuring almost seven feet by nine, this large oil on canvas must have been an arresting sight on the gallery's walls. It afforded the public a remarkable visual representation of Dublin's most notorious society, 'looking as unlike a blasphemous crew as can be conceived' in the opinion of one observer.[66] Also in the National Gallery is Worsdale's portrait of the Limerick Hellfire Club (see Plate 13), which had remained in the possession of the Croker family of Ballynagarde for over two centuries. In the 1950s it was bought by John L. Sweeney, whose wife bequeathed it to the gallery in 1987.[67] Regarded as the most important and aesthetically pleasing of these paintings, the Limerick club portrait has since been used as the cover illustration for a number of historical works.[68] A less well-known but equally striking conversation piece was Worsdale's *W. Domville and Friends at the Hellfire Club* (see Plate 3). While its early provenance is unknown, by the twentieth century it was in the personal collection of Lucius O'Callaghan, who served as director of the National Gallery between 1923 and 1927. Following O'Callaghan's death in 1954 the painting was auctioned by Christie's.[69] It was purchased by the American heiress Natalie Hays Hammond, in whose possession it remained until it was auctioned again by Christie, Manson & Woods in 1981. Its current whereabouts is unknown.[70]

Taken as a whole, these folkloric tales, antiques and artistic items constitute a rich corpus of hellfire club heritage. Ultimately, their popularity tells us more about how the hellfire clubs were perceived in later years than they do about the clubs themselves. Such interest, which endures to the present day, is reflected not only in folklore but also in a number of acclaimed works that draw on tales of the Dublin Hellfire Club. In Mia Gallagher's novel *HellFire* (2006), set in late twentieth-century Dublin, the central protagonist struggles to come to terms with a horrific experience she underwent on Mountpelier. Conor McPherson's award-winning play *The Seafarer* (2006) centres on a late-night card game between four protagonists and the Devil. Given the blurring of myth and reality that has characterized hellfire club folklore, it is unsurprising that the subject has provided such rich inspiration for these literary and theatrical works.

Chapter eight

Conclusion

Members of the Protestant elite of eighteenth-century Ireland were rooted in a culture of drunkenness, dissipation and violence. Possessing large disposable incomes and considerable leisure time, these gentlemen and noblemen chose to divert themselves through hedonistic indulgence and aggressive behaviour. Contemporary accounts of their drinking, gambling, profligacy and other excesses are manifold, as are references to instances of interpersonal violence and casual aggression. While the hellfire and rakish clubs engaged readily in such pursuits, they were not the only upper-class clubs to do so. Nor was it particularly unusual that hellfire club members had esoteric interests and may have engaged in mysterious rituals. Practices and ceremonies of this kind were integral to Freemasonry, and the Freemasons were one of the largest and most respectable associations in the country. What set the hellfire clubs apart from other eighteenth-century clubs was their interest in diabolism, their public articulation of blasphemous sentiments and their perpetration of violent atrocities. They associated themselves with hell and the Devil because they were attracted by the forbidden allure of diabolism, because they wished to intensify the aura of mystique that surrounded them, and because their appreciation of Enlightenment deism and atheism made them question the legitimacy of orthodox Christian belief. This stance brought them into conflict with the civil and ecclesiastic establishments, most notably in the case of the determined efforts that were made to apprehend Peter Lens for conduct that was not only blasphemous but also tantamount to devil worship. The authorities were keen to defend the established religion against blasphemy and sacrilege, not least because the legitimacy of the state was founded upon the legitimacy of that religion.

Strikingly, the hellfire clubs also suffered stern criticism from Jonathan Swift, George Berkeley and Edmund Burke, 'the great intellectual triumvirate of Ascendancy culture'.[1] That figures of such standing took the trouble to censure the hellfire clubs is indicative of the threat that the latter were perceived to pose to morality and politeness. Their dissipated and raucous ways seemed antithetical to the drive for 'improvement' being engineered by the more conscientious members of the upper classes. This occurred largely at an associational level, as a range of societies sought to address the economic and social problems that beset the country by advocating new industrial and agricultural techniques, philanthropic and charitable pursuits, and increased civility. Through such activities, they contributed to the development of civil society and the growth of democracy.[2] In dissenting from this culture of improvement the hellfire clubs seemed to oppose social development. However, they may have acted as a progressive force in a manner not envisaged by their contemporaries, or by later observers. Their attacks on institutional religion were a protest against the censorious measures that aimed to silence free-thinkers and the debate of religious issues. They were also influenced by a desire to move away from the 'superstitious' religiosity of the past towards a more scientific and rational society. This protest can be seen part as of a modernizing process that would culminate eventually in the separation of Church and State and the enshrinement in law of such values as civic and religious tolerance and freedom of speech. In this respect, the ethos of these groups was not entirely negative.

For the most part, however, the Irish hellfire clubs' intellectual dimensions were mere posturing. Their principal raison d'être was self-indulgence. In addition, both hellfire and rakish clubs displayed an extraordinary willingness to engage in violent and destructive behaviour. Although aggressive behaviour by members of the elite was not uncommon, the violence meted out by hellfire club members and groups such as the Pinkindindies was extreme even by contemporary standards. To an extent, such behaviour resulted from intoxication and the perpetrators' belief that their privileged position would allow them to circumvent retribution. The poorer and more vulnerable members of society were the chief sufferers of these excesses. Servants, prostitutes, unprotected women and unsuspecting country folk experienced abuse, rape, robbery and even murder at the hands of the Dublin Hellfire Club, Holy Fathers, Pinkindindies and Cherokees. Maltreatment of females was a recurring theme, from the Earl of Rosse's pursuit of Laetitia Pilkington, to the Pinkindindies' brutal assaults on prostitutes and maidservants, to the boorish conduct of the Cherokees. As Margaret Leeson's successful prosecution of Richard Crosbie shows, not all victims of such abuse were bereft of the means to avenge themselves on their tormentors. Yet this was the exception rather than rule; most of the misdeeds committed by members of hellfire and rakish clubs went unpunished. Lord Santry's crimes were probably the most shocking. His murder of at least two servants – one of which was carried out in a particularly savage and sadistic manner – and a range of other atrocities made him roundly hated in Dublin. When Santry's career of misdeeds was finally halted with his arrest for the killing of Laughlin Murphy, he avoided execution and was allowed to retire to Nottingham in relative comfort. Similarly, when Pinkindindies happened to be brought to trial, they were for the most part treated leniently. The experience of the hellfire and rakish clubs certainly supports the contention that in eighteenth-century Ireland, raucous and violent young gentlemen were rarely adequately, or at all, punished for their crimes. As Daniel Statt points out, 'in large measure impunity was their birthright, and license their prerogative'.[3]

In addition, the massive social inequalities that facilitated the hellfire clubs' excesses should not be ignored. Most hellfire club members, and many who belonged to rakish clubs, were the owners of or heirs to extensive properties, and much of the money that funded their hedonistic gatherings was derived from the labour of the impoverished, largely Catholic, lower classes. The latter lived hard and precarious lives and were particularly vulnerable in times of environmental and agricultural disaster. A few short years after the Dublin Hellfire Club's scandalous behaviour had shaken polite society, the lower classes suffered an unimaginable catastrophe. In the early months of 1740 the country was stricken by a great frost. Severe drought and floods followed, and mass deaths of livestock and the destruction of crops ushered in a devastating famine. Hundreds of thousands died as a result and 1741 entered folk memory as *bliain an áir*, the year of slaughter.[4] Like the Great Famine that followed a century later, this calamitous event resulted from the fundamental inequities of Irish society.

Nonetheless, the hellfire clubs have never failed to grip the popular imagination. It is difficult to conceive of any other eighteenth-century gentlemen's clubs that have had such a strong impact on local folklore, or that have occasioned so many tales of supernatural occurrences and otherworldly apparitions. This process was complemented by the survival of a range of physical objects associated with the clubs: putative relics, group portraits and isolated, ruinous meeting places. The latter are perhaps the most visible reminders of their existence, particularly the lodge on Mountpelier, which remains a popular destination for day trippers and curious visitors. In recent years, the lodge reacquired the reputation of a resort of fringe activities: late-night 'raves' are believed to have occurred there in the 1990s and early 2000s, despite the fact that its gloomy interior is anything but hospitable. Though less well known, its sister clubhouses in Askeaton and Doonass are also the subject of local attention. As long as these hollow and crumbling remains continue to mystify locals, visitors and passers-by, the Irish hellfire clubs will never be entirely forgotten.

Notes

1. Introduction

1. See Chapter 7 for a full discussion of the folklore of the Dublin Hellfire Club.
2. See Lady [Georgiana] Chatterton, *Rambles in the South of Ireland During the Year 1838* (London, 1839), vol. 2, pp.127–8 (Askeaton); Mark Bence-Jones, *A Guide to Irish Country Houses* (London, 1988), p.106 (Doonass); *Notes and Queries* (Series 1), 10 (26 August 1854), p.175 (Grangemellon).
3. See, for instance, Donald McCormick, *The Hell-Fire Club: The Story of the Amorous Knights of Wycombe* (London, 1958); Daniel P. Mannix, *The Hell-Fire Club* (London, 1961).
4. Works of fiction include Derek Wilson, *The Hellfire Papers* (London, 1995); Peter Straub, *The Hellfire Club* (London, 1996); Mia Gallagher, *HellFire* (Dublin, 2007). A 1961 film, *The Hellfire Club*, offered a Hammer-horror-style take on the subject, while a Hollywood film of the same name was in production in 2011. A heavy metal band known as the Electric Hellfire Club has attained a degree of fringe popularity. A Google search for 'hellfire club' conducted on 29 December 2011 returned approximately 1,360,000 results.
5. Lady Llanover (ed.), *The Autobiography and Correspondence of Mary Granville, Mrs Delany*, 2nd series (London, 1861–62), vol. 3, p.162; Louis C. Jones, *The Clubs of the Georgian Rakes* (New York, 1942), pp.37–44; Evelyn Lord, *The Hell-Fire Clubs: Sex, Satanism and Secret Societies* (London, 2008), pp.51–7.
6. *ODNB*, vol. 15, p.224. See also Lord, *Hell-Fire Clubs*, pp.97–155; Geoffrey Ashe, *The Hell-Fire Clubs: A History of Anti-Morality* (Stroud, 2000), *passim*; Arthur H. Cash, *John Wilkes: The Scandalous Father of Civil Liberty* (New Haven, CT, and London, 2006), pp.32–6.
7. Cash, *John Wilkes*, pp.33–5.
8. See Daniel Statt, 'The Case of the Mohocks: Rake Violence in Augustan London', *Social History*, 20, 2 (May 1995), pp.179–99; David Stevenson, *The Beggar's Benison: Sex Clubs of Enlightenment Scotland and their Rituals* (East Linton, 2001).
9. J–n O'C–nn–r [John O'Connor], *An Essay on the Rosary and Sodality of the Most Holy Name of Jesus...* (Dublin, 1772), p.113.
10. See, for instance, Lady Morgan, *The O'Briens and the O'Flahertys* (London, 1827–8), vol. 3, p.129; 'Oliver Moore', *The Staff Officer; Or, the Soldier of Fortune: A Tale of Real Life* (London, 1831), vol. 1, p.137.

11. See, for instance, K.L. Montgomery, 'Old Dublin Clubs and Coffee Houses', *New Ireland Review*, 6 (September 1896), pp.39–44; Joseph W. Hammond, *The Hell-Fire Club* (Dublin, n.d).

12. Jones, *Clubs of Georgian Rakes*, pp.56–83; Ashe, *Hell-Fire Clubs*, pp.60–2; Lord, *Hell-Fire Clubs*, pp.61–4, 196–203.

13. Peter Clark, *British Clubs and Societies 1580–1800: The Origins of an Associational World* (Oxford, 2000), p.61.

14. Máire Kennedy, 'Dublin's Coffee Houses of the Eighteenth Century', *Dublin Historical Record*, 58 (2010), p.29.

15. Roy Porter, *The Enlightenment*, 2nd edn (Basingstoke, 2001), pp.4–5.

16. Ophelia Field, *The Kit-Cat Club: Friends Who Imagined a Nation* (London, 2008), pp.242–65.

17. Porter, *Enlightenment*, p.6. See also Ian McBride, *Eighteenth-Century Ireland: The Isle of Slaves* (Dublin, 2009), p.53.

18. Robert J. Allen, *The Clubs of Augustan London* (Cambridge, MA, 1933), p.128; Porter, *Enlightenment*, p.34.

19. Stevenson, *Beggar's Benison*, p.83; Letter of I—h T—r, Dublin, 13 November 1728, in Wetenhall Wilkes, *An Essay on the Existence of a God: Particularly in Answer to Two Atheistical Letters . . .* (Belfast, 1730), pp.vii–viii.

20. Stevenson, *Beggar's Benison*, pp.83–4.

21. *ODNB*, vol. 58, p.367.

22. R.B., *The Hell-Fire-Club: Kept by a Society of Blasphemers. A Satyr . . .* (London, 1721), p.5. For general accounts of the club, see Jones, *Clubs of Georgian Rakes*, pp.37–44; Ashe, *Hell-Fire Clubs*, pp.40–50; Lord, *Hell-Fire Clubs*, pp.51–7.

23. Jones, *Clubs of Georgian Rakes*, p.43.

24. Daniel Defoe, *A Journal of the Plague Year*, reprint (London, 2003), pp.63–6. See also Allen, *Clubs of Augustan London*, pp.121–2.

25. Jones, *Clubs of Georgian Rakes*, p.38; [John] Oldmixon, *The History of England, during the Reigns of King William and Queen Mary, Queen Anne King George I . . .* (London, 1735), p.718.

26. R.B., *Hell-Fire-Club*, p.2; Allen, *Clubs of Augustan London*, pp.119–22.

27. Oldmixon, *History of England*, p.718. The 'Scowrers' were a late seventeenth-century group of rakes whose exploits inspired Thomas Shadwell's play *The Scowrers* (1691). See Statt, 'Case of the Mohocks', p.190.

28. Statt, 'Case of the Mohocks', passim and p.190.

29. Evelyn Lord, author of the most recent history of the British hellfire clubs, acknowledges that the Irish clubs were more 'full-blooded' than their English progenitors: Lord, *Hell-Fire Clubs*, p.61.

30. Edith Mary Johnston-Liik, *MPs in Dublin: Companion to History of the Irish Parliament, 1692–1800* (Belfast, 2006), p.5.

31. S.J. Connolly, *Religion, Law and Power: The Making of Protestant Ireland 1660–1760* (Oxford, 1992), p.43.

32. See R.F. Foster, *Modern Ireland, 1600–1972* (London, 1988), pp.173–6.

33. [Edward Lloyd], *A Description of the City of Dublin in Ireland ... by a Citizen of London ...* (London, 1732), p.21.

34. Johnston-Liik, *MPs in Dublin*, pp.3–5, 11.

35. McBride, *Eighteenth-Century Ireland*, p.38.

36. Foster, *Modern Ireland*, p.176; Toby Barnard, *Making the Grand Figure: Lives and Possessions in Ireland, 1641–1770* (London, 2004), p.289; Constantia Maxwell, *Dublin under the Georges 1714–1850* (London, 1936), pp.85–7. For a vivid description of such a banquet, see Jonah Barrington, *Personal Sketches and Recollections*, reprint (Dublin, 1998), pp.26–30.

37. Orrery to Mr Salkeld, Dublin, 4 May 1736, in Countess of Cork and Orrery (ed.), *The Orrery Papers* (London, 1903), vol. 1, p.157; Anne Conolly, quoted in Lena Boylan, 'The Conollys of Castletown', *Quarterly Bulletin of the Irish Georgian Society*, 9, 4 (October–December 1968), p.18.

38. Maxwell, *Dublin under the Georges*, p.84; Samuel Madden, *Reflections and Resolutions Proper for the Gentlemen of Ireland …* (Dublin, 1738), p.44.

39. Connolly, *Religion, Law and Power*, p.66.

40. Madden, *Reflections and Resolutions*, p.73.

41. As Edith Mary Johnston-Liik observed, 'there can be no clearer indication of the vast changes brought about by the social upheaval of the seventeenth century than the fact that every eighteenth-century Speaker [of the Irish parliament] came from a family which had emerged from obscurity in the seventeenth century, usually during the [Cromwellian] interregnum': Johnston-Liik, *MPs in Dublin*, p.7. However, it should be noted that the descendants of Cromwellian adventurers did not uniformly comprise elite society – a number of eighteenth-century noble families had been well established in the country since before the Cromwellian era: Toby Barnard, *A New Anatomy of Ireland: The Irish Protestants, 1649–1770* (London, 2003), p.22.

42. Connolly, *Religion, Law and Power*, pp.68–9; James Kelly, '*That Damn'd Thing Called Honour*': Duelling in Ireland, 1570–1860 (Cork, 1995), p.64; [Lloyd], *Description of the City of Dublin*, pp.16–17.

43. McBride, *Eighteenth-Century Ireland*, p.6; Connolly, *Religion, Law and Power*, p.57.

44. James Kelly and Martyn J. Powell, 'Introduction', in James Kelly and Martyn J. Powell (eds), *Clubs and Societies in Eighteenth-Century Ireland* (Dublin, 2010), p.24.

45. Patrick Walsh, 'Club Life in Late Seventeenth- and Early Eighteenth-Century Ireland: In Search of an Associational World, c. 1680 – c. 1730', in Kelly and Powell (eds), *Clubs and Societies*, pp.38–45; Clark, *British Clubs and Societies*, p.68.

46. Barnard, *Making the Grand Figure*, pp.292, 291; Martyn J. Powell, '"Beef, Claret and Communication": Convivial Clubs in the Public Sphere, 1750–1800', in Kelly and Powell (eds), *Clubs and Societies*, pp.359–61.

47. Maxwell, *Dublin under the Georges*, pp.84–5; Jacqueline Hill, 'Loyal Societies in Ireland, 1690–1790', in Kelly and Powell (eds), *Clubs and Societies*, pp.190, 193; James Kelly, '"The glorious and immortal memory": Commemoration and Protestant Identity in Ireland 1660–1800', *PRIA*, 94C, 2 (1994), pp.41–2; *Dublin Intelligence*, 30 May 1724.

48. Quoted in P. Walsh, 'Club Life', p.43; Countess of Cork and Orrery, *Orrery Papers*, vol. 1, p.157.

49. Éamonn Ó Ciardha, *Ireland and the Jacobite Cause, 1685–1766: A Fatal Attachment* (Dublin, 2002), p.169. See also P. Walsh, 'Club Life', p.43; R.B. McDowell, *Land and Learning: Two Irish Clubs* (Dublin, 1993), p.9.

50. [William King], *The Swan Tripe-Club in Dublin. A Satyr* ... (Dublin, 1706), p.5.
51. Toby Barnard, 'The Dublin Society and Other Improving Societies, 1731–85', in Kelly and Powell (eds), *Clubs and Societies*, pp.53–88, 68–72, 75.
52. Clark, *British Clubs and Societies*, p.71.
53. See Chapter 2.
54. *An Ample Discovery of the Damnable Cabal, Commonly Known by the Name of the Hell-fire Club, Kept in this City, Since the 17th of March Last* ... (Dublin, n.d.).
55. Statt, 'Case of the Mohocks', pp.180–1. For Samuel Johnson, the libertine was dedicated to 'irreligion and licentiousness', while the rake was 'a loose, disorderly, vicious, wild, gay, thoughtless fellow': ibid., p.181n.
56. Ibid., p.179.
57. See Chapter 7.

2. The Dublin Hellfire Club

1. *An Examination of Certain Abuses, Corruptions, and Enormities in the City of Dublin* (Dublin, 1732), p.8; Patrick Fagan, *The Second City: Portrait of Dublin 1700–1760* (Dublin, 1986), pp.19–20; William Laffan (ed.), *The Cries of Dublin &c. Drawn from the Life by Hugh Douglas Hamilton* (Dublin, 2003), p.138.
2. 'A Plan for Opening & Widening a Principal Avenue to the Castle', c. 1750. Reproduced in Pat Liddy, *Temple Bar – Dublin: An Illustrated History* (Dublin, 1992), p.36.
3. E. MacDowel Cosgrave, 'On Two Maps, Dated 1751 and 1753, of the Essex Bridge District, Dublin', *JRSAI*, 48 (1918), p.140; *The Georgian Society Records of Eighteenth Century Domestic Architecture and Decoration in Dublin* (Shannon, 1969), vol. 1, p.1; Kennedy, 'Dublin's Coffee Houses', p.30.
4. Laffan (ed.), *Cries of Dublin*, p.140; *The Whole Tryal and Examination of Mr Grace*; *The Whole Account of the Arraignment and Confinement of Thomas Grace, Coll. Luttrell's cousin* ... (Dublin, 1719).
5. *Four Letters Originally Written in French, Relating to the Kingdom of Ireland* ... (Dublin, 1739), p.24. When Essex Bridge was rebuilt in the 1750s this statue was moved to the Mansion House. It was later transported to England and is currently situated outside the Barber Institute of Fine Arts in Birmingham: Charles Brooking, *The City of Dublin, 1728*, introduction and notes by Maurice Craig (Dublin, 1983). Essex Bridge is now known as Grattan Bridge.
6. *PO*, 31 May–4 June 1737. This may have been the renowned Hackball, king of the beggars, who was hauled around on a wheelchair pulled variously by a mule, a pair of dogs or a boy: Laffan (ed.), *Cries of Dublin*, p.98.
7. *Four Letters Originally Written in French*, p.22.
8. *By-Laws, Rules and Orders, for the Better Regulating of Hackney-Coaches* ... (Dublin, 1729), pp.10, 14.
9. *A Humourous Description of the Manners and Fashions of the Inhabitants of the City of Dublin* (Dublin, 1734), p.4; see Laffan (ed.), *Cries of Dublin*, passim.
10. [Lloyd], *Description of the City of Dublin*, p.14. According to the army officer Samuel Bagshawe, as many as 600 to 800 people attended the balls that were held at Dublin Castle on Saturday evenings: Alan J. Guy (ed.), *Colonel Samuel Bagshawe and the Army of George II 1731–1762* (London, 1990), p.40.

11. J.L. McCracken, 'The Social Structure and Social Life, 1714–60', in T.W. Moody and W.E. Vaughan (eds), *A New History of Ireland IV: Eighteenth-Century Ireland 1691–1800* (Oxford, 1986), p.49.

12. W.J. Chetwode Crawley, *Caementaria Hibernica: Being the Public Constitutions That Have Served to Hold Together the Freemasons of Ireland* (Dublin, 1895–1900), vol. 2, p.13.

13. John Lodge, *The Peerage of Ireland, Or, a Genealogical History of the Present Nobility of that Kingdom* ... (London, 1754), vol. 2, p.75. The portrait is held at Birr Castle, residence of the current Earl of Rosse. It is reproduced in Anne Crookshank and the Knight of Glin, *Ireland's Painters 1600–1940* (New Haven, CT, Yale, 2002), p.23. A copy can be viewed in the Freemason's Hall, Molesworth Street, Dublin 2.

14. Letter of Viscount Rosse, Oxford, 7 April 1713, Birr Castle Archives, Rosse Papers, B/2/1; Joseph Foster, *Alumni Oxonienses: The Members of the University of Oxford 1500–1714 (L–R)* (Oxford, 1891–92), p.1123.

15. Letter of Viscount Rosse, 16 October 1713, Birr Castle Archives, Rosse Papers, B/2/2.

16. G.E. Cokayne [hereafter G.E.C.] *The Complete Peerage* (London, 1910–40), vol. 11, p.167.

17. *The Right Hon Richard Earl of Rosse... Appellant. Elizabeth Worsop... Worsop Bush and Noah Webb... Respondents. The Respondents' Case* [1741], p.2, BL, Add. Ms. 36154 ff.162–3).

18. G.E.C., *Complete Peerage*, vol. 11, p.167; *Journals of the House of Lords* (Dublin, 1779–1800), vol. 2, pp.545–7; *ODNB*, vol. 58, p.367.

19. G.E.C., *Complete Peerage*, vol. 11, p.167; John Heron Lepper and Philip Crosslé, *History of the Grand Lodge of Free and Accepted Masons of Ireland* (Dublin, 1925), p.130; Lodge, *Peerage* (1754), vol. 2, pp.75–6.

20. Crawley, *Caementaria Hibernica*, vol. 2, p.14; Lepper and Crosslé, *History of the Grand Lodge*, pp.131–2; Ó Ciardha, *Ireland and the Jacobite Cause*, p.108.

21. Seán Murphy, 'Irish Jacobitism and Freemasonry', *Eighteenth-Century Ireland*, 9 (1994), p.79; Lepper and Crosslé, *History of the Grand Lodge*, pp.70–1.

22. *Journals of the House of Lords*, vol. 3, p.10.

23. 'Notes on Burdy's *Life of Skelton*', p.130. Trinity College Dublin [hereafter TCD], Ms. 1091.

24. Clark, *British Clubs and Societies*, p.76; Petri Mirala, 'Masonic Sociability and its Limitations: The Case of Ireland', in Kelly and Powell (eds), *Clubs and Societies*, p.316; Porter, *Enlightenment*, p.36.

25. Crawley, *Caementaria Hibernica*, vol. 2, p.14; Lepper and Crosslé, *History of the Grand Lodge*, p.130.

26. *Dublin Weekly Journal*, 26 June 1725. See also Lepper and Crosslé, *History of the Grand Lodge*, pp.52–64; Fagan, *Second City*, pp.253–4. The King's Inns was at that time located on Inns Quay, the site of the present-day Four Courts: Lepper and Crosslé, *History of the Grand Lodge*, p.80.

27. Copy by John Lodge, c.1760, of an Act, c.1719, to allow payment of creditors of Richard, Earl of Rosse, NLI, Thomas Kemmis Papers, MS 15,419; Lepper and Crosslé, *History of the Grand Lodge*, p.132. On the Countess of Tyrconnell, see *DIB*, vol. 9, pp.238–9; *ODNB*, vol. 53, pp.688–9.

28. John Carteret Pilkington, *The Real Story of John Carteret Pilkington* (London, 1760), pp.142, 143.

29. Quoted in Lepper and Crosslé, *History of the Grand Lodge*, p.132; Obituary of the Earl of Rosse, 30 June [1741], Birr Castle Archives, Rosse Papers, B/2/5.

30. Samuel Burdy, *The Life of the Late Rev. Philip Skelton with Some Curious Anecdotes* (Dublin, 1792), p.38. Rosse is not named in the text. The author of the prank is identified as 'a late nobleman, a famous member of the hell-fire club'. Of the known members of the Dublin Hellfire Club, only Rosse and Henry, Baron Barry of Santry, held titles during Madden's lifetime (he died in 1765). The story evokes Rosse's character more than Santry's, and in any case the latter did not possess a house in Dublin. Rosse is also identified as the author of the prank in a late nineteenth-century manuscript, 'Notes on Burdy's *Life of Skelton*', p.130, TCD, Ms. 1091.

31. Madden, *Reflections and Resolutions*, pp.44, 73. Rosse was well acquainted with both Samuel Madden and his brother, John, the Dean of Kilmore, who was the victim of his last and most infamous practical joke. See 'Notes on Burdy's *Life of Skelton*', pp.130–1 and Chapter 3. On Samuel Madden see *DIB*, vol. 6, pp.218–9.

32. *ODNB*, vol. 60, p.340.

33. George Vertue, '*Note Books, III*', *Walpole Society*, 22 (1933–34), p.59; Norma Clarke, *Queen of the Wits: A Life of Laetitia Pilkington* (London, 2008), p.56; *The Celebrated Mrs. Pilkington's Jests; Or the Cabinet of Wit and Humour...*, 2nd edn (London, 1764), p.8.

34. Vertue, '*Note Books, III*', p.59; George C. Williamson (rev.), Bryan's *Dictionary of Painters and Engravers* (London, 1920–1), vol. 5, p.395; *ODNB*, vol. 60, p.340; Clarke, *Queen of the Wits*, p.57.

35. *National Gallery of Ireland Acquisitions 1986–88* (Dublin, 1988), p.71.

36. The painting was auctioned in New York by Christie, Manson & Woods International Inc. on 15 July 1981. I have been unable to establish its present whereabouts. I wish to thank the late Knight of Glin for drawing my attention to its existence and its resemblance to Kneller's work, and the late Arch Elias for his comments on it. Although the painting was at one time attributed to J. Fuller, the attribution was later revised: see Chapter 7.

37. This likeness bears a striking resemblance to a sketch 'said to be Mr Wm Domvile' in the Domvile family manuscripts, NLI, Domvile Papers, Ms. 9383 (see Plate 4); Francis Elrington Ball, 'Loughlinstown and its History', *JRSAI* (5th Series), 6 (1901), pp.80–1; Edith Mary Johnston-Liik, *History of the Irish Parliament 1692–1800* (Belfast, 2002), vol. 4, pp.72–3.

38. 'Hartley Hutchinson Esq; – Appel. William Domville Esq; – Respt. The Appellant's Case ... first day of March, 1744', NLI, Ms. 11,793 (13). Although regarded by his friends as a 'worthy and honest' man, Domvile was capable of antisocial behaviour; Jonathan Swift's comment that he was 'perfectly as fine a gentleman as I know' was meant ironically: Frederick Ryland (ed.), *Swift's Journal to Stella* (London, 1897), vol. 2, p.287; Irvin Ehrenpreis, *Swift: The Man, his Works, and the Age* (London, 1962–83), vol. 2, p.303.

39. Vertue, '*Note Books, III*', p.59; Clarke, *Queen of the Wits*, p.56.

40. His *Portrait of a Young Lady*, showing a young woman in an Irish setting, has been dated to 1725: *Irish Times*, 25 October 2003.

41. Anthony Pasquin [John Williams], *An Authentic History of the Professors of Painting, Sculpture, & Architecture, Who Have Practised in Ireland . . .* (London [1796]), p.21. Blayney had been obliged to petition Parliament for financial assistance during the reign of Queen Anne (1702–14) and in 1724 he found it necessary to sell part of his County Monaghan estates to settle his debts: E. Rowley-Morris, *The Family of Blayney* (London, [1890]), pp.16–17; D.W. Hayton, *Ruling Ireland, 1685–1742: Politics, Politicians and Parties* (Woodbridge, 2004), p.109; *Dublin Intelligence*, 31 March 1724. See also Barnard, *New Anatomy of Ireland*, p.26.

42. Clarke, *Queen of the Wits*, p.56; Ralph Straus, *The Unspeakable Curll: Being Some Account of Edmund Curll, Bookseller* (London, 1927), pp.163–5; Curll, quoted in Straus, *Unspeakable Curll*, pp.163–4; *ODNB*, vol. 14, p.719.

43. Clarke, *Queen of the Wits*, pp.56–7, 73–5, 90–7.

44. Ibid., pp.73, 74, 148–9. On Walpole, see *DIB*, vol. 9, pp.727–8.

45. A.C. Elias (ed.), *Memoirs of Laetitia Pilkington* (Athens, GA, 1997), vol. 2, pp.451–2; James Worsdale, *A Cure for a Scold* (London [1735]). This is available in facsimile reprint in Walter H. Rubsamen (arr.), *The Ballad Opera, Vol. 4: The Medical and Legal Professions* (New York and London, 1974).

46. John Bayly to Edward Walpole, 11 August 1737, John Bayly Letter-Book, NLI, microfilm, P. 4068.

47. Elias (ed.), *Laetitia Pilkington*, vol. 2, pp.501, 611; Jonathan Swift to John Barber, 9 March 1737/38, in David Woolley (ed.), *The Correspondence of Jonathan Swift, D.D.* (Frankfurt am Main, 1999–2007), vol. 4, p.503.

48. Pilkington, *Real Story*, p.143.

49. *Catalogue of Pictures and Other Works of Art in the National Gallery of Ireland* (Dublin, 1928), p.383.

50. Ibid., p.383.

51. John Brooks (after Francis Bindon), *Richd St George Esqr Brigr. Genl in his Majesty King George the IIds Forces*, published 1744, NGI 10,044. Reproduced in Nicola Figgis and Brendan Rooney, *Irish Paintings in the National Gallery of Ireland, Volume I* (Dublin, 2001), p.82.

52. *Burke's Peerage*, 104th edn (London, 1967), p.2198; Johnston-Liik, *History of the Irish Parliament*, vol. 6, p.217; Deed relative to appointment of Richard St George as Colonel, 27 June 1737, NLI, D. 22,683.

53. Hayton, *Ruling Ireland*, p.268; *ODNB*, vol. 44, pp.810–11; Johnston-Liik, *History of the Irish Parliament*, vol. 6, p.88.

54. John Ponsonby, *The Ponsonby Family* (London, 1929), p.45; *DEP*, 3–7 June 1735, 19–22 June 1736.

55. Johnston-Liik, *History of the Irish Parliament*, vol. 3, p.423; Percival Wood Clement, *Ancestors and Descendants of Robert Clements* (Philadelphia, [1937]), vol. 2, p.889; A.P.W. Malcomson, *The Clements Archive* (Dublin, 2010), p.709; A.P.W. Malcomson, *Nathaniel Clements: Government and the Governing Elite in Ireland, 1725–75* (Dublin, 2005), p.38.

56. 'A Letter to the Right Reverend the Lord Bishop of Cloyne, by a Gentleman in

the Army, in the Year 1739', in *The Harleian Miscellany: Or, a Collection of Scarce, Curious and Entertaining Pamphlets and Tracts...* (London, 1745), vol. 3, p.173.

57. Malcomson, *Nathaniel Clements*, p.38.

58. *ODNB*, vol. 34, pp.810–11; *DIB*, vol. 5, pp.605–6; John Lodge, *The Peerage of Ireland, or, a Genealogical History of the Present Nobility of that Kingdom* (London, 1789), vol. 3, pp.411–12.

59. *DIB*, vol. 5, p.606; *Whole Tryal and Examination of Mr Grace*; *The Historical Register, Containing an Impartial Relation of all Transactions, Foreign and Domestick ... Volume XV. For the Year 1730* (London [1730]), p.110. Stafford Street is now known as Wolfe Tone Street.

60. Francis Hardy, *Memoirs of the Political and Private Life of James Caulfield, First Earl of Charlemont* (London, 1812), vol. 1, p.263; Jones, *Clubs of Georgian Rakes*, p.71; John Ingamells, *A Dictionary of British and Irish Travellers in Italy 1701–1800* (London, 1997), p.617.

61. Lionel Cust, *History of the Society of Dilettanti* (London, 1898), pp.4, 7–9.

62. A.P.W. Malcomson, *The Pursuit of the Heiress: Aristocratic Marriage in Ireland 1740–1840* (Belfast, 2006), p.46; *PO*, 23–27 August 1737.

63. G.E.C., *Complete Peerage*, vol. 3, pp.23–4; Lepper and Crosslé, *History of the Grand Lodge*, p.149.

64. Hardy, *Memoirs of the Political and Private Life*, vol. 1, p.263.

65. *Journal of the House of Lords*, vol. 3, p.381 and passim.

66. Blind Quay is now known as Exchange Street Upper. For an early eighteenth-century map of the area, see 'A Survey of Cork Hill & Part of Castle Street from the End of Crane Lane to the Castle Gate' [1710], Dublin City Library and Archive, Gilbert Manuscripts, Ms. 195.

67. Powell, '"Beef, Claret and Communication"', p.361; *The Ordinary of Newgate, his Account ... on Monday the 9th of this Instant October 1732, Being the Eight Execution in the Mayoralty of the Rt. Hon. Sir Francis Child, Knt* (London, 1732), p.31.

68. *Irish Quarterly Review*, 2, 6 (1852), p.327n; *DEP*, 25–29 April 1738, 30 January–3 February 1738/39; *DNL*, 25–29 April 1738; *PO*, 24–27 June 1738, 8–11 December 1739.

69. One of the Eagle's drawers was a man named James Timms, who 'always behaved honestly'. However, Timms later moved to London, where he was sentenced to death in 1741 for assaulting a constable: *Proceedings at the Sessions of Peace, Oyer and Terminer for the City of London ...* (London, 1741), pp.4–5.

70. Betty Elzea, *Glass* (Philadelphia, PA, 1984), p.24. The glass is currently in the Philadelphia Museum of Art (see Chapter 7).

71. 'Master of the Revels' was also a title held by people who were in positions of authority in theatrical affairs. In 1741 Dublin's Master of the Revels, Luke Gardiner, appointed Worsdale his deputy (see Chapter 4).

72. Stevenson, *Beggar's Benison*, passim; Cash, *John Wilkes*, pp.32–5; Ashe, *Hell-Fire Clubs*, pp.119–35.

73. *Ample Discovery*.

74. 'Notes on Burdy's *Life of Skelton*', p.33.

75. The printer is identified as 'G.F. in Warborows [Werburgh] Street'. This may have been George Faulkner, who had published last speeches and other material of

voyeuristic appeal in the 1720s: see James Kelly, *Gallows Speeches from Eighteenth-Century Ireland* (Dublin, 2001), pp.29–30. My thanks to James Kelly for his comments on the *Ample Discovery* broadsheet.

76. He was said to be 'the agent of [Rosse's] gallantry', i.e. his pimp: Pilkington, *Real Story*, p.143.

77. Elias (ed.), *Laetitia Pilkington*, vol. 1, p.92. See also Clarke, *Queen of the Wits*, p.129.

78. See Elias (ed.), *Laetitia Pilkington*, vol. 1, p.115.

79. Ibid. vol. 1, p.67; vol. 2, pp.445–6. See also W.G. Strickland, *A Dictionary of Irish Artists* (Dublin and London, 1913), vol. 2, pp.563–4; *ODNB*, vol. 60, p.340.

80. Jones, *Clubs of Georgian Rakes*, pp.73–4.

81. Pilkington, *Real Story*, p.143.

82. MacDowel Cosgrave, 'On Two Maps', pp.140–1; Sean Murphy, 'Municipal Politics and Popular Disturbances 1660–1800', in Art Cosgrove (ed.), *Dublin Through the Ages* (Dublin, 1988), p.80. On the inactivity or apathy of the watch, see *DEP*, 17–20 February 1738/39.

83. *Irish Quarterly Review*, 2, 6 (June 1852), p.327n; Fagan, *Second City*, pp.75–6; *DNL*, 28 February–4 March 1738. See *A Directory of Dublin for the Year 1738* (Dublin, 2000), pp.137–8 for a list of establishments on Cork Hill at this time.

84. *By-Laws, Rules and Orders*, p.9.

85. John T. Gilbert, *A History of the City of Dublin* (Dublin, 1854–9), vol. 2, p.21; Fagan, *Second City*, p.50.

86. [King], *Swan Tripe-Club*, p.5.

87. *Dublin Weekly Journal*, 13 November 1725, 27 November 1725; Kelly, 'That Damn'd Thing', pp.77–8.

88. Horace Walpole to Lady Ossory, 16 March 1773, in W.S. Lewis et al. (eds), *The Yale Edition of Horace Walpole's Correspondence* (Oxford, 1937–83), vol. 32, p.107.

89. *Notes and Queries* (Series 2), 10 (28 July 1860), p.77; William Butler Odell, *Essay on Duelling, in Which the Subject is Morally and Historically Considered...* (Cork, 1814), p.19.

90. On at least one occasion, Lady Santry visited her son at school and used her influence to obtain a free day for the pupils. The poetess Mary Barber commemorated the occasion in verse: Mary Barber, *Poems on Several Occasions* (London, 1734), p.95.

91. Margaret, Countess of Orrery, to Earl of Orrery, 4 November 1738, NLI, Orrery Papers, microfilm, P. 792. The reference to 'Mrs Coghill' is an intimation that Bridget Domvile should have chosen to marry the respectable lawyer Marmaduke Coghill (1673–1739), rather than become the wife of a peer who was an inveterate drinker.

92. Marmaduke Coghill to Edward Southwell, 14 January 1734 [1735], in D.W. Hayton (ed.), *Letters of Marmaduke Coghill 1722–1738* (Dublin, 2005), p.153; *DEP*, 4–7 January 1734/35, 25–28 January 1734/35.

93. 'Some of Lord Santry's Accounts & Rentals from 1701 to 1750', Domvile Papers, NLI, Ms. 9367; *DEP*, 7–11 October 1735; *Journals of the House of Lords*, vol. 3, p.301.

94. *PO*, 5–9 April 1737; *An Analysis of the Philosophical Works of Lord Bolingbroke ... to which is Prefixed, a Parallel of Earl Ferrers's Case, with that of Lord Santry...* (London, 1760), p.iii.

95. Jonathan Swift to Lady Santry [February 1737], in Woolley (ed.), *Correspondence of Jonathan Swift*, vol. 4, pp.389–90.

96. *PO*, 7–10 May 1737; G.E.C., *Complete Peerage*, vol. 1, p.449; *Analysis of the Philosophical Works*, pp.iv, vi.

97. *Analysis of the Philosophical Works*, p.v.

98. Andrew O'Reilly, *Reminiscences of an Emigrant Milesian* (London, 1853), vol. 3, p.290.

99. [Michael Banim], 'Record of H–l F–e [Hell Fire] Club', NLI, Ms. 25,527 (2); Gilbert, *History of the City of Dublin*, vol. 1, pp.94–6. The area in which Saul's Court was situated is now occupied by the western end of Lord Edward Street (laid out in the 1880s) and adjoining buildings.

100. O'Reilly, *Reminiscences*, vol. 3, p.290. On 28 January 1739 there was a fire at Mr Saul's premises which consumed much of his merchandise and obliged several individuals 'to leap out of the windows to save themselves, and some were very much bruised in the fall'. However, this must have been a separate incident, as by this time, Santry had been taken into custody for another murder. See *DEP*, 27–30 January 1738/39.

101. *DNL*, 6–9 May 1738.

3. The Demise of the Hellfire Club

1. *Journals of the House of Lords*, vol. 3, p.401; 'Report of the Lords' Committees for Religion', in ibid., p.414.

2. Jonathan Swift to John Barber, 9 March 1737/38, in Woolley (ed.), *Correspondence of Jonathan Swift*, vol. 4, p.503; [George Berkeley], *A Miscellany, Containing Several Tracts on Various Subjects* (London, 1752), p.80n.

3. *ODNB*, vol. 54, pp.814–7; 'A Letter … by a Gentleman in the Army, in the Year 1739', in *Harleian Miscellany*, vol. 3, p.169.

4. *ODNB*, vol. 54, p.815.

5. 'Letter … by a Gentleman in the Army…1739', pp.175–6, 171.

6. *ODNB*, vol. 54, p.895; *DIB*, vol. 9, p.397; David Berman, 'Enlightenment and Counter-Enlightenment in Irish Philosophy', *Archiv Für Geschichte der Philosophie*, 64 (1982), p.152.

7. Quoted in Graham Gargett, 'Voltaire's View of the Irish', in Graham Gargett and Geraldine Sheridan (eds), *Ireland and the French Enlightenment 1700–1800* (London, 1999), p.156.

8. 'Letter … by a Gentleman in the Army…1739', p.176.

9. David Berman, *Berkeley and Irish Philosophy* (London and New York, 2005), p.107.

10. Quoted in *Irish Quarterly Review*, 3, 10 (June 1853), p.267.

11. Berman, *Berkeley and Irish Philosophy*, p.108; *Irish Quarterly Review*, 3, 10 (June 1853), p.267.

12. 'Letter … by a Gentleman in the Army…1739', p.170.

13. *ODNB*, vol. 33, pp.380–2; Vertue, 'Note Books, III', p.106.

14. Elias (ed.), *Laetitia Pilkington*, vol. 1, p.110; vol. 2, pp.498–9.

15. George Berkeley, *A Discourse Addressed to Magistrates and Men in Authority Occasioned by the Enormous Licence and Irreligion of the Times* (Cork, 1738), p.40.

16. *Journals of the House of Lords*, vol. 3, p.414.

17. Ada Peter, *Sketches of Old Dublin* (Dublin, 1907), p.283. This table was acquired by the National Museum of Ireland (NMI) in 1904: *Irish Times*, 30 March 1904. A sideboard carved with what looks like a satyr's head, currently held by NMI (cat. no. 1904-73), may be the item referred to.

18. *Irish Quarterly Review*, 3 (1853), p.267n.

19. *Re Sir Compton Meade Domvile, Bart., Deceased: Catalogue of the Unique and Historic Collection … to be Sold by Auction … 4th July 1944* (Battersby & Co. Auctioneers, Dublin, 1944), p.5 (copy of catalogue in the Hellfire Club File, Dublin City Archive). This may not have been the only such item in existence. Denis Florence MacCarthy (1817–82) remembered seeing a snuffbox bearing a similar inscription that had been made from an oaken statue of the Devil. This statue once stood at the entrance to 'Hell', an area adjoining Fishamble Street and Christchurch. See Denis Florence MacCarthy, *Shelley's Early Life from Original Sources* (London, 1872), p.237. The story is corroborated in the recollections of John Burke, a nineteenth-century resident of the Dublin Liberties: 'John Burke's Recollections', *Dublin Historical Record*, 47, 1 (1994), p.106. Hellfire club relics are discussed more fully in Chapter 7.

20. Pilkington, *Real Story*, p.143.

21. *DEP*, 3–6 June 1738.

22. *Ample Discovery*.

23. See Robin Briggs, *Witches and Neighbours: The Social and Cultural Context of European Witchcraft*, 2nd edn (Oxford, 2002); Brian P. Levack, *The Witch-Hunt in Early Modern Europe*, 3rd edn (Harlow, 2006); Gareth J. Medway, *Lure of the Sinister: The Unnatural History of Satanism* (New York, 2001).

24. Berman, 'Enlightenment and Counter-Enlightenment', p.163; David Nash, *Blasphemy in the Christian World: A History* (Oxford, 2007), p.4.

25. Berkeley, *Discourse Addressed*, pp.40–1.

26. *The Works of George Berkeley, D.D., Late Bishop of Cloyne in Ireland…* (London, 1784), p.xx; *Journal of the House of Lords*, vol. 3, p.401; *DEP*, 25–28 February 1737 [1738]; *The Irish Blasters: Or, the Votaries of Bacchus* (Dublin, 1738), Preface.

27. Jonathan Swift to John Barber, 9 March 1737/38, in Woolley (ed.), *Correspondence of Jonathan Swift*, vol. 4, p.503.

28. *Journal of the House of Lords*, vol. 3, p.414.

29. Ibid. p.417; *DNL*, 25–28 March 1738.

30. John T. Gilbert and Rosa Mulholland Gilbert (eds), *Calendar of Ancient Records of Dublin* (Dublin, 1889–1944), vol. 8, p.304; Strickland, *Dictionary of Irish Artists*, vol. 2, pp.17–18.

31. Elias (ed.), *Laetitia Pilkington*, vol. 2, pp.500–1; *DEP*, 3–7 January 1737 [1738].

32. Hayton, *Ruling Ireland*, p.267; Malcomson (ed.), *Clements Archive*, pp.194, 708.

33. *DEP*, 3–6 June 1738. 'Mr Frankland' may have been Frederick Frankland, a Revenue Commissioner and probable moralist who was the dedicatee of a tract against the consumption of alcoholic spirits: see William Henry, *An Earnest Address to the People of Ireland Against the Drinking of Spirituous Liquors* (Dublin, 1753).

34. See, for instance, Lord Doneraile's reaction to Laetitia Pilkington's anti-panegyric on him in Clarke, *Queen of the Wits*, p.207.

35. Edward Madden to Santry, 10 July 1744, NLI, Ms 11,793(20).

36. *DEP*, 9–13 August 1737. The riot occurred as part of the factional rivalry of the Ormond and Liberty Boys, which gained momentum in Dublin during the 1730s: see James Kelly, *The Ormond and Liberty Boys: Factional Riot in Eighteenth-Century Dublin* (Dublin, 2005), p.32.

37. Neal Garnham, 'The Trials of James Cotter and Henry, Baron Barry of Santry: Two Case Studies in the Administration of Criminal Justice in Eighteenth-Century Ireland', *IHS*, 31 (1998–9), p.332; Petition of Santry to Lords Justices and General Governors of Ireland [1739], PRONI, Wilmot Papers, T/3019/195. Strangely, it seems that Murphy – or an individual bearing the same name – had been the subject of legal proceedings a few weeks prior to the Palmerstown incident. In late June or early July 1738, one 'Laughlin Murphy, alias Everard' was tried at the Court of Oyer and Terminer for housebreaking and sentenced to be transported. It is uncertain, therefore, why Murphy was in Palmerstown, apparently at liberty, on 9 August: *PO*, 27 June–1 July 1738.

38. Garnham, 'Trials of James Cotter', p.332; J. Roderick O'Flanagan, *The Lives of the Lord Chancellors... of Ireland* (London, 1870), vol. 2, pp.67–8.

39. Garnham, 'Trials of James Cotter', pp.332–3; *PO*, 26–29 August 1738. The Carlow Races were then regarded as one of the country's principal race meetings: see Robert Hitchcock, *An Historical View of the Irish Stage, From the Earliest Period Down to the Close of the Season 1788...* (Dublin, 1788–94), vol. 1, p.101.

40. See Statt, 'Case of the Mohocks', p.185.

41. Lords Justices to Lord Lieutenant, 10 November 1738, PRONI, Wilmot Papers, T/3019/180; BL, Newcastle Papers, Add. Ms. 35586 f.134; Petition of Henry, Lord Baron of Santry, to the Lords Justices, 1738, PRONI, Wilmot Papers, T/3019/181.

42. D. Ryder and J. Strange [to Duke of Newcastle], 23 January 1738 [1739], TNA, State Papers, SP63/417/36); Garnham, 'Trials of James Cotter', pp.331–2.

43. Richard Mathew to Lord Fitzwilliam, 21 April 1739, NAI, Pembroke Estate Papers, 97/46/1/2/4/4); see also *DEP*, 13–17 March 1738/39, 21–24 April 1739; *DG*, 21–24 April 1739.

44. *PO*, 24–28 April 1739; Gilbert, *History of the City of Dublin*, vol. 3, pp.88–95; Garnham, 'Trials of James Cotter', pp.332–4; Affidavit relating to the death of Laughlin Murphy, 1738, NLI, D23,076.

45. Garnham, 'Trials of James Cotter', p.333; Tickell to Walpole, 28 April 1739, PRONI, Wilmot Papers, T/3019/193.

46. Letter of Thomas Rundle, Bishop of Derry, to Mr Richardson, n.d., in George-Monck Berkeley, *Literary Relics: Containing Original Letters...* (London, 1789), pp.412–14.

47. O'Flanagan, *Lives of the Lord Chancellors*, vol. 2, p.72; *Analysis of the Philosophical Works*, p.v.

48. O'Flanagan, *Lives of the Lord Chancellors*, vol. 2, p.72; Representation of Lords Triers to Lords Justices and General Governor of Ireland on Behalf of Santry, PRONI, Wilmot Papers, T/3019/196); *FDJ*, 28 April–1 May 1739; Petition of Santry to Lords Justices General and General Governors of Ireland, PRONI, Wilmot Papers, T/3019/195.

49. *DG*, 1–5 May 1739; *PO*, 1–5 May 1739; *DEP*, 19–22 May 1739, 22–26 May 1739. No documented evidence has been found to support the oft-cited story that Sir Compton Domvile obtained a reprieve for his nephew by threatening to cut off Dublin's water supply.

50. *PO*, 19–22 May 1739; Archbishop Boulter, quoted in Johnston-Liik, *History of the Irish Parliament*, vol. 1, p.328n.

51. Garnham, 'Trials of James Cotter', pp.335–6; Declaration of Sir Compton Domvile and Richard Wingfield, 1 December 1741, NLI, Ms. 11,793 (2). See also NLI, Ms. 11,793(1).

52. Madden to Domvile, 25 November 1740, NLI, Ms. 11,793(3).

53. Santry [to Lady Domvile], 24 July 1743, NLI, Ms. 11,793 (20).

54. Edward Madden to Santry, 10 July 1744, NLI, Ms. 11,793 (20); Garnham, 'Trials of James Cotter', pp.335–6; Madden to Santry, 10 July 1744.

55. Letters of Lord Santry, Nottingham, 17 July 1745, 22 December 1746, 11 February 1748/9, NLI, Ms. 11,793(20).

56. G.E.C., *Complete Peerage*, vol. 1, p.449.

57. Letters of Lord Santry, 11 February 1748/49, 22 December 1746, NLI, Ms. 11,793(20).

58. Letter of Lord Santry, n.d; see also Letter of Lord Santry [to Lady Domvile], 24 July 1743, NLI, Ms. 11,793(20).

59. *FDJ*, 2–6 April 1751; *Exshaw's Magazine*, March 1751, p.167; Robert Somerville-Woodward, *Ballymun: A History* (Ballymun, [c. 2002]), vol. 1, p.57 (unpublished study). Reference copies are available in Trinity College Dublin and Ballymun Library, Dublin.

60. *County Magazine*, July 1788, p.100.

61. Vertue, 'Note Books, III', p.106; Elias (ed.), *Laetitia Pilkington*, vol. 2, pp.498–9; *ODNB*, vol. 33, p.382.

62. 'The Several Answer of Edward Kean Esquire One of the Defendants to the Amended Bill of Complaint of the Right Honble Richard, Earl of Ross[e], Complt', 10 January 1752, pp.1–2, NAI, M. 5762(1). See also Barnard, *New Anatomy of Ireland*, p.27.

63. *FJ*, 27–30 July 1771.

64. 'The Joint and Several Answers of...Richard Earl of Ross[e]...and...Lady Elizabeth Parsons his Daughter...to the Bill of Complaint of...William Lord Berkely of Stratton', 5 December[?] 1740, TNA, C11/2081/15; 'Richard Earl of Rosse...Appellant. Elizabeth Worsop [et al.]...Respondents: The Appellant's Case' [1741], Hardwicke Papers, BL, Add. Ms. 36154 ff.160–1.

65. Nathaniel Salmon, *A Short View of the Families of the Present Irish Nobility...* (London, 1759), p.44.

66. David Dickson, *Arctic Ireland: The Extraordinary Story of the Great Frost and Forgotten Famine of 1740–41* (Belfast, 1997); Letter of Edward Madden, 19 December 1740, NLI, Ms. 11,793.

67. Crawley, *Caementaria Hibernica*, vol. 2, p.15.

68. Pilkington, *Real Story*, pp.143–7. The story was repeated in various late eighteenth-century anthologies of wit and humour including *The Entertaining Medley: Being a Collection of Genuine Anecdotes...* (London, 1767), pp.96–102;

The New Story-Teller: Or, Historical Medley (Newcastle, 1782), pp.173–6; Mr Addison, *A Collection of Interesting Anecdotes, Memoirs, Allegories, Essays, and Poetical Fragments...* (London, 1793), pp.28–31.

69. Barnard, 'Dublin Society', p.70.
70. Malcomson, *Nathaniel Clements*, pp.38–41; Clement, *Ancestors and Descendents*, vol. 2, pp.889–91.
71. Walpole, *Correspondence*, vol. 17, pp.450–1n; J. Potter, Dublin Castle, to R. Wilmot, 2 July 1741, PRONI, Wilmot Papers, T/3019/306; Dickson, *Arctic Ireland*, pp.55–6.
72. Quoted in Clement, *Ancestors and Descendents*, vol. 2, p.890; *ODNB*, vol. 44, p.811; Henry Ponsonby to Viscount Duncannon, 10 October 1744, NLI, Ms. 22,735.
73. *ODNB*, vol. 44, p.811; Ponsonby, *Ponsonby Family*, p.45.
74. Malcomson, *Nathaniel Clements*, pp.38–41; Clement, *Ancestors and Descendents*, vol. 2, pp.890–1; Horace Walpole to Horace Mann, 11 May 1745, in Lewis et al. (eds), *Walpole's Correspondence*, vol. 19, p.42.
75. Deeds relative to military appointments of Richard St George, NLI, D. 22,685; 22,686; 22,687; Johnston-Liik, *History of the Irish Parliament*, vol. 6, pp.217–19.
76. 'Deposition of Edward Palmer, Coleshire, Co. of Warwick', Depositions taken at Sutton Coldfield 27 September 1762. Richard Bisse Riland, Clerk v. Simon Luttrell Esq., TNA, E134/3Geo3/Mich1.
77. Letter of Duke of Newcastle to Luttrell, 25 March 1759, BL, Add. Ms. 32889 f.237; G.E.C., *Complete Peerage*, vol. 3, p.23; Jones, *Clubs of Georgian Rakes*, pp.72–4.
78. See Charles Jenkinson, *Life History and Remarkable Pedigree of the Rt. Hon. Simon, Lord Irnham* (London, 1769); [William Combe], *The Diaboliad, a Poem: Dedicated to the Worst Man in His Majesty's Dominions* (London, 1777).
79. *DNB*, vol. 22, p.538.
80. *ODNB*, vol. 34, p.812; *DIB*, vol. 5, pp.606–7.
81. Jenkinson, *Life History*, p.22; John Cannon (ed.), *The Letters of Junius* (Oxford, 1978), p.317; [Combe], *Diaboliad*, passim.
82. Hardy, *Memoirs of the Political and Private Life*, vol. 1, p.265.
83. G.E.C., *Complete Peerage*, vol. 3, p.24n.
84. Malcomson, *Pursuit of the Heiress*, pp.12–13; Henry Lawes Luttrell, quoted in ibid., p.13.
85. *ODNB*, vol. 34, p.812; *Between the Hon. Henry Lawes Luttrell, and Francis M'Farland – Appellants, and the Right Hon. Simon Lord Irnham – Respondent...* [London, 1778], p.1.
86. *FJ*, 10–12 October 1775.
87. Henry MacDougall, *Sketches of Irish Political Characters, of the Present Day...* (London, 1799), pp.39–40; Irnham, quoted in Malcomson, *Pursuit of the Heiress*, p.13.
88. *DNB*, vol. 12, p.300. It was also said that Henry Lawes Luttrell 'sent word that if he (the father) could prevail on any gentleman to be his second, he would fight him with all his heart': A. Francis Steuart (ed.), *The Last Journals of Horace Walpole during the Reign of George III from 1771–1785* (London, 1910), vol. 1, p.xix.

89. G.E.C., *Complete Peerage*, vol. 3, p.23.

90. R.R. Madden, *The United Irishmen: Their Lives and Times*, new edn (New York [c. 1916]), vol. 3, pp.258–60; *ODNB*, vol. 34, p.813; *DIB*, vol. 5, p.607; J.F. Kenny, 'The Annals of a Hated Race', *New Ireland Review* 23 (March–August 1905), pp.275–6.

4. Regional Hellfire Clubs

1. Gilbert, *History of the City of Dublin*, vol. 3, p.256; Elias (ed.), *Laetitia Pilkington*, vol. 2, p.353.

2. Clarke, *Queen of the Wits*, p.108.

3. James Kelly, '"Drinking the Waters": Balneotherapeutic Medicine in Ireland, 1660–1850', *Studia Hibernica*, 35 (2008–09), p.117.

4. Clarke, *Queen of the Wits*, pp.136–8; Elias (ed.), *Laetitia Pilkington*, vol. 1, pp.95, 99–101, 104–13, 115.

5. The portrait is in the National Gallery of Ireland (cat. no. NGI 4523). See *National Gallery of Ireland Acquisitions 1986–88*, p.69.

6. Johnston-Liik, *History of the Irish Parliament*, vol. 3, p.543; *PO*, 23–26 November 1734; Johnston-Liik, *History of the Irish Parliament*, vol. 3, pp.543–4.

7. Johnston-Liik, *History of the Irish Parliament*, vol. 6, p.138. By 1878 the Dunraven estates extended to 14,298 acres in Limerick alone: U.H. Hussey de Burgh, *The Landowners of Ireland: An Alphabetical List of the Owners of Estates of 500 Acres or £500 Valuation and Upwards...* (Dublin [1878]), p.141.

8. On Royse, see Toby Barnard, *The Abduction of a Limerick Heiress: Social and Political Relations in Mid-Eighteenth Century Ireland* (Dublin, 1998), pp.23–4, 27.

9. *Burke's Landed Gentry of Ireland*, 4th edn (London, 1958), p.64.

10. Johnston-Liik, *History of the Irish Parliament*, vol. 6, p.128; *PO*, 24–27 February 1739; *National Gallery of Ireland Acquisitions 1986–88*, p.68.

11. Barnard, *Abduction of a Limerick Heiress*, pp.17, 27; *National Gallery of Ireland Acquisitions 1986–88*, p.69; *Burke's Irish Family Records* (London, 1976), p.136.

12. J. Anthony Gaughan, *The Knights of Glin: A Geraldine Family* (Dublin, 1978), pp.70–6.

13. Anne Crookshank and the Knight of Glin, *Irish Portraits 1660–1860* (London, c.1969), pp.40–1. The beckoning figure bears a resemblance to the mezzotint of Robert Edge Pine's portrait of Worsdale (see Plate 14).

14. Barnard, *Abduction of a Limerick Heiress*, p.49.

15. Ibid., p.47.

16. Daniel Hayes, *The Works in Verse of Daniel Hayes, Esq....*, 2nd edn (Limerick, 1785), p.26. See Crookshank and Knight of Glin, *Irish Portraits 1660–1860*, p.41.

17. Hayes, *Works of Verse*, p.26, p.24.

18. Gaughan, *Knights of Glin*, p.70.

19. Barnard, *Abduction of a Limerick Heiress*, p.49.

20. The Knight of Glin, interview with the author, 24 March 2005; William Laffan (ed.), *Painting Ireland: Topographical Views from Glin Castle* (Tralee, Co. Kerry, 2006), p.77.

21. Chatterton, *Rambles in the South of Ireland*, vol. 2, pp.127–8. My thanks to the late

Knight of Glin for bringing this to my attention.

22. Irish Folklore Collection, Schools' Manuscripts for Askeaton School, Co. Limerick 1935–38, IFC UCD, 503: 159–60.

23. 'The Pilgrim's Grave', *Duffy's Fireside Magazine*, January 1853, p.67. 'Damer's estate' is a reference to the property that the land agent and moneylender Joseph Damer (c. 1630–1720) acquired at Shronell, County Tipperary, following the Restoration. Damer was remembered as a notorious miser and references to 'Damer's gold' abounded in Munster folklore. Joseph's nephew (also called Joseph Damer) built the Damer House in Roscrea, County Tipperary: *DIB*, vol. 3, pp.34–5. Coincidentally, the Dublin Hellfire Club portrait was exhibited at the Damer House for a time in the late twentieth century, on loan from the National Gallery of Ireland. It was claimed that it fell from the wall in the course of an alleged haunting. See *Irish Independent*, 28 October 1995.

24. *Evangelical Magazine*, 19 (1811), p.265.

25. *ODNB*, vol. 60, p.340; Crookshank and Knight of Glin, *Ireland's Painters*, p.48; Strickland, *Dictionary of Irish Artists*, vol. 2, p.563.

26. T.J.Walsh, *Opera in Dublin 1798–1820: Frederick Jones and the Crow Street Theatre* (Oxford, 1993), p.5; T.J. Walsh, *Opera in Dublin: The Social Scene 1705–1797* (Dublin, 1973), pp.59, 70–1.

27. Pasquin, *Authentic History*, p.21; Williamson (rev.), *Bryan's Dictionary of Painters*, vol. 5, p.395; Clarke, *Queen of the Wits*, p.229.

28. *ODNB*, vol. 60, p.340; Elias (ed.), *Laetitia Pilkington*, vol. 1, pp.274–7; vol. 2, pp.663–5. On the relationship between Worsdale and Laetitia Pilkington in London, see Clarke, *Queen of the Wits*, pp.229–37.

29. *The Tryal of John Cather, Adam Nixon, David Alexander, and Patrick Cain . . . on Friday the 5th of July, 1751 . . .* , 2nd edn (Dublin, 1751), passim. See also Elias (ed), *Laetitia Pilkington*, vol. 2, p.452; *DIB*, vol. 9, pp.727–8.

30. John Timbs, *Lives of Wits and Humourists* (London, 1862), vol. 1, pp.198–200; Clarke, *Queen of the Wits*, p.231.

31. The original painting appears to have been lost; however, there are copies of a mezzotint by W. Dickinson in the National Gallery of Ireland (NGI 10,686) and the National Portrait Gallery, London (NPG D4914).

32. *ODNB*, vol. 60, p.340; Horace Walpole, *Anecdotes of Painting in England* (London, 1786), vol. 4, p.119.

33. Vertue, '*Note Books*, III', p.59; Elias (ed), *Laetitia Pilkington*, vol. 1, pp.275, 277, 347.

34. *New York Times*, 18 February 2007.

35. Arthur P.I. Samuels, *The Early Life, Correspondence and Writings of the Rt. Hon. Edmund Burke . . .* (Cambridge, 1923), pp.323–4. See p.88 in this volume.

36. Bence-Jones, *Guide to Irish Country Houses*, p.106; Kate O'Brien, *My Ireland* (London, 1962), p.177.Thanks to Cos Egan for bringing this to my attention and for taking me to visit the remains of the tower.

37. Journal of Daniel Augustus Beaufort, July–August 1788, pp.61, 68, TCD, Ms. 4029; *DIB*, vol. 6, pp.413–14. A medieval promontory fort previously occupied the site on which the tower stands. See T.J. Westropp, 'Ancient Place-Names, Brugh of the Boyne and Others', *JRSAI* (5th series), 36, 1 (1906), p.83.

38. Johnston-Liik, *History of the Irish Parliament*, vol. 6, p.229; Ingamells, *Dictionary*, pp.740, 837.

39. Horace Walpole to Sir Horace Mann, 4 June 1749, in Lewis et al. (eds), *Walpole Correspondence*, vol. 20, p.64; George Anne Bellamy, *An Apology for the Life of George Anne Bellamy*... (London, 1785), vol. 2, pp.89–90, 90–2.

40. Réamonn Ó Muirí, 'Lt John Lindley St Leger, United Irishman', *Seanchas Ardmhacha: Journal of the Armagh Diocesan Historical Society*, 11, 1 (1983–4), p.173.

41. Kelly, *'That Damn'd Thing'*, p.70; HMC, *The Manuscripts and Correspondence of James, First Earl of Charlemont* (London, 1891–94), vol. 1, pp.190–1; *PO*, 25–29 December 1753.

42. *Notes and Queries* (Series 1), 10 (26 August 1854), p.175; Liam Price (ed.), *An Eighteenth Century Antiquary: The Sketches, Notes and Diaries of Austin Cooper (1759–1830)* (Dublin, 1942), p.91; A.A. Weldon, 'A Slight Sketch of Grangemellon and the Story of St Leger's Castle', *JCKAS*, 1, 2 (1892), p.96.

43. *WHM*, July 1795, p.56.

44. Weldon, 'Grangemellon', p.100. It is likely that stories of the club that once met there, and the names of St Leger's club-mates, were passed down to Weldon from his forebears. See ibid., p.101.

45. Henry B. Swanzy, 'Dixon of Kilkea Castle', *JCKAS*, 9, 5 (1920), pp.392–4; Lord Walter Fitzgerald, 'William Fitzgerald of Castleroe, and his Tomb in the Kilkea Churchyard', *JCKAS*, 3 (1899–1902), pp.249–51.

46. Johnston-Liik, *History of the Irish Parliament*, vol. 4, p.375.

47. Fitzgerald, 'William Fitzgerald of Castleroe', p.251.

48. Bellamy, *Apology*, vol. 2, p.92; Malcomson, *Nathaniel Clements*, p.398.

49. Lord Walter FitzGerald, 'Kilkea Castle', *JCKAS*, 2, 1 (1896), p.20; Barrington, *Personal Sketches*, p.212.

50. Kelly, *'That Damn'd Thing'*, p.150; Jonah Barrington, *Historic Memoirs of Ireland; Comprising Secret Records of the National Convention, the Rebellion, and the Union*... (London, 1835), vol. 2, p.27. On Bagenal, see also William J. O'Neill Daunt, *Ireland and her Agitators* (Dublin, 1845), pp.8–12; Johnston-Liik, *History of the Irish Parliament*, vol. 3, pp.122–4; *DIB*, vol. 1, pp.214–5.

51. Fitzgerald, 'William Fitzgerald of Castleroe', p.251.

52. Ó Muirí, 'Lt John Lindley St Leger', p.173; Fitzgerald, 'William Fitzgerald of Castleroe', p.251.

53. Mary Leadbeater, *The Leadbeater Papers: A Selection from the Mss. and Correspondence of Mary Leadbeater*, 2nd edn (London, 1862), vol. 1, p.124; ibid, pp.124–5.

54. A similar case occurred in 1809, when Captain William Perry, an officer in the Clare Militia, repented for a 'career of wickedness' in the days prior to his death. He claimed to have belonged to a society of atheists and deists who 'were bound to work all manner of iniquity to the extent of their power, and to utter all possible blasphemies against God': *Evangelical Magazine*, 19 (1811), pp.265–8.

55. Weldon, 'Grangemellon', pp.100–1; Fitzgerald, 'William Fitzgerald of Castleroe', pp.249–51.

56. *Notes and Queries* (Series 1), 10 (4 November 1854), p.376. This correspondent mistakenly identified St Leger's son, Colonel John Hayes St Leger (1756–1800), as the club's initiator.

57. Fitzgerald, 'William Fitzgerald of Castleroe', p.251.

58. Hugh Fenning, 'Letters from a Jesuit in Dublin on the Confraternity of the Holy Name, 1747–1748', *Archivium Hibernicum* 29 (1971), pp.133–54.

59. O'C–nn–r [O'Connor], *Essay on the Rosary and Sodality*, p.113; *FJ*, 9–12 March 1771, 2–4 April 1771.

60. *FJ*, 9–12 March 1771.

61. Ibid.

62. Quoted in Hugh Fenning, *The Irish Dominican Province, 1698–1797* (Dublin, 1990), p.502; Thomas Wall, *The Sign of Doctor Hay's Head: Being Some Account of the Hazards and Fortunes of Catholic Printers and Publishers…* (Dublin, 1958), pp.85–6.

63. It has been described as 'the most substantial devotional work written by any Irish Dominican' prior to the twentieth century (Fenning, *Irish Dominican Province*, p.394).

64. O'C–nn–r [O'Connor], *Essay on the Rosary and Sodality*, pp.112–4.

65. *FJ*, 20–23 April 1771; Meade Swift, *The Miscellaneous Works of Mr Meade Swift, Senr in Prose and Verse* (Dublin, 1772), pp.98–101.

66. *FJ*, 2–4 April 1771, 9–12 March 1771; See Kelly, *'That Damn'd Thing'*, p.94 and passim.

67. *FJ*, 2–4 April 1771.

68. Kelly, *'That Damn'd Thing'*, pp.151–7.

69. William Laffan (ed.), *Miscelanea Structura Curiosa* (Tralee, Co. Kerry, 2005), passim.

70. William Laffan, 'From Paper to Pillar, "Miscelanea Structura Curiosa" and the Cumberland Column', in Laffan (ed.), *Miscelanea Structura Curiosa*, pp.19, 20.

71. Toby Barnard, 'Chearnley and his Contexts: Family Neighbours and Gardens', in Laffan (ed.), *Miscelanea Structura Curiosa*, p.49.

72. Laffan, 'From Paper to Pillar', p.20; Lord, *Hell-Fire Clubs*, pp.137–40.

73. The clockcase is depicted on the back cover of volume 5 of the original edition of this work: see *Georgian Society Records of Eighteenth-Century Domestic Architecture and Decoration in Ireland* (Dublin, 1909–13), vol. 5.

74. *The Reformer*, 7 April 1748, quoted in Samuels, *Edmund Burke*, pp.323–4.

75. This notion forms the basis of a nineteenth-century fictional narrative, in which Lucifer makes known 'his intention of testing the claim to preeminence of the metropolitan [i.e. Dublin] hl [hell] fire Club over the provincial clubs he patronised': 'Record of the Hell Fire Club', NLI, Ms. 25,527(2). See Chapter 7.

76. *Irish Quarterly Review*, 2, 7 (1852), p.528.

77. O'Reilly, *Reminiscences*, vol. 3, p.289. Born in County Westmeath, O'Reilly was a United Irishman who went into exile in Paris after 1798. He later became the Paris correspondent of *The Times*, in which capacity he 'rendered such signal service in exposing a great financial fraud that a tablet recording his services was put up in Lloyd's Marine Office': Kevin Whelan, 'Introduction to Section VII', in Thomas Bartlett, David Dickson, Dáire Keogh and Kevin Whelan (eds), *1798: A Bicentenary Perspective* (Dublin, 2003), p.529n; Douglas Hyde and D.J. O'Donoghue, *Catalogue of the Books & Manuscripts Comprising the Library of the Late Sir John T. Gilbert* (Dublin, 1918), p.615. O'Reilly was a brother of the

scholar and lexicographer Edward O'Reilly (1765–1830), for whom see *DIB*, vol. 7, pp.850–2.

78.   Lady Morgan, *O'Briens and the O'Flahertys*, vol. 3, p.129.

79.   Daunt, *Ireland and her Agitators*, p.131; J.E. Walsh, *Ireland Sixty Years Ago*, 3rd edn (Dublin, 1851), pp.17–18; *Irish Quarterly Review*, 2, 7 (1852), pp.528–31; James J. Gaskin, *Varieties of Irish History; From Ancient and Modern Sources and Original Documents* (Dublin, 1869), pp.419–20.

80.   See Kelly, *'That Damn'd Thing'*, pp.127–90.

5. The Pinkindindies

1.   *FJ*, 18–20 January 1785. Clontarf Island no longer exists, having been subsumed into the reclaimed land around East Wall.

2.   'Commemorative Statue for Ranelagh', press release, Ranelagh Arts Festival, 2008, http://www.ranelagharts.org/2008_statue.php (accessed 3 August 2011); *Irish Times*, 29 September 2008; *Irish Independent*, 29 September 2008.

3.   Maxwell, *Dublin under the Georges*, pp.149–53.

4.   See Kelly, *Ormond and Liberty Boys*, passim and p.48.

5.   Vincent Morley, *Irish Opinion and the American Revolution, 1760–1783* (Cambridge, 2002), pp.92–3; Stanley H. Palmer, *Police and Protest in England and Ireland 1780–1850* (Cambridge, 1988), p.93; Morley, *Irish Opinion and the American Revolution*, pp.90–4, 128–9, 181–2, 256. See also *FJ*, 12–14 January 1775; *HJ*, 11–14 December 1778; *FDJ*, 22–25 January 1780.

6.   See, for instance, *FJ*, 1–5 March 1768, 15–17 July 1773, 12–14 January 1775, 2–5 September 1775; Morley, *Irish Opinion and the American Revolution*, p.91.

7.   *A Classical Dictionary of the Vulgar Tongue*, 3rd edn (London, 1796).

8.   See Stat. 13 & 14 Geo. 3, cap. 45. sect. 1 and Stat. 17 & 18 Geo. 3, cap. 11. sect. 1, in *An Abridgement of the Publick Statutes of Ireland, Now in Force and of General Use . . .* (Dublin, 1786), vol. 1.

9.   Allen, *Clubs of Augustan London*, pp.106–7; Statt, 'Case of the Mohocks', p.190.

10.   *Gentleman's Magazine*, 25 (1755), pp.64–5.

11.   Fagan, *Second City*, pp.101–8; Kelly, *Ormond and Liberty Boys*, p.28; Constantia Maxwell, *A History of Trinity College Dublin 1591–1892* (Dublin, 1946), pp.133–4.

12.   Barrington, *Personal Sketches*, p.270.

13.   *Register of Censures and Degrees, Trinity College Dublin, 1740–1890*, TCD, MUN/V/5/4 (22).

14.   *WHM*, October 1774, p.567; *FJ*, 31 August–2 September 1780.

15.   *FJ*, 11–14 February 1775; Maxwell, *History of Trinity College Dublin*, p.134.

16.   Notice of Censure of Emmanuel Thompson, 16 February 1775, TCD, MUN V/5/4 (24); *FJ*, 25–28 February 1775, 2–4 March 1775, 7–9 March 1775.

17.   *DIB*, vol. 2, p.1035; *WHM*, January 1785, p.1; Georges Dames Burtchaell and Thomas Ulick Sadlier (eds), *Alumni Dublinensis: A Register of the Students, Graduates, Professors and Provosts of Trinity College in the University of Dublin (1593–1860)* (Dublin, 1935), vol. 1, p.196.

18.   Barrington, *Personal Sketches*, p.197.

19. Ibid., pp.197–9. On Daly, see *DIB*, vol. 3, pp.31–2.

20. Barrington, *Personal Sketches*, p.197; *WHM*, January 1785, p.1.

21. Mary Lyons (ed.), *The Memoirs of Mrs. Leeson, Madam 1727–1797* (Dublin, 1995), pp.69, 79; Burtchaell and Sadleir (eds), *Alumni Dublinensis*, vol. 1, p.196; vol. 2, p.326.

22. See Register of Censures and Degrees, 28 January 1740/41–14 June 1890, passim, TCD, MUN/V/5/4.

23. J.D. Herbert, *Irish Varieties, for the Last Fifty Years: Written from Recollections* (London, 1836), p.77, 79–81; *FJ*, 24 July 1794.

24. A contemporary dictionary of colloquialisms defined 'pinking' as 'to stab or wound with a small sword: probably derived from the holes formerly cut in both men and women's clothes, called pinking' (*Classical Dictionary of the Vulgar Tongue*). The name has many variant spellings; other contemporary versions include Pink-in-dindies and Pinking-dindies.

25. Herbert, *Irish Varieties*, p.78.

26. Lyons (ed.), *Memoirs of Mrs. Leeson*, p.69.

27. MacDowel Cosgrave, 'On Two Maps', p.141.

28. *HJ*, 5–7 July 1779; *FDJ*, 18–20 March 1779; Gilbert, *History of the City of Dublin*, vol. 2, p.165.

29. *HJ*, 29 September–1 October 1779; Herbert, *Irish Varieties*, p.78; *DEP*, 15 May 1779.

30. Herbert, *Irish Varieties*, pp.77–8; *FJ*, 31 October–3 November 1778.

31. Herbert, *Irish Varieties*, pp 78–9.

32. *FJ*, 31 October–3 November 1778; *DEP*, 13 October 1778. See also *FJ*, 19–22 December 1778.

33. *FJ*, 31 October–3 November 1778; *WHM*, June 1779, p.374; *DEP*, 10 June 1779.

34. Herbert, *Irish Varieties*, p.78; *WHM*, July 1779, pp.429–30; *FDJ*, 4–6 January 1780.

35. *HJ*, 4–7 February 1780; see also *DEP*, 23 January 1779. See David Fleming, 'Public Attitudes to Prostitution in Eighteenth-Century Ireland', *Irish Economic and Social History*, 32 (2005), pp.1–18.

36. *FJ*, 22–24 June 1780, 29 June–1 July 1780; Herbert, *Irish Varieties*, p.78. A policeman was fined and jailed for this practice in 1787: *FJ*, 22–24 May 1787.

37. *DEP*, 19 September 1778; *WHM*, October 1774, p.568.

38. Drogheda Street occupied the middle section of present-day O'Connell Street, between the Henry Street and Abbey Street junctions.

39. *DIB*, vol. 5, p.415; *ODNB*, vol. 33, pp.153–4; *Peg Plunket, or the Dublin Courtezans: A Musical Whim, in Two Acts*, NLI, microfilm, P. 544. Original in BL, Add. Ms. 25,992.

40. *HJ*, 22–24 February 1779; Lyons (ed.), *Memoirs of Mrs. Leeson*, p.69; Barrington, *Personal Sketches*, p.197.

41. *HJ*, 22–24 February 1779, 7–9 July 1779; Lyons (ed.), *Memoirs of Mrs. Leeson*, pp.69–70.

42. *DEP*, 14 January 1779, 23 January 1779. On Katherine Netterville, see Lyons (ed.), *Memoirs of Mrs. Leeson*, pp.xiii–xiv.

43. Lyons (ed.), *Memoirs of Mrs. Leeson*, pp.70–1.

44. *HJ*, 7–9 July 1779; *DEP*, 29 July 1779.
45. *DEP*, 8 July 1779.
46. Lyons (ed.), *Memoirs of Mrs. Leeson*, pp.70–1.
47. James Kelly, 'The Abduction of Women of Fortune in Eighteenth-Century Ireland', *Eighteenth-Century Ireland*, 9 (1994), p.39. See also James Kelly, '"A most inhuman and barbarous piece of villainy": An Exploration of the Crime of Rape in Eighteenth-Century Ireland', *Eighteenth Century Ireland*, 10 (1995), pp.78–107.
48. *FJ*, 14–16 December 1784.
49. *DEP*, 24 June 1779; *FJ*, 25–28 September 1779.
50. *FJ*, 1–3 June 1780, 29 June–1 July 1780.
51. *FJ*, 22–24 June 1780. On the abduction of heiresses, see Kelly, 'Abduction of Women of Fortune'.
52. *FJ*, 26–29 February 1780; *HJ*, 28 February–1 March 1780; *HJ*, 22–25 September 1780.
53. *DEP*, 27 February 1779; *FDJ*, 25–27 February 1779; *SNL*, 3 March 1779.
54. Jim Herlihy, *The Dublin Metropolitan Police: A Short History and Genealogical Guide* (Dublin, 2001), p.3; *The Dublin Cries, or a Representation of the Various Cries and Callings throughout … Dublin* (c. 1773), reproduced in Laffan (ed.), *Cries of Dublin*, p.52.
55. *WHM*, February 1782, p.112; *WHM*, December 1780, p.688.
56. *WHM*, June 1779, p.374.
57. Contemporary newspapers give many instances of such procrastination. In February 1779 a man named John Fallon was attacked and robbed on Ormond Quay while a watchman, 'standing almost at his side, never offered to stir'. In March of the following year a gentleman who was attacked by three men outside Smock Alley Theatre called in vain for the assistance of a watchman, 'who was a calm spectator of the whole transaction': *DEP*, 27 February 1779; *FDJ*, 23–25 March 1780. See also *HJ*, 11–14 December 1778.
58. *HJ*, 17 December 1784.
59. See, for instance, *DEP*, 25 March 1780; *FJ*, 29 June–1 July 1780, 13–15 July 1780, 1–3 August 1780, 29–31 August 1780; *HJ*, 13–15 September 1780.
60. Kelly, *Ormond and Liberty Boys*, p.28; Minutes of the Board, Trinity College Dublin, 7 July 1775, TCD, MUN V/5/3 p.320.
61. Statt, 'Case of the Mohocks', pp.192–3.
62. Herbert, *Irish Varieties*, p.77. An exception to the rule may have occurred on 6 December 1778, when a group of students, possibly Pinkindindies, were worsted in a clash with the watch of St Bride's parish: *FJ*, 8–10 December 1778.
63. Lyons (ed.), *Memoirs of Mrs. Leeson*, p.70; *DEP*, 19 September 1778; *FJ*, 17–19 September 1778: my thanks to Martyn Powell for bringing this to my attention.
64. *FJ*, 29 January–1 February 1780.
65. *FDJ*, 11–13 May 1779; *DEP*, 25 January 1780; *HJ*, 24–26 January 1780.
66. *FJ*, 11–13 May 1780, 18–20 May 1780; *FJ*, 22–25 October 1785.
67. *HJ*, 23–26 June 1780.
68. *FDJ*, 22–24 February 1780, 30 May–1 June 1780.
69. *FJ*, 31 October–3 November 1778, 19–22 December 1778.
70. *FJ*, 10–13 October 1778, 19–22 December 1778.

71. Statt, 'Case of the Mohocks', p.190; *FJ*, 27–29 July 1780.

72. Proclamation of Provost and Senior Fellows, 29 November 1779 in Register of Censures and Degrees, Trinity College Dublin, 1740–1890, TCD, MUN/V/5/4 (29).

73. *FJ*, 11–13 May 1780.

74. *DEP*, 5 June 1779; J.E. Walsh, *Ireland Sixty Years Ago*, pp.100–1; *DIB*, vol. 8, p.561.

75. *FJ*, 14–16 December 1784.

76. *FJ*, 15–17 June 1780, 27–29 July 1780; *DEP*, 20 June 1780. On Mary Hall, see Lyons (ed.), *Memoirs of Mrs. Leeson*, pp.86–7, 172–3. While the area around Mecklenburgh Street (later renamed as Tyrone Street and then as Railway Street) was well known in the late nineteenth and early twentieth centuries as the 'Monto' red-light district, it is clear that prostitutes were already active there in the late eighteenth century. On the 'Monto', see Maria Luddy, *Prostitution and Irish Society, 1800–1940* (Cambridge, 2007), pp.33–5; Diarmuid Ferriter, *Occasions of Sin: Sex and Society in Modern Ireland* (London, 2009), pp.29–30, 148–52.

77. *FJ*, 10–12 April 1781.

78. *FJ*, 19–21 September 1782, 24–26 October 1782. My thanks to Martyn Powell for bringing these references to my attention.

79. *FJ*, 14–16 December 1784, 18–20 April 1786.

80. Palmer, *Police and Protest*, p.93.

81. Herlihy, *Dublin Metropolitan Police*, pp.5–6; *FJ*, 10–13 May 1788.

82. Thomas Bartlett (ed.), *Revolutionary Dublin, 1795–1801: The Letters of Francis Higgins to Dublin Castle* (Dublin, 2004), pp.25–6; *DIB*, vol. 4, p.682; *Advice to the University of Dublin . . .* (Dublin, 1791), p.44.

83. *FJ*, 5–7 October 1786.

84. *FJ*, 24 July 1794; *HJ*, 25 July 1794, 30 July 1794, 5 August 1794, 19 August 1795; Herbert, *Irish Varieties*, pp.79–81; Brian Henry, *Dublin Hanged: Crime, Law Enforcement and Punishment in Late Eighteenth-Century Dublin* (Dublin, 1994), pp.144–5.

85. TCD, MUN/V/5/3, p.410.

86. *DIB*, vol. 2, p.1036; John Burke, *A Genealogical and Heraldic History of the Commoners of Great Britain and Ireland* (London, 1836–38), vol. 4, p.349; *WHM*, January 1785, pp.1–2.

87. Barbara Traxler Brown, 'French Scientific Innovation in Late-Eighteenth-Century Dublin: The Hydrogen Balloon Experiments of Richard Crosbie (1783–1785)', in Gargett and Sheridan (eds), *Ireland and the French Enlightenment*, pp.108–9, 119; *FJ*, 23–25 September 1784.

88. *FJ*, 4–6 January 1785, 18–20 January 1785; Deirdre Kelly, *Four Roads to Dublin: A History of Rathmines, Ranelagh and Leeson Street* (Dublin, 1995), p.47; Lyons (ed.), *Memoirs of Mrs. Leeson*, p.71.

89. *FJ*, 18–20 January 1785.

90. Brown, 'French Scientific Innovation', p.109; Barrington, *Personal Sketches*, p.197.

91. L.T.C. Rolt, *The Balloonists: The History of the First Aeronauts* (Stroud, 2006), p.99; *The Times*, 19 May 1785; *WHM*, May 1785, pp.278–80.

92. *DIB*, vol. 2, p.1036; Gilbert, *History of the City of Dublin*, vol. 3, pp.279–81.

93. P[atrick] Fitzgerald, *The History, Topography, and Antiquities, of the County and City of Limerick . . .* (Dublin, 1827), vol. 2, p.486; Charlemont to Alexander H. Haliday, 17 June 1786, in HMC, *The Manuscripts and Correspondence of James, First Earl of Charlemont* (London, 1891–94), vol. 2, p.39. For a comprehensive account of Crosbie's aeronautical career, see Bryan MacMahon, *Ascend or Die: Richard Crosbie Pioneer of Balloon Flight* (Dublin, 2010). For other accounts, see Brown, 'French Scientific Innovation'; F.E. Dixon, 'Ballooning in Dublin', *Dublin Historical Record*, 14, 1 (June 1955), pp.2–11.

94. MacMahon, *Ascend or Die*, pp.167–81; quoted in ibid, p.181.

95. Ibid., pp.182–5; *The Asiatic Journal & Monthly Miscellany* (London, 1824), p.101.

96. Morgan, *O'Briens and O'Flahertys*, vol. 3, p.129; Daunt, *Ireland and her Agitators*, p.118; J.E. Walsh, *Ireland Sixty Years Ago*, pp.17–18.

6. Daly's Club, 'Buck' Whaley and the Cherokees

1. *FJ*, 15–17 1784, 24–26 June 1784.

2. *DIB*, vol. 9, p.266.

3. R.B. McDowell, 'Parliamentary Independence, 1782–9', in T.W. Moody and W.E. Vaughan (eds), *A New History of Ireland IV: Eighteenth-Century Ireland 1691–1800* (Oxford, 1986), p.274; *DIB*, vol. 9, p.266.

4. In 1786 Fitzgerald was tried and executed for his part in the murder of Patrick Randle McDonnell: Kelly, *'That Damn'd Thing'*, p.157; *DIB*, vol. 3, p.844.

5. Martyn J. Powell, 'The Society of Free Citizens and Other Popular Political Clubs', in Kelly and Powell (eds), *Clubs and Societies*, pp.257–8; quoted in ibid., p.257.

6. Sir Lewis Namier and John Brooke, *The History of Parliament: The House of Commons 1754–1790* (London, 1964), vol. 3, p.160; Countess of Drogheda, *The Family of Moore* (Dublin, 1906), p.131.

7. Horace Walpole to Lady Ossory, 12 November 1784, in Lewis et al. (eds), *Walpole Correspondence*, vol. 33, p.447; Lady Mary Coke, quoted in ibid., p.447n.

8. Powell, '"Beef, Claret and Communication"', pp.359, 363.

9. R.B. McDowell, *Land and Learning: Two Irish Clubs* (Dublin, 1993), p.15.

10. Montgomery, 'Old Dublin Clubs', p.39.

11. See, for instance, Sir Edward Sullivan (ed.), *Buck Whaley's Memoirs Including His Journey to Jerusalem . . .* (London, 1906), pp.273–4.

12. Charles Lever, *The Knight of Gwynne* (London, 1872), pp.77–84.

13. *DIB*, vol. 6, p.620; *ODNB*, vol. 38, p.917; Johnston-Liik, *History of the Irish Parliament*, vol. 5, p.294; Drogheda, *Family of Moore*, p.132.

14. Lyons (ed.), *Memoirs of Mrs. Leeson*, pp.216–17; *Celebrated Mrs. Pilkington's Jests*, pp.47–8. On William Alexander English, see Kelly, *'That Damn'd Thing'*, pp.150–1; Johnston-Liik, *History of the Irish Parliament*, vol. 4, pp.113–14.

15. McDowell, *Land and Learning*, p.15; R.B. McDowell, 'Ireland in 1800', in Moody and Vaughan (eds), *New History of Ireland IV*, p.684.

16. Sullivan (ed.), *Buck Whaley's Memoirs*, p.8. Richard Chapel Whaley is sometimes also identified as a member of the Dublin Hellfire Club. This may result from a confusion of father and son.

17. Ibid., pp.10–32.
18. Ibid., p.34. That St Leger and Whaley knew one another is clear from the latter's memoirs, where Whaley refers to a gambling session in England to which he was accompanied by 'Col St L—': ibid., p.273.
19. Sullivan (ed.), *Buck Whaley's Memoirs*, p.34. The Marquis of Grandison promised to pay Whaley £455 should he succeed in completing the journey and issued a promissory note to that effect on 22 February 1788 (NLI, Ms. 10,750). However, as this was only a small proportion of the total amount staked, there must have been a large number of significant individual wagers.
20. Sullivan (ed.), *Buck Whaley's Memoirs*, passim.
21. Ibid., p.270.
22. *DIB*, vol. 9, pp.864–5; Sullivan (ed.), *Buck Whaley's Memoirs*, p.xxviii.
23. See, for instance, *Notes and Queries* (Series 3), 2 (23 August 1862), p.149; *Weekly Irish Times*, 24 December 1904. More recently, Whaley appears in Mia Gallagher's novel *HellFire*, set in present-day Dublin. For the protagonist, Lucy Dolan, he is a near-mythical figure who gambled with the Devil to acquire his money, his townhouse and 'his lodge in the country they useta call the HellFire Club': Gallagher, *HellFire: A Novel* (London, 2007), p.70. Whaley is also commemorated by the Dublin nightclub that bears his name, situated not far from his old residence on St Stephen's Green.
24. Price (ed.), *Eighteenth-Century Antiquary*, p.43.
25. 'Moore', *Staff Officer*, vol. 1, pp.137–8.
26. Morgan, *O'Briens and O'Flahertys*, vol. 3, p.129.
27. *FJ*, 28 February–1 March 1792, 17–20 March 1792.
28. *WHM*, April 1792, p.289.
29. 'Moore', *Staff Officer*, vol. 1, p.137. These colours were known as the 'Devil's livery' (see *DEP*, 25 January 1780). In a fictional account of the Dublin Hellfire Club written in the nineteenth century, the Devil's livery as worn by a servant of the club is described as 'a black coat with red cuffs and collar black vest red small clothes and black hose': [Michael Banim], 'Record of H–l F–e [Hell Fire] Club', NLI, Ms 25,527 (2).
30. 'Moore', *Staff Officer*, vol. 1, p.137.
31. *FJ*, 29–31 March 1792.
32. J[ohn] Long, *Voyages and Travels of an Indian Interpreter and Trader, Describing the Manners and Customs of the North American Indians...* (London, 1791); William Bartram, *Travels through North and South Carolina, Georgia, East and West Florida, the Cherokee Country...* (London, 1792).
33. *The Times*, 30 October 1790, 1 November 1790, 27 December 1790, 18 March 1791; *FJ*, 26 February–1 March 1791. Bowles's memoirs were published early in 1791. See *The Times*, 20 January 1791; *Authentic Memoirs of William Augustus Bowles, Esquire, Ambassador from the United Nations of Creeks and Cherokees...* (London, 1791).
34. *Finn's Leinster Journal*, 10–13 November 1790.
35. *FJ*, 13–15 March 1792; *WHM*, April 1792, p.290.
36. Members of the club performed in a 1793 production of *The Beggar's Opera* (see Gilbert, *History of the City of Dublin*, vol. 1, p.87) and appeared in performances

at the Music Hall in Fishamble Street: see Lady Morgan, *Lady Morgan's Memoirs: Autobiography, Diaries and Correspondence* (London, 1862), vol. 1, pp.113–14; Herbert, *Irish Varieties*, p.259.

37. Lord, *Hell-Fire Clubs*, p.35; Allen, *Clubs of Augustan London*, pp.105–18. See also Statt, 'Case of the Mohocks', p.179.

38. 'Moore', *Staff Officer*, vol. 1, pp.137–8; O'Reilly, *Reminiscences*, vol. 3, pp.276–7.

39. Johnston-Liik, *History of the Irish Parliament*, vol. 6, pp.14–16.

40. Ibid., vol. 3, pp.345, 349, 355–6; Malcomson, *Pursuit of the Heiress*, p.89; quoted in ibid, p.89.

41. Lyons (ed.), *Memoirs of Mrs. Leeson*, p.130.

42. Morgan, *Memoirs*, vol. 1, p.114; Barrington, *Personal Sketches*, p.91.

43. O'Reilly, *Reminiscences*, vol. 3, p.277; *DIB*, vol. 6, p.424; O'Reilly, *Reminiscences*, vol. 3, p.278.

44. O'Reilly, *Reminiscences*, vol. 3, p.278; R.G.Thorne (ed.), *The History of Parliament: The House of Commons 1790–1820* (London, 1986), vol. 4, pp.569–70; *DIB*, vol. 6, pp.424–5.

45. MacDougall, *Sketches of Irish Political Characters*, p.56; G.E.C., *Complete Peerage*, vol. 3, pp.411–12; Johnston-Liik, *History of the Irish Parliament*, vol. 3, p.323.

46. Quoted in Johnston-Liik, *History of the Irish Parliament*, vol. 3, pp.453–4.

47. G.E.C., *Complete Peerage*, vol. 5, pp.100–11. In October 1789, Erroll was found guilty of assaulting Philip Glenville at the Theatre Royal on Crow Street and fined five marks (*FJ*, 24–27 October 1789).

48. Johnston-Liik, *History of the Irish Parliament*, vol. 4, p.130; *Georgian Society Records*, vol. 4, pp.93–4; Johnston-Liik, *History of the Irish Parliament*, vol. 3, p.402.

49. Burtchaell and Sadleir (eds), *Alumni Dublinensis*, vol. 3, p.871; Lyons (ed.), *Memoirs of Mrs. Leeson*, p.112.

50. *DIB*, vol. 1, pp.469, 463–4, 467–8.

51. *WHM*, April 1792, p.289; *FJ*, 13–15 March 1792; 'Moore', *Staff Officer*, vol. 1, p.137. The *Hibernian Magazine* elsewhere described the uniform as being 'of red and blue' (*WHM*, May 1792, p.475). A Dame Street hosier was employed to make matching stockings – 'black, with red clocks, curiously designed': *FJ*, 29–31 March 1792.

52. O'Reilly, *Reminiscences*, vol. 3, pp.278–9.

53. The caricatures, entitled *How to Ride with Elegance thro' the Streets* and *A Pair of Polished Gentlemen*, were published in London by H. Humphrey in 1800 and 1801 respectively. My thanks to James Kelly for bringing this to my attention. At least two other likenesses of Montague Mathew are also extant: a drawing by James Petrie reproduced in Barrington's *Historic Memoirs of Ireland*, vol. 1, p.337 (a print of which is in the National Gallery, NGI 10,936), and a full-length etching showing Mathew declaiming (NGI 10,659).

54. O'Reilly, *Reminiscences*, vol. 3, p.279.

55. *WHM*, April 1792, pp.289–90.

56. Jean Agnew (ed.), *The Drennan-McTier Letters* (Dublin, 1998–99), vol. 1, p.575; Kelly, 'That Damn'd Thing', pp.203, 208, 241–2.

57. 'Moore', *Staff Officer*, vol. 1, p.137.

58. *WHM*, May 1792, p.475; *DEP*, 24 March 1792.

59. McDowell, 'Ireland in 1800', pp.669–70.

60. Ian Campbell Ross, 'The Early Years of the Dublin Lying-In Hospital', in Ian Campbell Ross (ed.), *Public Virtue, Public Love: The Early Years of the Dublin Lying-In Hospital* (Dublin, 1986), p.50; T. Percy C. Kirkpatrick, *The Book of the Rotunda Hospital: An Illustrated History of the Dublin Lying-In Hospital . . .* (London, 1913), pp.95–104.

61. Minutes of meeting, 24 December 1791, in Rotunda Minute Book, 1756–98, p.500, NLI, P. 5646.

62. Minutes of meeting, 3 February 1792, in ibid., p.505.

63. De Latocnaye, *A Frenchman's Walk through Ireland 1796–7*, trans. John Stevenson (Belfast, 1984), p.24.

64. *DEP*, 18 February 1792.

65. *WHM*, April 1792, pp.289, 290.

66. *FJ*, 9–11 February 1792; Minutes of meeting, 20 February 1792, in Rotunda Minute Book, p.508; *HJ*, 5 March 1792.

67. *HJ*, 11 April 1792; *DEP*, 12 April 1792.

68. *WHM*, May 1792, p.475; *WHM*, April 1792, p.290.

69. Minutes of meeting, 10 April 1792 in Rotunda Minute Book, p.511; Minutes of meeting, 17 April 1792 in ibid., p.512; *DEP*, 24 April 1792.

70. Minutes of meeting, 10 April 1792 in Rotunda Minute Book, p.511; *WHM*, April 1792, p.290.

71. Minutes of meeting, 17 April 1792 in Rotunda Minute Book, p.512; see also *HJ*, 18 April 1792; *FDJ*, 17–19 April 1792.

72. *WHM*, April 1792, p.290.

73. *FJ*, 24–26 April 1792. On Miss Groves, see Lyons (ed.), *Memoirs of Mrs. Leeson*, pp.192–3, 198.

74. *FJ*, 5–8 May 1792, 13–16 October 1792.

75. *DEP*, 31 March 1792; *HJ*, 30 March 1792.

76. *FDJ*, 26–28 April 1792; *FJ*, 24–26 April 1792. See also James Kelly, 'The Bar Club, 1787–93: A Dining Club Case Study', in Kelly and Powell (eds), *Clubs and Societies*, p.390.

77. See Kelly, '*That Damn'd Thing*', pp.230–1, 238–9.

78. *WHM*, April 1792, facing p.289; *FJ*, 17–19 May 1792.

79. *FDJ*, 26–28 April 1792; *DEP*, 3 June 1792.

80. Morgan, *Memoirs*, vol. 1, p.114. Residence at Kilkenny did not guarantee a quiet life. Around 1793, Lord Thurles, his father and his brother were arraigned for breaking the windows of Dr Duffy, a Kilkenny apothecary who had offended the family. They were successfully defended by Jonah Barrington, who was conscious that he had rendered a considerable service: 'The conviction of the Earl of Ormonde for a nocturnal outrage in his own town, would have been to him a source of the utmost dismay.' Barrington, *Personal Sketches*, pp.88–91.

81. 'Moore', *Staff Officer*, vol. 1, p.138.

82. A.P.W. Malcomson, *Archbishop Charles Agar: Churchmanship and Politics in Ireland, 1760–1810* (Dublin, 2002), p.131.

83. Letter to Edward Cooke, 26 May 1798, NAI, Rebellion Papers, 620/36/72; Thomas Pakenham, *The Year of Liberty: The Story of the Great Irish Rebellion of 1798*

(London, 2000), pp.310–11; Edward Cooke to William Wickham, 31 August 1798, in Charles Ross (ed.), *Correspondence of Charles, First Marquis Cornwallis* (London, 1859), vol. 2, p.395. The loyalty of the Kilkenny militia was questionable; United Irishmen were believed to have infiltrated its ranks. See David Ryan, 'Disaffection and Rebellious Conspiracy in the Loughrea area, 1791–1804', in Joseph Forde, Christina Cassidy, Paul Manzor and David Ryan (eds), *The District of Loughrea, Vol. 1: History 1791–1918* (Loughrea, Co. Galway, 2003), p.19.

84. Johnston-Liik, *History of the Irish Parliament*, vol. 3, p.355; Barrington, *Personal Sketches*, p.91.

85. *Georgian Society Records*, vol. 4, pp.93–4; Johnston-Liik, *History of the Irish Parliament*, vol. 4, pp.130–1.

86. Thorne, *History of Parliament*, vol. 4, pp.568–70; O'Reilly, *Reminiscences*, vol. 3, p.281.

87. *WHM*, October 1792, p.382; Johnston-Liik, *History of the Irish Parliament*, vol. 3, pp.402–3.

88. Johnston-Liik, *History of the Irish Parliament*, vol. 5, pp.210–11; Thorne, *History of Parliament*, vol. 4, 568–9; O'Reilly, *Reminiscences*, vol. 3, pp.279–81.

89. *ODNB*, vol. 13, pp.76–8.

90. Kelly, 'Bar Club', p.377; Kirkpatrick, *Rotunda Hospital*, p.125.

91. 'Moore', *Staff Officer*, vol. 1, p.137.

92. Morgan, *O'Briens and O'Flahertys*, vol. 3, p.129; J. Roderick O'Flanagan, *The Irish Bar: Comprising Anecdotes, Bon-Mots, and Biographical Sketches of the Bench and Bar of Ireland*, 2nd edn (London, 1879), p.6.

7. The Hellfire Myth

1. *Gentleman's and Citizen's Almanack, for the Year ... 1799 ...* (Dublin, 1799); John James McGregor, *New Picture of Dublin: Comprehending a History of the City ...* (Dublin, 1821), p.311.

2. Kelly, '*That Damn'd Thing*', p.223.

3. Peter Somerville-Large, *Dublin: The Fair City*, rev. edn (London, 1996), p.174.

4. See NLI, PD 450 TA (before) and PD 451 TA (after).

5. Gearóid Ó Tuathaigh, *Ireland before the Famine 1798–1848* (Dublin, 1990), p.37.

6. McDowell, 'Ireland in 1800', p.712.

7. James Kelly, 'The Decline of Duelling and the Emergence of the Middle Class in Ireland', in Fintan Lane (ed.), *Politics, Society and the Middle Class in Modern Ireland* (Basingstoke, 2010), pp.99–100, p.90.

8. Kelly, '*That Damn'd Thing*', pp.223–5; McGregor, *New Picture of Dublin*, pp.311–12.

9. W.E.H. Lecky, *A History of Ireland in the Eighteenth Century* (London, 1913), vol. 1, pp.323–4; J.E. Walsh, *Ireland Sixty Years Ago*, p.17.

10. Pilkington, *Real Story*, pp.143–5; Gilbert, *History of the City of Dublin*, vol. 3, pp.252–4.

11. Daunt, *Ireland and her Agitators*, p.118.

12. Morgan, *O'Briens and O'Flahertys*, vol. 2, p.37; vol. 3, p.129; Gerald Griffin, *The Collegians: A Tale of Garryowen* (Dublin, 1847), pp.40–1.

13. *Tales and Stories of Ireland: By Carleton, Lover and Mrs Hall* (Halifax, 1852), pp.103–23; William Carleton, *Tales and Stories of the Irish Peasantry* (New York, 1860), pp.249–50.

14. Odell, *Essay on Duelling*, p.19; *Notes and Queries* (Series 2), 10, 28 July 1860), p.77.

15. Thomas Taylor, *An Answer to Second Part of Mr Paine's Age of Reason* (Manchester, 1796), p.55. See also Bernard Escarbelt, 'Michael Banim: "The Hell Fire Club"', *Études Irlandaises*, 1 (1976), p.54; *Tales and Stories of Ireland*, p.105.

16. O'Reilly, *Reminiscences*, vol. 3, pp.289–90.

17. *Hibernicus; Or Memoirs of an Irishman, Now in America* (Pittsburgh, 1828), p.88.

18. J.E. Walsh, *Ireland Sixty Years Ago*, pp.17–18; R. Chambers (ed.), *The Book of Days: A Miscellany of Popular Antiquities in Connection with the Calendar* (London and Edinburgh, 1863–64), vol. 1, p.559; Gaskin, *Varieties of Irish History*, pp.418–9; Montgomery, 'Old Dublin Clubs', p.42.

19. *Glasgow, Past and Present: Illustrated in Dean of Guild Court Reports, and in the Reminiscences and Communications of Senex, Aliquis, J.B. &c.* (Glasgow, 1851), vol. 1, p.208.

20. Unpublished essays of R.R. Madden, RIA, Ms. 24 O 6 (157–201). This version was published in 1976: see Escarbelt, 'Michael Banim', pp.51–61; 'Record of H–l F–e [Hell Fire] Club', NLI, Ms. 25,527(2).

21. 'Record of H–l F–e [Hell Fire] Club.'

22. E. Catterson Smith, 'Romances of Illustrious Irish Houses: No. 1. – How an Irish Peerage was Lost', *Lady of the House*, 15 September 1891, p.9; Hammond, *Hell-Fire Club*, pp.8–10; Irish Folklore Collection, Schools' Manuscripts for Glenasmole School, Rathfarnham Parish, Co. Dublin, 1 October 1937–20 December 1938, IFC UCD, 795:15. See also Irish Countrywomen's Association, *A Local History of Ballymun and Glasnevin* (Dublin, 1985), p.4.

23. Chambers, *Book of Days*, vol. 1, p.559; Peter, *Sketches of Old Dublin*, p.282; Hammond, *Hell-Fire Club*, pp.10–16; *Irish Times*, 27 April 1931; Jones, *Clubs of Georgian Rakes*, pp.76–7.

24. The ingredients for scaltheen were identified as 'half a pint of whiskey, half a pound of butter and six eggs'. Another recipe involved boiling whiskey, water, sugar, butter and pepper together: George A. Little, *Malachi Horan Remembers* (Dublin, 1943), pp.52, 153. See also Diarmaid Ó Muirithe, *Words We Don't Use (Much Anymore)* (Dublin, 2011), pp.263–4.

25. Ó Muirithe, *Words We Don't Use*, p.264.

26. Little, *Malachi Horan Remembers*, p.52.

27. Chambers, *Book of Days*, vol. 1, p.559; Hammond, *Hell-Fire Club*, p.7.

28. Chambers, *Book of Days*, vol. 1, p.559.

29. Ibid., p.559; E.L. Murphy, 'The Hell Fire' (undated newspaper cutting, c. early twentieth century), NLI, Ms. 11,664. See also Hammond, *Hell-Fire Club*, pp.6–7.

30. See Kelly, 'Bar Club', p.374.

31. See Lord, *Hell-Fire Clubs*, p.54.

32. Wharton's father acquired the estate in 1692 through his marriage to Lucy, daughter of Sir Adam Loftus, Viscount Lisburne: *ODNB*, vol. 58, p.381.

33. *ODNB*, vol. 58, p.367; E. Beresford Chancellor, *The Lives of the Rakes* (London, 1924–25), vol. 3, pp.213–14; 'A List of Deeds & Papers Relating to the Title and

Purchase of Rathfarnham Estate Delivered from Right Honble William Conolly Esqr. The [—] Day of June 1724—', NLI, Conolly Papers, P. 6796; Boylan, 'Conollys of Castletown', pp.4–6; Patrick Walsh and A.P.W. Malcomson (eds), *The Conolly Archive* (Dublin, 2010), pp.x, 61–2.

34.　According to Austin Cooper, the house was 'built by the late Mr Connolly', though it is unclear whether he meant the original William 'Speaker' Conolly, or his nephew, also William, who inherited the estate following his uncle's death in 1729: Price (ed.), *Eighteenth Century Antiquary*, p.43.

35.　Michael Fewer, 'The Hellfire Club, Co. Dublin', *History Ireland*, 18, 3 (May–June 2010), p.29.

36.　The outline of this cairn, approximately twenty-six yards in diameter, is still visible. As Liam Price indicated, it may have encompassed a souterrain or cist: Christiaan Corlett and Mairéad Weaver (eds), *The Price Notebooks* (Dublin, 2002), vol. 2, pp.373–4. See also William Domville Handcock, *History and Antiquities of Tallaght*, 2nd edn (Dublin, 1899), pp.86–90.

37.　Handcock, *Tallaght*, p.88; Paul Ferguson, *The A to Z of Georgian Dublin: John Rocque's Maps of the City in 1756 and the County in 1760* (Lympne Castle, Kent, 1998), pp.49–50.

38.　Fewer, 'Hellfire Club', p.29; James Howley, *The Follies and Garden Buildings of Ireland* (New Haven, CT, and London, 1993), p.209.

39.　NLI, Ms. 25,527(1), pp.152, 154. See Francis Elrington Ball, *A History of the County Dublin* (Dublin, 1905), vol. 3, p.40, for a cruder version of the front view. Sir William Betham's sketch of 1841 depicts the lodge in a ruinous condition with a section of the enclosing semicircular wall still in situ: NLI, PD TX 1959 (60). See Plate 30.

40.　This claim has repeatedly been made, most recently in a television documentary on the Dublin Hellfire Club broadcast on TG4 on 8 December 2011 and 4 January 2012. See also Ball, *History of the County Dublin*, vol. 3, p.40; *Irish Times*, 25 September 1963; Fewer, 'Hellfire Club', p.29. In fact, Cobbe died of a fever in Montpellier, France, on 15 July 1751: *FDJ*, 10–13 August 1751; *Exshaw's Magazine*, August 1751, p.447.

41.　Handcock, *Tallaght*, p.87; Weston St John Joyce, *The Neighbourhood of Dublin*, 2nd edn (Dublin, 1921), p.121. Dollymount House was constructed by Henry Loftus, 1st Earl of Ely. A marginal note in the manuscript version of Handcock's *History and Antiquities of Tallaght* suggests that a hellfire club met there 'under the presidency of Lord Ely': NLI, Ms. 25,527(1), p.46. However, there is no contemporary evidence to verify such a claim, and Handcock himself chose to omit it from the published version of his work.

42.　'Rent Roll of the Estate of the Rt. Honble Thomas Conolly Esqr...for the Half Year Ended at 1 Nov. 1764', NLI, Conolly Papers, P. 6796.

43.　Price (ed.), *Eighteenth Century Antiquary*, p.43.

44.　Peter O'Shaughnessy (ed.), *Rebellion in Wicklow: General Joseph Holt's Personal Account of 1798* (Dublin, 1998), p.56. On the United Irish presence in the Mountpelier area, see *FJ*, 7 July 1798, 21 July 1798.

45.　*FJ*, 8 December 1801. Incidentally, White also purchased Luttrellstown Castle, the one-time residence of the Dublin Hellfire Club member Simon Luttrell, in

1799: *DIB*, vol. 9, p.892.

46. [J. Coad], *The Angling Excursions of Gregory Greendrake, Esq. in Ireland* (Dublin, 1826), p.122.

47. Handcock, *Tallaght*, 2nd edn, p.88. It is uncertain which member of the club 'lived not far off'. There may have been some confusion between Lord Santry and his uncle, Sir Compton Domvile, whose residence at Templeogue was within five miles of Mountpelier.

48. See, for instance, W.J. Fitzpatrick, *The Life of the Very Rev. Thomas N. Burke, OP* (London, 1885), pp.183, 215; Smith, 'Romances of Illustrious Irish Houses: No. 1', p.9; 'How I Lost Nora, or a Night on Mountpelier', *Weekly Irish Times*, 17 December 1892, 24 December 1892; Montgomery, 'Old Dublin Clubs', p.133; Ball, *History of the County Dublin*, vol. 3, p.40; Joyce, *Neighbourhood of Dublin*, p.123; Hammond, *Hell-Fire Club*.

49. 'A Letter to the...Bishop of *Cloyne*', in *Harleian Miscellany*, vol. 3, p.173. A similar story was told in a 2005 Dublin radio programme on the Hellfire Club, although in this version a cat rather than a goose is said to have come down the chimney ('City Edition', Newstalk 106, 8 August 2005). Thanks to Declan Carty for providing me with an audio copy of this programme.

50. Irish Folklore Collection, Glenasmole School, IFC UCD, 795:15.

51. Lords Justices to Lord Lieutenant, 10 November 1738, PRONI, Wilmot Papers, T/3019/180. Domvile received an annual payment of £50 for maintaining the water course running through his estate at Templeogue, and a further £100 'for widening the course and putting the whole into a state of thorough repair': Dublin Assembly Rolls, 1731, in Gilbert (ed.), *Calendar of Ancient Records*, vol. 8, pp.34–6. There is a manuscript map of the waterworks at Templeogue House in the National Library of Ireland: NLI, 16 G. 42(12).

52. Irish Folklore Collection, Schools Manuscripts, Edmonstown School, Co. Dublin, 14 June 1934–11 November 1939, IFC UCD, 797:52. For similar accounts, see IFC UCD, 797: 202, 231.

53. Éilís Ní Anluain, 'The Cardplayers and the Devil', *Béaloideas*, 59 (1991), pp.45–54; Rose-Marie and Rainer Hagen, *What Great Paintings Say* (Köln, 2003), vol. 2, p.236. Thanks to Professor Daithí Ó hÓgáin and Emer Ní Cheallaigh for providing information on this subject.

54. See Peter, *Sketches of Old Dublin*, p.282; Hammond, *Hell-Fire Club*, pp.10–16; *Irish Times*, 27 April 1931; D.A. Chart, *The Story of Dublin* (London, 1907), p.309 (imitation of hell); IFC UCD, 795:15, *Irish Times*, 25 September 1963; Richard Jones, *Haunted Britain and Ireland* (London, 2001), pp.124–5 (burning of servant); Jones, *Clubs of Georgian Rakes*, pp.76–7 (cat and the clergyman).

55. See, for instance, newspaper cuttings collected in NLI, Ms. 11,664.

56. *Official Catalogue, Loan Museum of Art Treasures, Industrial Exhibition Palace, Dublin, 1873* (Dublin, 1873), p.153; Henry Naylor, 'Eighteenth Century Dublin Silver (Part 1)', *Dublin Historical Record*, 12 (1951), p.17; Ida Delamer and Conor O'Brien, *500 Years of Irish Silver: An Exhibition at the National Museum of Ireland* (Bray, Co. Wicklow, 2005), p.120.

57. *Official Catalogue, Loan Museum of Art Treasures*, p.153; Ball, 'Loughlinstown', p.82; Declaration of Sir Compton Domvile, 6 August 1764, NLI, Ms. 10,811.

58. Kurt Ticher Papers, NAI, 2002/KT/199(1); Tony Sweeney, *Irish Stuart Silver* (Blackrock, Co. Dublin, 1995), pp.110–11; *Irish Times*, 5 February 1937; Naylor, 'Eighteenth Century Dublin Silver', p.17.

59. *Re Sir Compton Meade Domvile, Bart., Deceased. Catalogue...*, pp.5–6.

60. William F. Dennehy, *Record: The Irish International Exhibition, 1907* (Dublin, 1909), p.clviii.

61. Miles Collection, Wadsworth Atheneum, 1971.102. My thanks to Thomas Sinsteden for identifying the current whereabouts of this item and for his kind responses to my queries on hellfire club punchbowls.

62. *Irish Times*, 30 April 1904; *Georgian Society Records*, vol. 5 (back cover). For Alfred E. Jones, see his entry in the Irish Architectural Archive's online *Dictionary of Irish Architects 1720–1940*, www.dia.ie/architects/view/2840 (accessed 3 August 2011).

63. Dennehy, *Irish International Exhibition*, p.clix.

64. Philadelphia Museum of Art, George H. Lorimer Collection, 1953-29-20. See Elzea, *Glass*, pp.5, 24.

65. AP [Ada Peter], 'The Hell-Fire Club', *Weekly Irish Times*, 6 August 1904.

66. *Catalogue of Pictures and Other Works of Art in the National Gallery of Ireland*, p.383; Chart, *Story of Dublin*, p.252. The painting has recently been restored.

67. *National Gallery of Ireland Acquisitions 1986–88*, p.69.

68. See, for instance, Connolly, *Religion, Law and Power*; Barnard, *Abduction of a Limerick Heiress*; Ted Murphy, *A Kingdom of Wine: A Celebration of Ireland's Winegeese* (Cloghroe, Co. Cork, 2005).

69. The auction took place on 12 October 1956. In the accompanying catalogue, the painting is given the title *Portraits of W. Domville, Esq., and a Group of His Friends*, and attributed to J. Fuller. However, annotations to a copy of the catalogue held by the National Portrait Gallery in London indicate that the curator who visited the sale doubted that attribution. The annotations also estimate the date of the work as between 1710 and 1720: *Catalogue of the Collection of Pictures...the Property of the Late Lucius O'Callaghan...* (London, 1956), p.29; email from Paul Cox, Assistant Curator, National Portrait Gallery, 22 July 2009, in response to author's query.

70. *Old Master Paintings...which will be sold on Wednesday, July 15, 1981...* (New York, 1981), p.59. An inquiry to Christie's New York offices as to the painting's current whereabouts proved inconclusive.

8. Conclusion

1. Foster, *Modern Ireland*, p.175.

2. Barnard, 'Dublin Society', p.58; Kelly and Powell, 'Introduction', in Kelly and Powell (eds), *Clubs and Societies*, pp.17–18, 30.

3. Statt, 'Case of the Mohocks', pp.185–6. Even today, society affords a certain tolerance to upper-class excess. It is perhaps instructive that the current British Prime Minister, Chancellor of the Exchequer and Mayor of London are all ex-members of Oxford University's controversial Bullingdon Club, which distinguishes itself through wanton acts of vandalism and the wreckage of restaurants and dining rooms.

4. Dickson, *Arctic Ireland*; Connolly, *Religion, Law and Power*, p.48.

Bibliography

Primary Sources

Manuscript Sources
Birr Castle Archives, County Offaly
Rosse Papers. B/2/1–2, 5.

British Library, London
Letter of Duke of Newcastle to Simon Luttrell, 25 March 1759. Add. Ms. 32889 f.237.
'The Right Hon Richard Earl of Ross, in the Kingdom of Ireland, Appellant. Elizabeth Worsop, otherwise Wood Widow, Worsop Bush and Noah Webb, Esqrs. – Respondents.' Add. Ms. 36154, ff.160–3.

Department of Irish Folklore, University College Dublin
Irish Folklore Collection: Schools' Manuscripts for Askeaton School, Co. Limerick. IFC 503; Glenasmole School, Co. Dublin. IFC 795; Edmonstown School, Co. Dublin. IFC 797.

Dublin City Library and Archive
Hellfire Club File.
'A Survey of Cork Hill & Part of Castle Street from the End of Crane Lane to the Castle Gate' [1710]. Gilbert Manuscripts, Ms. 195.

The National Archives, Kew, London
'Deposition of Edward Palmer, Coleshire, Co. of Warwick', Depositions Taken at Sutton Coldfield 27 September 1762. Richard Bisse Riland, Clerk v. Simon Luttrell Esq. E134/3Geo3/Mich1.
'The Joint and Several Answers of ... Richard Earl of Ross[e] ... and ... Lady Elizabeth Parsons his Daughter ... to the Bill of Complaint of ... William Lord Berkely of Stratton', 5 December 1740. C11/2081/15.
State Papers. SP 36.

National Archives of Ireland, Dublin
Calendar of Miscellaneous Letters Prior to 1760. 2/447/23.

Kurt Ticher Papers. 2002/KT/199(1).
'Lease from Simon Luttrell Esqr. to William Sheppard Esqr. of Parts of the Lands of Esker in the Co. of Dublin . . . from First May 1735 . . .'. M. 7036(9).
Pembroke Estate Papers. 97/46/1.
'The Several Answer of Edward Kean...to the Amended Bill of Complaint of the Right Honble Richard, Earl of Rosse . . .', 1752. M. 5762(1).

National Gallery of Ireland, Dublin
Hellfire Club File.

National Library of Ireland, Dublin
Affidavit Relating to the Death of Laughlin Murphy, 1738. D. 23,076.
Conolly Papers. P. 6796 (Microfilm).
Copy by John Lodge, c. 1760, of an Act, c. 1719, to Allow Payment of Creditors of Richard, Earl of Rosse. Thomas Kemmis Papers. Ms. 15,419.
Correspondence of and Documents Relating to Sir Compton Domvile, William Domvile, Edward Madden and Lord Santry, 1740–49. Ms. 11,793(1–20).
Declaration of Sir Compton Domvile, 6 August 1764. Ms. 10,811.
Deeds Relative to Appointments of Richard St George. D. 22,681–7.
Domvile Papers. Mss. 9367, 9370, 9371, 9381, 9383 and 11,840.
John Bayly Letter-Book. P. 4068 (Microfilm).
Letter of Henry Ponsonby to Viscount Duncannon, 10 October 1744. Ms. 22,735.
Manuscript Papers of William Domville Handcock. Ms. 25,527(1–2).
Marquis of Grandison Promissory Note, 22 February 1788. Ms. 10,750.
Newspaper Cuttings on Dublin Clubs and Societies. Ms. 11,664.
Orrery Papers. P. 792 (Microfilm).
Peg Plunket, or the Dublin Courtezans: A Musical Whim, in Two Acts. P. 544. Microfilm. Original in British Library. Add. Ms. 25,992.
Plan of Templeogue Waterworks. 16 G. 42 (12).
Rotunda Minute Book, 1756–98. P. 5646 (Microfilm).

Public Record Office of Northern Ireland
Transcripts of State Papers Relating to Ireland in the Public Record Office [London] 1736–38. T/778/1.
Typed Copy of the Succession of Colonels from Quarters of the Army in Ireland, 1739. T/470/14.
Wilmot Papers. T/3019.

Royal Irish Academy
Unpublished Essays of R.R. Madden. Ms. 24 O 6 (157–201).

Trinity College Dublin
Journal of Daniel Augustus Beaufort, July–August 1788. Ms. 4029.
Minutes of the Board, Trinity College Dublin. MUN V/5/3.
Notes on Burdy's *Life of Skelton*. Ms. 1091.
Register of Censures and Degrees, Trinity College Dublin, 1740–1890. MUN/V/5/4.

Newspapers and Periodicals:
County Magazine
Dublin Courant
Dublin Evening Post
Dublin Gazette
Dublin Intelligence
Dublin News Letter
Dublin Weekly Journal
Evangelical Magazine
Exshaw's Magazine
Faulkner's Dublin Journal
Finn's Leinster Journal
Freeman's Journal
Gentleman's Magazine
Hibernian Journal
London Gazette
Pue's Occurrences
Saunders' News Letter
The Times
Walker's Hibernian Magazine

Printed Sources, Edited and Calendared Documents

An Abridgement of the Publick Statutes of Ireland, Now in Force and of General Use … , 2 vols (Dublin, 1786).

An Ample Discovery of the Damnable Cabal, Commonly Known by the Name of the Hell-Fire Club, Kept in this City, Since the 17th of March Last … (Dublin, n.d.). The only known copy is in the National Library of Ireland. LO, folder 9/28.

An Analysis of the Philosophical Works of Lord Bolingbroke … to which is Prefixed, a Parallel of Earl Ferrers's Case, with that of Lord Santry … (London, 1760).

R.B., *The Hell-Fire-Club: Kept by a Society of Blasphemers. A Satyr* … (London, 1721).

Barrington, J., *Historic Memoirs of Ireland; Comprising Secret Records of the National Convention, the Rebellion, and the Union* … , new edn, 2 vols (London, 1835).

Barrington, J., *Personal Sketches and Recollections*, reprint (Dublin, 1998).

Bellamy, G.A., *An Apology for the Life of George Anne Bellamy* … , 6 vols (London, 1785).

Berkeley, G., *A Discourse Addressed to Magistrates and Men in Authority Occasioned by the Enormous Licence and Irreligion of the Times* (Cork, 1738).

Berkeley, G.-M., *Literary Relics: Containing Original Letters…* (London, 1789).

Between the Hon. Henry Lawes Luttrell, and Francis M'Farland – Appellants, and the Right Hon. Simon Lord Irnham – Respondent… (London, 1778).

Brooking, C., *The City of Dublin, 1728*, with introduction and notes by Maurice Craig (Dublin, 1983).

Burdy, S., *The Life of the Late Rev. Philip Skelton with Some Curious Anecdotes* (Dublin, 1792).

By-Laws, Rules and Orders, for the Better Regulating of Hackney-Coaches… (Dublin, 1729).

By the Lord Lieutenant and Council of Ireland a Proclamation Promising a Reward for Apprehending Peter Lens, Late of Dublin, Painter (Dublin [1738]).

Cannon, J. (ed.), *The Letters of Junius* (Oxford, 1978).

The Celebrated Mrs. Pilkington's Jests; Or the Cabinet of Wit and Humour..., 2nd edn (London, 1764).

[Combe, W.], *The Diaboliad, a Poem. Dedicated to the Worst Man in His Majesty's Dominions* (London, 1777).

Cork and Orrery, Countess of (ed.), *The Orrery Papers*, 2 vols (London, 1903).

Elias, A.C. (ed.), *Memoirs of Laetitia Pilkington*, 2 vols (Athens, GA, 1997).

An Examination of Certain Abuses, Corruptions, and Enormities in the City of Dublin (Dublin, 1732).

Four Letters Originally Written in French, Relating to the Kingdom of Ireland... (Dublin, 1739).

Gilbert, J.T. and Mulholland Gilbert, R. (eds), *Calendar of Ancient Records of Dublin*, 19 vols (Dublin, 1889–1944).

Hardy, F., *Memoirs of the Political and Private Life of James Caulfield, First Earl of Charlemont*, 2 vols (London, 1812).

The Harleian Miscellany: Or, a Collection of Scarce, Curious and Entertaining Pamphlets and Tracts..., 3 vols (London, 1745).

Hayes, D., *The Works in Verse of Daniel Hayes, Esq. ... ,* 2nd edn (Limerick, 1785).

Hayton, D.W. (ed.), *Letters of Marmaduke Coghill 1722–1738* (Dublin, 2005).

Herbert, J.D., *Irish Varieties, for the Last Fifty Years: Written from Recollections* (London, 1836).

Hibernicus; Or Memoirs of an Irishman, Now in America (Pittsburgh, 1828).

HMC, *The Manuscripts and Correspondence of James, First Earl of Charlemont*, 2 vols (London, 1891–94).

HMC, *Manuscripts of the Earl of Egmont: Diary of Viscount Percival Afterwards First Earl of Egmont*, 3 vols (London, 1920–23).

A Humorous Description of the Manners and Fashions of the Inhabitants of the City of Dublin (Dublin, 1734).

The Irish Blasters: Or, the Votaries of Bacchus (Dublin, 1738).

Jenkinson, C., *Life History and Remarkable Pedigree of the Rt. Hon. Simon, Lord Irnham* (London, 1769).

Journals of the House of Lords, 8 vols (Dublin, 1779–1800).

[King, W.], *The Swan Tripe-Club in Dublin: A Satyr...* (Dublin, 1706).

Leadbeater, M., *The Leadbeater Papers: A Selection from the Mss. and Correspondence of Mary Leadbeater*, 2nd edn, 2 vols (London, 1862).

Lewis, R., *The Dublin Guide; Or a Description of the City of Dublin* (Dublin, [1787]).

Lewis, W.S. et al. (eds), *The Yale Edition of Horace Walpole's Correspondence*, 48 vols (Oxford, 1937–83).

Llanover, Lady (ed.), *The Autobiography and Correspondence of Mary Granville, Mrs Delany*, 2nd series, 3 vols (London, 1861–62).

[Lloyd, E.], *A Description of the City of Dublin in Ireland...by a Citizen of London...* (London, 1732).

Lyons, M. (ed.), *The Memoirs of Mrs Leeson, Madam 1727–1797* (Dublin, 1995).

MacDougall, H., *Sketches of Irish Political Characters, of the Present Day...* (London, 1799).

Madden, S., *Reflections and Resolutions Proper for the Gentlemen of Ireland...* (Dublin, 1738).

McGregor, J.J., *New Picture of Dublin: Comprehending a History of the City...* (Dublin, 1821).

A Miscellany, Containing Several Tracts on Various Subjects (London, 1752).

'Moore, O.', *The Staff Officer; Or, the Soldier of Fortune: A Tale of Real Life*, 3 vols (London, 1831).

Morgan, Lady [S.], *The O'Briens and the O'Flahertys*, 4 vols (London, 1827–28).

Morgan, Lady [S.], *Lady Morgan's Memoirs: Autobiography, Diaries and Correspondence*, 2 vols (London, 1862).

O'C–nn–r [O'Connor], J., *An Essay on the Rosary and Sodality of the Most Holy Name of Jesus...* (Dublin, 1772).

O'Reilly, A., *Reminiscences of an Emigrant Milesian*, 3 vols (London, 1853).

O'Shaughnessy, P. (ed.), *Rebellion in Wicklow: General Joseph Holt's Personal Account of 1798* (Dublin, 1998).

Pilkington, J.C., *The Real Story of John Carteret Pilkington* (London, 1760).

Price, L. (ed.), *An Eighteenth Century Antiquary: The Sketches, Notes and Diaries of Austin Cooper (1759–1830)* (Dublin, 1942).

Sullivan, Sir E. (ed.), *Buck Whaley's Memoirs Including his Journey to Jerusalem...* (London, 1906).

Vertue, G., 'Note Books, III', *Walpole Society*, 22 (1933–34).

Ward, E., *The Secret History of Clubs: Particularly the Kit-Cat, Beef-Stake, Vertuosos, Quacks, Knights of the Golden Fleece, Florists, Beaus, &c ...* (London, 1709).

Wilkes, W., *An Essay on the Existence of a God: Particularly in Answer to Two Atheistical Letters...* (Belfast, 1730).

Woolley, D. (ed.), *The Correspondence of Jonathan Swift*, 4 vols (Frankfurt am Main, 1999–2007).

Worsdale, J., *A Cure for a Scold* (London [1735]). Available in facsimile reprint in Walter H. Rubsamen (arr.), *The Ballad Opera, Vol. 4: The Medical and Legal Professions* (New York and London, 1974).

Secondary Sources

Selected Books and Articles

Allen, R.J., *The Clubs of Augustan London* (Cambridge, MA, 1933).

Ashe, G., *The Hell-Fire Clubs: Sex, Rakes and Libertines*, rev. edn (Stroud, 2005). First published in 1974 as *Do What You Will: A History of Anti-Morality*, and reissued in 2000 as *The Hell-Fire Clubs: A History of Anti-Morality*.

Ball, F.E., *A History of the County Dublin*, 6 vols (Dublin, 1905).

Barnard, T., *The Abduction of a Limerick Heiress: Social and Political Relations in Mid-Eighteenth Century Ireland* (Dublin, 1998).

Barnard, T., 'Hamilton's "Cries of Dublin": The Society and Economy of Mid-Eighteenth-Century Dublin', in Laffan (ed.), *Cries of Dublin &c.* (2003), pp.26–37.

Barnard, T., *A New Anatomy of Ireland: The Irish Protestants, 1649–1770* (London, 2003).

Barnard, T., 'The Dublin Society and Other Improving Societies, 1731–85', in Kelly and Powell (eds), *Clubs and Societies* (2010), pp.53–88.

Berman, D., 'Enlightenment and Counter-Enlightenment in Irish Philosophy', *Archiv für Geschichte der Philosophie* 64 (1982), pp 148–65.

Berman, D., *Berkeley and Irish Philosophy* (London and New York, 2005).

Brown, B.T., 'French Scientific Innovation in Late-Eighteenth-Century Dublin: The Hydrogen Balloon Experiments of Richard Crosbie (1783–1785)', in G. Gargett and G. Sheridan, *Ireland and the French Enlightenment 1700–1800* (London, 1999), pp.107–26.

Cash, A.H., *John Wilkes: The Scandalous Father of Civil Liberty* (New Haven, CT, and London, 2006).

Catterson Smith, E., 'Romances of Illustrious Irish Houses: No. 1: How an Irish Peerage was Lost', *Lady of the House*, 15 September 1891.

Chambers, R. (ed.), *The Book of Days: A Miscellany of Popular Antiquities in Connection with the Calendar*, 2 vols (London & Edinburgh, 1863–64).

Chancellor, E.B., *The Lives of the Rakes*, 6 vols (London, 1924–25).

Chatterton, Lady [G.], *Rambles in the South of Ireland during the Year 1838*, 2 vols (London, 1839).

Chetwode Crawley, W.J., *Caementaria Hibernica: Being the Public Constitutions That Have Served to Hold Together the Freemasons of Ireland*, 3 vols (Dublin, 1895–1900).

Clark, P., *British Clubs and Societies 1580–1800: The Origins of an Associational World* (Oxford, 2000).

Clarke, N., *Queen of the Wits: A Life of Laetitia Pilkington* (London, 2008).

Connolly, S.J., *Religion, Law and Power: The Making of Protestant Ireland 1660–1760* (Oxford, 1992).

Craig, M., *Dublin 1660–1860* (London, 1992). First published 1952.

Crookshank A. and the Knight of Glin, *Irish Portraits 1660–1860* (London [c. 1969]).

Crookshank A. and the Knight of Glin, *The Painters of Ireland c. 1660–1920* (London, 1978).

Crookshank A. and the Knight of Glin, *Ireland's Painters 1600–1940* (Yale, 2002).

Dickson, D., *Arctic Ireland: The Extraordinary Story of the Great Frost and Forgotten Famine of 1740–41* (Belfast, 1997).

Escarbelt, B. 'Michael Banim: "The Hell Fire Club"', *Études Irlandaises* 1 (1976), pp.51–61.

Fagan, P., *The Second City: Portrait of Dublin 1700–1760* (Dublin, 1986).

Fewer, M.,'The Hellfire Club, Co. Dublin', *History Ireland*, 18, 3 (May–June 2010), p.29.

Field, O., *The Kit-Cat Club: Friends Who Imagined a Nation* (London, 2008).

Fitzgerald, C.W., Duke of Leinster, *The Earls of Kildare and their Ancestors from 1057 to 1773*, 2 vols (Dublin, 1858–62).

Fleming, D., 'Public Attitudes to Prostitution in Eighteenth-Century Ireland', *Irish Economic and Social History*, 32 (2005), pp.1–18.

Foster, R.F., *Modern Ireland 1600–1972* (London, 1988).

Garnham, N., *The Courts, Crime and the Criminal Law in Ireland 1692–1760* (Dublin, 1996).

Garnham, N., 'The Trials of James Cotter and Henry, Baron Barry of Santry: Two Case Studies in the Administration of Criminal Justice in Eighteenth-Century Ireland', *Irish Historical Studies*, 31, 123 (May 1999), pp.328–42.

Gaskin, J.J., *Varieties of Irish History: From Ancient and Modern Sources and Original Documents* (Dublin, 1869).

Gilbert, J.T., *A History of the City of Dublin*, 3 vols (Dublin, 1854–59).

Hammond, J.W., *The Hell-Fire Club* (Dublin, n.d.).

Handcock, W.D., *The History and Antiquities of Tallaght*, 2nd edn (Dublin, 1899). First published 1876.

Hayton, D.W., *Ruling Ireland, 1685–1742: Politics, Politicians and Parties* (Woodbridge, 2004).

Howley, J., *The Follies and Garden Buildings of Ireland* (New Haven, CT, and London, 1993).

Jones, L.C., *The Clubs of the Georgian Rakes* (New York, 1942).

Joyce, W.S., *The Neighbourhood of Dublin* (Dublin, 1988). First published 1912.

Kelly, J., *'That Damn'd Thing Called Honour': Duelling in Ireland, 1570–1860* (Cork, 1995).

Kelly, J., *Gallows Speeches from Eighteenth-Century Ireland* (Dublin, 2001).

Kelly, J., *The Ormond and Liberty Boys: Factional Riot in Eighteenth-Century Dublin* (Dublin, 2005).

Kelly, J., 'The Bar Club, 1787–93: A Dining Club Case Study', in Kelly and Powell (eds), *Clubs and Societies* (2010), pp.373–91.

Kelly, J., 'The Decline of Duelling and the Emergence of the Middle Class in Ireland', in F. Lane (ed.), *Politics, Society and the Middle Class in Modern Ireland* (Basingstoke, 2010), pp.89–106.

Kelly, J. and Powell, M.J. (eds), *Clubs and Societies in Eighteenth-Century Ireland* (Dublin, 2010).

Kelly, J. and Powell, M.J. 'Introduction', in Kelly and Powell (eds), *Clubs and Societies* (2010), pp.17–35.

Kirkpatrick, T.P.C., *The Book of the Rotunda Hospital: An Illustrated History of the Dublin Lying-in Hospital . . .* (London, 1913).

Laffan, W. (ed.), *The Cries of Dublin &c. Drawn from the Life by Hugh Douglas Hamilton* (Dublin, 2003).

Laffan, W. (ed.), *Miscelanea Structura Curiosa* (Tralee, Co. Kerry, 2005).

Lecky, W.E.H., *A History of Ireland in the Eighteenth Century*, 5 vols (London, 1913).

Lepper J.H. and Crosslé, P., *History of the Grand Lodge of Free and Accepted Masons of Ireland* (Dublin, 1925).

Lord, E., *The Hell-Fire Clubs: Sex, Satanism and Secret Societies* (London, 2008).

MacDowel Cosgrave, E., 'On Two Maps, Dated 1751 and 1753, of the Essex Bridge District, Dublin', *JRSAI*, 48 (1918), pp.140–9.

MacMahon, B., *Ascend or Die: Richard Crosbie Pioneer of Balloon Flight* (Dublin, 2010).

Malcomson, A.P.W., *Nathaniel Clements: Government and the Governing Elite in Ireland, 1725–75* (Dublin, 2005).

Malcomson, A.P.W., *The Pursuit of the Heiress: Aristocratic Marriage in Ireland 1740–1840* (Belfast, 2006).

Maxwell, C., *Dublin under the Georges 1714–1850* (London, 1936).

McBride, I., *Eighteenth-Century Ireland: The Isle of Slaves* (Dublin, 2009).

McCracken, J.L., 'The Social Structure and Social Life, 1714–60', in Moody and Vaughan (eds), *New History of Ireland IV* (1986), pp.31–56.

McDowell, R.B., 'Ireland in 1800', in Moody and Vaughan (eds), *New History of Ireland IV* (1986), pp.657–712.

McDowell, R.B., *Land and Learning: Two Irish Clubs* (Dublin, 1993).

Montgomery, K.L., 'Old Dublin Clubs and Coffee Houses', *New Ireland Review*, 6

(September 1896–February 1897).

Namier, Sir L. and Brooke, J., *The History of Parliament: The House of Commons 1754–1790*, 3 vols (London, 1964).

National Gallery of Ireland Acquisitions 1986–1988 (Dublin, 1988).

Ní Anluain, E., 'The Cardplayers and the Devil', *Béaloideas*, 59 (1991), pp.45–54.

Notes and Queries (Series 1), 10 (1854); (Series 2), 5 (1858), 10 (1860); (Series 3), 2 (1862).

O'Flanagan, J.R., *The Lives of the Lord Chancellors...of Ireland*, 2 vols (London, 1870).

O'Neill Daunt, W.J., *Ireland and her Agitators* (Dublin, 1845).

Oxmantown, Lord, 'The Hell-Fire Club', *Irish Times*, 25 September 1963.

Peter, A., *Sketches of Old Dublin* (Dublin, 1907).

Ponsonby, J., *The Ponsonby Family* (London, 1929).

Porter, R., *The Enlightenment*, 2nd edn (Basingstoke, 2001).

Powell, M.J., '"Beef, Claret and Communication": Convivial Clubs in the Public Sphere, 1750–1800', in Kelly and Powell (eds), *Clubs and Societies* (2010), pp.353–72.

Statt, D., 'The Case of the Mohocks: Rake Violence in Augustan London', *Social History*, 20, 2 (May 1995), pp.179–99.

Stevenson, D., *The Beggar's Benison: Sex Clubs of Enlightenment Scotland and their Rituals* (East Linton, 2001).

Story of Killakee House and the Hell Fire Club (Killakee, Co. Dublin, n.d.).

Walsh, J.E., *Ireland Sixty Years Ago*, 3rd edn (Dublin, 1851).

Walsh, P. 'Club Life in Late Seventeenth- and Early Eighteenth-Century Ireland: In Search of an Associational World, c. 1680–c. 1730', in Kelly and Powell (eds), *Clubs and Societies* (2010), pp.36–49.

Weldon, A.A., 'A Slight Sketch of Grangemellon, and the Story of St Leger's Castle', *JCKAS*, 1 (1891–95), pp.95–101.

Reference Works

Burtchaell, G.D. and Sadleir, T.U. (eds), *Alumni Dublinensis: A Register of the Students, Graduates, Professors and Provosts of Trinity College in the University of Dublin (1593–1860)*, 3 vols (Dublin, 1935).

Cokayne, G.E., *The Complete Peerage*, 13 vols in 14 parts (London, 1910–40).

The Georgian Society Records of Eighteenth Century Domestic Architecture and Decoration in Dublin, 5 vols (Shannon, 1969). First published 1909–13.

Johnston-Liik, E.M., *History of the Irish Parliament 1692–1800*, 6 vols (Belfast, 2002),

Matthew, H.C.G. and Harrison, B. (eds), *Oxford Dictionary of National Biography*, 60 vols (Oxford, 2004).

McGuire, J. and Quinn, J. (eds), *Dictionary of Irish Biography from the Earliest Times to the Year 2002*, 9 vols (Cambridge, 2009).

Stephen, L. and Lee, S. (eds), *The Dictionary of National Biography from the Earliest Times to 1900*, 22 vols (Oxford, 1959–60).

Strickland, W.G., *A Dictionary of Irish Artists*, 2 vols (Dublin and London, 1913).

Thorne, R.G. (ed.), *The History of Parliament: The House of Commons 1790–1820*, 5 vols (London, 1986).

Williamson, G.C. (rev.), *Bryan's Dictionary of Painters and Engravers*, 5 vols (London, 1919–21).

Index